HISTORY'S GREATEST SCANDALS

HISTORY'S GREATEST SCANDALS

Shocking Stories of Powerful People

Ed Wright

THUNDER BAY
P · R · E · S · S
San Diego, California

CONTENTS

INTRODUCTION

Being the best, the brightest, the richest or the most powerful is no guarantee against screwing up. Contained within these pages is a collection of history's greatest scandals, which have caused the stellar careers of many high achievers to be sullied and even destroyed. You will find murder, fraud, blackmail, perversion and treason permeating through to the highest echelons of society.

Although we live in a cynical era, surrounded by spin doctors and billion-dollar dodges such as Enron, we continue to be intrigued by scandal. It seems where there is large-scale society there will always be scandal. People competing for advantage are tempted to break the rules and others are unable to control their natures, while scandal, or even just the whiff of it, can be a tool of the envious to bring the innocent down.

US President Bill Clinton, impeached for perjury and obstruction of justice, following Monicagate, 1998.

Scandal is a jewel of many facets. Greed, lust, envy, incompetence and sheer perversity are just some of its motivating factors. Undoubtedly sex is one of the most common desires that lead to corruption. The British Profumo affair is a classic example, where a short, pudgy, powerful man was brought down by his lust for youth and beauty. Similarly, a blow-job almost cost Bill Clinton the American presidency and blighted much of his second term. Mind you, Clinton was not the first American president to get into trouble over his love affairs. Thomas Jefferson was attacked by his Federalist opponents for having fathered children to one of his black slaves, while Warren Harding's mistress tried to blackmail him into German-friendly policies with the revelation of their secret love affair.

However, some of the most sensational sex scandals in recent times have involved preachers. The wonderful world of televange-lism, where telegenic preachers gorge themselves on the contributions of their flocks while fraternising with prostitutes and secretaries, is a personal favourite of the media. Swaggart and Bakker are two who have scammed in the name of God and have been caught with their pants down.

As voyeurs and gossip-mongers, we are particularly fascinated when a sex scandal has the taint of perversity about it. For many years, homosexuality was considered deviant (often condemned by people such as Swaggart and Bakker who scandalised themselves the way God intended them to). Being a Methodist minister didn't prevent Canaan Banana, Zimbabwe's inaugural President, from drugging and raping his male staff. Firmly in the closet was composer Pyotr Tchaikovsky, who was traumatised by his homosexuality to the extent he may have beenpersuaded to commit suicide after being threatened with the revelation of his sexual inclinations. Similarly, the former British Liberal Party leader Jeremy Thorpe resorted to unorthodox means to conceal his sexual past when he put a hit out on a former male lover.

Other characters in these pages are far more bizarre in their sexual predilections. Australian composer, Percy Grainger, was literally whipped towards success by his Aryan-minded, strong-wristed mother. Then there is the Marquis de Sade, from whom the term sadism is derived. His mother-in-law had him locked up for a variety of sexual behaviours which included cutting into a servant girl's buttocks with a knife. One of the rumours about Catherine the Great was that she liked to have sex with a stallion. But perhaps this is just a case of scandalmongering by her enemies.

President Ferdinand Marcos and his wife, Imelda, treated the treasury of the Philippines as their personal bank account.

It seems as humans we are programmed to lust after forbidden fruit. Roman Polanski, whose life is full of terrible stories, drugged and raped a 13-year-old girl. But given his background, perhaps this behaviour may have been a twisted kind of quest for the innocence his own childhood never afforded him.

Sex scandals are usually initiated by a transgression against values of a society at a given point in history. Sleeping with a 13-year-girl 200 years ago would have scarcely raised an eyebrow, while homosexuality is broadly accepted in the western world today where it was once a capital crime. The unfortunate tale of Edward VIII reminds us how important social context is in the realm of scandal. As the King of England he was forced to abdicate because the love of his life had previously been divorced.

Sometimes sex can lead to murder. When US Senator Dan Sickles discovered that his wife had been sleeping with the son of the author of the *Star Spangled Banner*, he packed three pistols, confronted the man in the street and murdered him. He was acquitted at his trial on the grounds of temporary insanity. Here the scandal is as much about how he got away with it as the act itself. Meanwhile, US Vice President Aaron Burr, who killed Alexander Hamilton in a duel, was hounded out of politics by his enemies, even though the act – although tragic – was legal.

An angry crowd protests against the possible abdication of King Edward VIII, clearly laying the blame on the shoulders of his mistress, the divorcée Wallis Simpson.

Murders are not always planned, however. The Italian painter, Caravaggio, killed an adversary in a swordfight after a heated quarrel, while Lord Lucan allegedly smashed in his children's nanny's head with a metal pipe for no apparent reason.

Once you've killed someone, however, there are usually consequences. Rather than face execution or jail, Caravaggio and Lucan spent the rest of their lives on the run.

Of course running away is not always successful, even with the best possible preparation. Running away from business problems and probably his wife, British politician John Stonehouse faked his own drowning then migrated to Australia under a new identity. Paradoxically, he was only caught because the Australian police mistook him for the aforementioned Lord Lucan. When the writing was on the wall for 19th-century British tycoon Jabez Spencer Balfour, whose profligate business practices had cost many ordinary Britons their homes, savings and in some cases even their lives, he decided to slip away to Argentina, where he was pursued for 3 years by the British police. Nothing spices up a good scandal like a good escape story.

Industrialist Howard Hughes died in a state of such pitiful neglect that his corpse was unrecognisable, and had to be fingerprinted to prove its identity.

But what about when the scandal is built upon escapism from the very beginning? One of the most remarkable tales here is of Therese Daurignac, the motherless peasant girl, who utilised her captivating powers of imagination to build castles in the air that eventually translated into actual property and a salon that was frequented by the most important people in France. She was a natural born scammer. Still, once she had started she couldn't stop: her greed caught up with her and brought the fragile edifice tumbling down.

Perhaps the most unusual incentives for scandal come from those who become spies. Here the motivation can be ideology, the thrill of leading a double life, or sheer boredom. Adding more spice is the danger of needing recognition for ones activities. Anthony Blunt was Keeper of the Queen's pictures, yet at the same time was the best of the influential Cambridge spy circle, while Vladimir Petrov and his glamorous wife were tempted into defection by the Australian good life. For some, however, the good life is not enough. Sir John Kerr's sacking of Australian Prime Minister Gough Whitlam was as much a case of a thwarted ego seeking his place in history as Whitlam's mismanagement of the economy.

It would be interesting to know the amount of times the perpetrators of these scandals said to themselves, 'If only I'd stopped while the going was good'. But greed is incessant: feed the monster and it is bound to want more. For some, such as the eccentric genius, aviator and tycoon Howard Hughes, their natures are bound up in obsessions that are beyond their control. In a strange way, perhaps these are the happiest of the people in these pages. For them 'being' itself is scandalous. The others have to deal with the knowledge that they had a choice. However, it's only a scandal if you get caught.

POLITICAL
MISCONDUCT

On 9 August 1974, US President Richard Nixon stands
at a podium reading a farewell speech to his staff,
following his resignation from the White House.

MOTIVATION

anger
charity
envy
faith
gluttony
greed
hope
lust
pride
sloth

A QUESTION OF PATERNITY: THOMAS JEFFERSON AND SALLY HEMINGS

MAIN CULPRIT:
Thomas Jefferson (1743–1826), 3rd President of the United States of America (1801–19)

SCANDAL:
Reputedly fathered as many as six children with one of his slaves, Sally Hemings

WHY:
After his wife died he was drawn to Sally, his wife's illegitimate half-sister

It is well known that the man, whom it delighteth the people to honor, keeps, and for many years past has kept, as his concubine, one of his own slaves. Her name is SALLY. The name of her eldest son is TOM. His features are said to bear a striking, although sable resemblance to those of the President himself.

– James T. Callender, *Richmond Recorder*, 1 September 1802

Teams of geneticists have spent years trying to prove whether the descendants of Sally Hemings are also the descendants of Thomas Jefferson, pictured here c.1799.

If he had it to do over again, Thomas Jefferson probably would have appointed James T. Callender Postmaster of Richmond, Virginia. After all, it was – and still is – expected that a newly elected president will reward his friends and allies with cushy government jobs.

As a journalist with a genuine gift for vitriol, Callender had been an especially useful friend to Jefferson. In 1797, when Jefferson was battling his political nemesis Alexander Hamilton, Callender had published shocking newspaper articles that exposed Hamilton's many adulteries. The next year, when Jefferson found himself at odds with his old friend John Adams, Callender brought out an inflammatory pamphlet that derided President Adams as a 'hideous hermaphroditical character which has neither the force and firmness of a man, nor the gentleness and sensibility of a woman'. Jefferson bankrolled the publication that made that attack on Adams; furthermore, he went on record endorsing it as a work certain to 'inform the thinking part of the nation'.

But by 1802 Jefferson, for a variety of motives, had decided to distance himself from Callender. Jefferson was now president and wanted to project an aura of dignity, and Callender, whose penchant for heavy drinking had degenerated into full-blown alcoholism, made him a less-than-reliable character. Perhaps more to the point, Jefferson had become tired of Callender's endless string of letters begging for handouts of $50 or $100 – a Jefferson associate recalled the president cursing Callender as 'a damned eternal mendicant'.

Sally Hemings's mother, Betty, was a bright mulatto woman, and Sally mighty near white ... Sally was very handsome, long straight hair down her back.

– Recollection of Isaac Jefferson, former Monticello slave, 1847

When Jefferson turned down Callender's request to be made Postmaster of Richmond, Callender rebelled against his old patron. He joined Jefferson's political rivals, the Federalists, and began looking around for some scandal from Jefferson's private life that he could expose in Federalist newspapers. He found one very quickly. It had been whispered in Virginia society that Thomas Jefferson had a lover – a slave woman named Sally Hemings, and that Jefferson was the father of her six children. In the *Richmond Recorder*, 1 September 1802, Callender exposed Thomas Jefferson's best-kept secret. 'It is well known,' he wrote, 'that the man, whom it delighteth the people to honor, keeps, and for many years past has kept, as his concubine, one of his own slaves. Her name is SALLY. The name of her eldest son is TOM. His features are said to bear a striking, although sable resemblance to those of the President himself.'

Other Federalist papers across the United States seized the story and ran with it. In a matter of weeks, there was scarcely a soul in the country who had not heard that Thomas Jefferson was sleeping with one of his own slaves.

Thomas and Martha

On New Year's Day 1772, 28-year-old Thomas Jefferson married Martha Wayles Skelton, a 24-year-old widow. Jefferson was a lawyer, a burgess (or legislator) in the Virginia Assembly, and a landowner who was designing an elegant Palladian-style house for himself, called Monticello, atop the little mountain that overlooked his 2000-hectare estate. From a matrimonial point of view, Jefferson was a good catch, but Martha was an even better one, as she came from a very wealthy family. Her father, John Wayles, had made a fortune in the slave trade and, at his death, Martha stood to inherit cash, land and slaves.

Monticello, Thomas Jefferson's beloved mountaintop home, where descendants of Jefferson are buried in the private burial ground. However, the Monticello Association has not allowed the descendants of Sally Hemings to be buried here.

On his wedding day, Thomas Jefferson was a good-looking young man, around 2 metres tall with a ruddy complexion, clear blue eyes and sandy hair with red highlights. As for Martha, unfortunately no portrait of her has ever been found. Recollections from her family, friends and slaves at Monticello all agree that she was 'low' in stature – perhaps only around 1.5 metres tall – and that her eyes were hazel, her hair a deep red and that she was lithe and lovely. Martha had lost her first husband after only 22 months of marriage and her first child, a 4-year-old boy, not long after.

After the wedding at the plantation home of Martha's parents, the newlyweds set out for Jefferson's estate. While on the road they were caught in a blizzard which slowed their progress. By the time they reached Monticello it was late at night, and all the servants had gone to bed.

At that time Jefferson was living in a small – 20 x 20 metres – one-room brick house on the estate, while his slaves were building his mansion house. Into this cold, dark place Jefferson brought his bride. On their arrival he built a fire, lit a few candles and rummaged around until, behind some books, he found half a bottle of wine. That is how Thomas and Martha Jefferson began their life together – sipping leftover wine before a roaring fire in a tiny house perched on the edge of their mountain.

Eighteen months later John Wayles died and Martha inherited not only 4500 hectares of land but also 135 of her father's slaves. Among them was a light-skinned woman of mixed origin, Betty Hemings, and her ten young children. Betty Hemings had been John Wayles's mistress, and six of the ten children were Martha Jefferson's half-brothers and sisters. Among them was a baby girl, just a little over a year old, named Sally.

By all accounts, Thomas and Martha Jefferson were deeply in love. And while their love matured, their fortunes increased. At home, Jefferson pressed forward with building their splendid new house, Monticello, while in the wider world he was busy building a reputation as the most polished spokesman for the cause of American independence. However, in spite of all this good fortune and happiness, the Jeffersons were often in mourning. Of their six children, three died as infants and one as a toddler. Worse still, with each pregnancy, Martha Jefferson grew physically weaker.

On 8 May 1782, Martha gave birth to a daughter whom the Jeffersons named Lucy Elizabeth. Twelve days later Jefferson wrote to his friend James Madison, 'Mrs Jefferson has added another daughter to our family. She has ever since and still continues very dangerously ill'.

Martha Jefferson lingered for 4 months and, during the whole time, her husband was never out of earshot. He moved into a tiny room, almost a closet, adjacent to his wife's room. Betty Hemings was one of the house servants who tended Martha.

One day, shortly before she died, Martha Jefferson asked for pen, ink, paper and a copy of Laurence Sterne's novel *Tristam Shandy*. It had been a favourite of the Jeffersons, and now she turned the pages to an especially poignant passage. Grasping the pen she copied out these lines from the novel: 'Time wastes too fast: every letter I trace tells me with what rapidity life follows my pen. The days and hours of it are flying over our heads like clouds of a windy day never to return – everything presses on.' Jefferson then took the pen from his wife to copy the rest of the passage: 'And every time I kiss thy hand to bid adieu, every absence which follows it, are preludes to that eternal separation which we are shortly to make'.

Thomas Jefferson preserved this paper for the rest of his life. After his own death his family found it in a secret drawer in his writing desk. Its worn and dog-eared condition showed that Jefferson had read and reread it many times. And tucked away within the folds of the paper were locks of hair belonging to Martha Jefferson and two of the babies the Jeffersons had lost.

The end came on the morning of 6 September 1782. As she lay dying, Martha begged Jefferson not to remarry, saying she could not die happy if she thought her children would have a stepmother ruling over them. Taking his wife's hand in his, Jefferson swore solemnly never to marry again. And, being a man of his word, he kept that promise.

A Place Apart

Sally Hemings was 9 years old when her mistress and half-sister, Martha Jefferson, died. As a Hemings she enjoyed privileges that the other slaves at Monticello did not. While most of Jefferson's slaves performed the heavy, dirty outdoor work of the plantation, the members of the Hemings family worked either in the house or as Monticello's skilled craftspeople. Even in appearance the Hemings family occupied a place apart: while the plantation slaves wore ill-fitting clothes made from coarse fabric, the Hemingses wore well-tailored clothes made of fine linen and cotton. In 1847, the 72-year-old Isaac Jefferson, a former slave at Monticello, dictated a memoir to a man named Charles Campbell. Isaac described Betty Hemings as 'a bright mulatto woman', meaning that she was light skinned. As for Betty's daughter Sally, Isaac said she was 'mighty near white ... very handsome, [with] long straight hair down her back'.

In 1784, when Sally was only 11 years old, she received her first position of responsibility within the inner circle of the Jefferson family when she became the companion and caretaker for Thomas Jefferson's 6-year-old daughter, Maria. In 1787, Jefferson, who was now serving as the United States ambassador to France, sent for Maria and Sally to join him and his eldest daughter, Martha, in Paris. Soon after she arrived, Jefferson promoted Sally to serve as lady's maid to Martha and Maria. As their personal maid, Sally may have moved into the *Abbaye Royale de Panthemont*, the Paris convent school where the Jefferson girls boarded. What is certain is that Jefferson arranged for Sally to be taught the art of needlework as well as techniques for laundering fine clothes – skills required of any lady's maid. There is no hint in any document to suggest that Thomas Jefferson began a love affair with the teenage Sally Hemings while they were in France. In 1789 they all returned home to Monticello where Sally continued to serve the Jeffersons.

A PLEA FROM JEFFERSON

I plead guilty to one of their charges, that when young and single, I offered love to a handsome lady. I acknowledge its incorrectness. It is the only one founded on truth among all their allegations against me ...

– From a letter by Thomas Jefferson to Robert Smith, Secretary of the Navy, 1 July 1805

In 1795 Sally Hemings gave birth to her first child, a girl, whom she named Harriet. The child died when she was just 2 years old, but five other children followed – a son, Beverly (1798); a daughter who died in infancy (1799); a second Harriet (1801); a son, Madison (1805); and aother son, Eston (1808). Sally Hemings never married, nor was she linked to any black man at Monticello or from the surrounding neighbourhood. For 200 years the persistent rumours in the Monticello region and the oral tradition among the descendants of Sally Hemings have agreed that the father of all of Sally's children was Thomas Jefferson.

All the official sources testify that after the death of his wife Thomas Jefferson remained a celibate and lonely man. However, the sources also tell us that Sally Hemings was a young, lovely woman who was not attached to any man – and that she was a part of the Jefferson family circle of trusted servants. There is one point which none of the surviving records mentions: did Sally Hemings resemble her half-sister Martha Wayles Jefferson? We do not know, as no-one has ever found a portrait of either woman. To suggest that Jefferson began an affair with Sally because she reminded him of his late wife is pure speculation. But as speculation goes, it is particularly intriguing.

The DNA Test

For nearly 200 years Jefferson biographers have wrestled with the contradictory testimony about the Thomas Jefferson–Sally Hemings story.

Jefferson's eldest grandson, Thomas Jefferson Randolph, lived at Monticello, managed the farm and was executor of his grandfather's will. He stated that he had 'never seen a motion, or a look, or a circumstance which led him to suspect for an instant that there was a particle of familiarity between Mr Jefferson and Sally Hemings … and that no person ever at Monticello dreamed of such a thing'. Randolph believed that Peter Carr (the son of Jefferson's sister) was the father of Sally's children and that accounted for the resemblance of the Hemings children to the Jeffersons.

In 1873, S. F. Wetmore, editor of the *Pike County Republican* newspaper, interviewed Madison Hemings. During that interview Madison referred to 'my father, Thomas Jefferson', claiming that his mother had told him he was the son of the famous American founding father.

As for Thomas Jefferson, he alluded to the scandal only obliquely in an 1805 letter. 'I plead guilty to one of [the Federalists'] charges', Jefferson wrote, 'that when young and single, I offered love to a handsome lady. I acknowledge its incorrectness. It is the only one founded on truth among all their allegations against me.'

The scandal remained in the realm of gossip and speculation until 1998 when a team of geneticists led by Dr Eugene Foster, a pathologist from the University of Virginia (a school founded by Thomas Jefferson), collected DNA samples from the descendants of Field Jefferson (Thomas Jefferson's uncle), John Carr (the grandfather of Jefferson's Carr nephews), Eston Hemings (Sally's youngest son) and Thomas Woodson (whose descendants claimed that he was Sally Hemings's first child by Thomas Jefferson). Since Thomas Jefferson and his wife Martha had no sons that survived infancy, there are no direct male-line descendants from Thomas Jefferson himself. This point became important later during DNA testing.

Dr Foster and his team were searching for the Jefferson Y chromosome – the chromosome a father passes on to his son and which is the marker of paternity – in the various Jefferson–Hemings–Woodson descendants. After studying the DNA samples, the geneticists made three discoveries:

1. There is no link between the descendants of Field Jefferson and Thomas Woodson. Although the Woodson family have insisted that they are descended from Thomas Jefferson and Sally Hemings, there is no documentary evidence from the period to suggest that Woodson was Sally's child, and now there is no DNA evidence to support the claim either.

2. There is no link between the descendants of John Carr and Sally Hemings. This eliminates Thomas Jefferson Randolph's claim that Jefferson's nephew, Peter Carr, was the father of Sally Hemings's children.

3. The geneticists did find the Jefferson Y chromosome in the DNA sample of Eston Hemings's male descendants. The DNA evidence, combined with documentary evidence that shows that Thomas Jefferson was at Monticello at least 9 months prior to the birth of all six of Sally Hemings's children, led Dr Foster and his team to conclude that 'the simplest and most probable' interpretation of the data is that Thomas Jefferson was the father of Eston Hemings, and probably Sally Hemings's other five children as well.

GENETICISTS TO THE RESCUE?

After much DNA testing, the geneticists found the Jefferson Y chromosome in the DNA sample of the male descendants of Eston Hemings (Sally Hemings's youngest son). However, this does not prove that Jefferson was the father, simply that it was possible and, perhaps, given other documented and anecdotal evidence, even probable.

Nonetheless, the study is not without its problems. Since Thomas Jefferson fathered no sons, the DNA study could only look for the general Jefferson family Y chromosome, not the one that belonged uniquely to Thomas Jefferson.

Objections to the Study

In response to the Foster study, the Thomas Jefferson Foundation – the organisation that owns and operates Jefferson's estate, Monticello, and which has become the premier institution in the United States for the study of every aspect of Thomas Jefferson's life – sponsored its own examination of the DNA report, as well as historical documents and oral histories related to the Jefferson–Hemings case. In January 2000 the Foundation issued a report which stated, 'The DNA study, combined with multiple strands of currently available documentary and statistical evidence, indicates a high probability that Thomas Jefferson fathered Eston Hemings, and that he most likely was the father of all six of Sally Hemings's children appearing in Jefferson's records'.

Along with the main report of the Thomas Jefferson Foundation that accepted Dr Foster's DNA study, there was also a minority report that questioned the geneticists' conclusions. The main objection of the authors of the minority report was Dr Foster's use of the phrase 'high probability' and the Jefferson Foundation's use of the phrase 'most likely'. Since there are no direct male descendants of Thomas and Martha Jefferson, and because there were approximately twenty-five Jefferson males living in Virginia during the period when Sally Hemings had her children, the best that could be said, the minority report argued, was that Dr Foster's 'DNA studies enhance the possibility' that Thomas Jefferson was the father of Eston Hemings. Furthermore, the report continued, 'the findings do not prove that Thomas Jefferson was the father of Eston' – let alone the five other children of Sally Hemings.

Aside from highlighting the shades of meaning between the terms 'probability' and 'possibility', the Minority Report Committee has a point. Although Dr Foster and the Jefferson Foundation have been cautious in their conclusions, the phrases 'high probability' and 'most likely' take them as close as they dare to saying the result of the DNA tests are conclusive. Certainly the general public has understood the Foster and the Foundation reports to mean that it is an established fact that Thomas Jefferson had a long-running affair with his slave Sally Hemings, and together they produced six children. The authors of the minority report argue, however, that, based on the incomplete DNA samples available (that is, none from Thomas Jefferson himself), the best that can be said is that Jefferson may indeed have been the father of Eston Hemings. But, the minority report authors argue that the evidence is inconclusive. Furthermore, given the absence of any concrete evidence, to assert that Thomas Jefferson fathered the five other Hemings children is pure conjecture.

And so the gossip that has titillated historians, biographers and the general public for 200 years continues. But while the debate rages on, the Monticello Association, an organisation of Thomas Jefferson's lineal descendants, is taking a wait-and-see approach. Until conclusive evidence is available, the Monticello Association refuses to accept the membership applications of descendants of Sally Hemings, nor will the Association permit Hemings's descendants to be buried with Thomas Jefferson in the Monticello graveyard, the private burial ground reserved exclusively for members of the Jefferson family.

What Happened to Sally Hemings's Children?

Harriet I (1795–97) As the dates indicate, the first child born to Sally Hemings died young, at just 2 years of age.

Beverly (1798–after 1822) Jefferson had Sally's first son trained as a woodworker. He must have also been a talented musician because one of the Jefferson's grand-daughters mentioned that, at family parties, Beverly always supplied the dance music. Beverly was so fair skinned that he could pass as white. Jefferson never formally granted Beverly his freedom but, in 1822, the young man left Monticello to live as a white man. He moved to Maryland where he married a white woman. They had one child, a daughter, but Beverly Hemings's line appears to have died out. The date of his death is unknown.

Daughter (1799–1800) This child died in infancy. Her name has not been found in any of the surviving Jefferson documents.

Harriet II (1801–after 1822) Until she was 14 years old Harriet spent most of her time in and around Monticello, doing no work, but instead running the occasional errand for the Jefferson family. As a teenager she was given the highly coveted light work of spinning and weaving in the plantation 'cloth factory'. Like her brother Beverly she could pass for white. Jefferson never formally freed Harriet either but, in 1822, she left the plantation and settled in Washington DC, where she married a white man. The couple had children, but geneaologists have been unable to find any living descendants. Her date of death is unknown, but her brother Madison said in 1873 that he had not heard from his sister Harriet in 10 years.

Madison (1805–77) Like his older brother, Beverly, Madison was trained as a woodworker. He was light skinned, but not as fair as Beverly and Harriet. In his will, Jefferson freed Madison, his younger brother Eston and their mother Sally. After Jefferson's death the family lived in Charlottesville, Virginia, where Madison married a free woman of mixed race. After Sally's death in 1835, Madison, his wife and their children moved to southern Ohio, where they farmed. In a lengthy memoir published in the *Pike County Republican* on 13 March 1873, Madison stated that Thomas Jefferson was his father. Madison and his wife had ten children, and have many descendants living today.

Eston (1808–56) Of all the Hemings boys, Eston was the most gifted wood-worker, renowned in later life for his fine cabinet making. He was also an accomplished violinist who formed his own dance band after he moved to Ohio. Eston was freed in Thomas Jefferson's will, married a free woman of mixed race, and after the death of his mother, Sally, moved with his family to southern Ohio. Later the family moved to Madison, Wisconsin, where Eston died and lies buried.

MOTIVATION

anger
charity
envy
faith
gluttony
greed
hope
lust
pride
sloth

TEMPERANCE IN ALL THINGS: JABEZ SPENCER BALFOUR

MAIN CULPRIT:
Jabez Spencer Balfour (1843–1916), British Liberal Member of Parliament, financier and property developer

SCANDAL:
Ran up a massive debt of £7 million then skipped town to Buenos Aires, leaving thousands of angry investors penniless

WHY:
His greed led to corruption and his arrogance made him believe the law didn't apply to him

You will never be able to shut from your ears the cries of the widows and orphans you have ruined.
– Justice Bruce, at Balfour's sentencing

An illustration depicting Jabez Spencer Balfour in the cells at Bow Street Police Station, London, after his arrest for conspiracy and fraud, 1895.

On 28 November 1895, a small, almost fantastically portly man with ruddy cheeks, cropped whiskers and a chin-concealing beard sat in court awaiting sentence. His name was Jabez Spencer Balfour and he had just been successfully prosecuted by none other than Sir Richard Webster, the British Attorney General, on charges of fraud. Balfour was a former Liberal member of parliament, Mayor of Croydon and an agitator for the liberal, temperance and non-conformist causes. Yet it was his

business career, as a financier and property developer, that landed him in the dock. His preposterous exuberance, talent for financial chicanery and bluster, and abuse of the public's trust, ruined thousands of investors, large and small. Some of them committed suicide, while others, who had saved hard for their retirements, were doomed to the Dickensian prospect of the workhouse. One newspaper of the time even went so far as to claim that Balfour 'had wrought more woe and misery in English households than anything that has happened since the South Sea Bubble'.

The youngest of seven children and highly intelligent, at an early age Balfour's mother had an insight into the amoral potential of his gift for persuasive public speaking.

Dressed in the best suit money could buy and determined not to reveal his anxiety, Balfour waited patiently while Justice Gainsford Bruce, his former parliamentary colleague, albeit a Conservative, passed sentence on his co-accused. Balfour expected he would get around eight years. When Bruce prefaced the sentence with the grave observation that those in high social positions should be equally accountable before the law as the common thief, Balfour's natural optimism dimmed. He was given two 7-year sentences, to be served consecutively – almost twice as long as he had anticipated. Balfour remained determined to put on a brave face. His lawyer rushed out of the court to buy sandwiches and champagne, which he brought to the room where Balfour waited, before he was packed off to prison. It was the last drop of wine that would pass the famed temperance campaigner and wine connoisseur's lips for 12 years.

Origins of a Scoundrel

That Jabez Spencer Balfour ever reached the upper echelons of British society was rather remarkable in itself. His mother, Clara, was the illegitimate child of an Isle of Wight butcher and cattle dealer. When her father died, 9-year-old Clara and her mother, Sarah, aged 29, moved to London where Sarah scratched an unhappy living from needlework. At the age of 15, Clara married Jimmy Balfour, 12 years her senior, the master of a rag-and-bone shop who was prone to getting on the grog a little too often. Clara found a career for herself on the public lecture circuit where she talked persuasively on the evils of drink. She also converted her husband into a temperance lecturer – one who spoke from personal experience to people living in some of London's roughest areas.

Jabez, born in 1843, was the youngest of seven children. By the time he came along the family was doing quite well. Jimmy had become a minor official in the House of Commons, and Clara was known as one of Britain's leading temperance lecturers. In demand throughout England, Wales and Ireland, she drew large audiences and an excellent salary. Her speeches were as popular for their style as their content. Young Jabez often accompanied her on tour and Clara was aware of his precocity. Yet while she was certain of his intelligence, she was already worried about his moral fibre, claiming in a letter to her eldest son, James, that Jabez 'will either be good or evil – there is nothing negative about him'. It is possible that, as a professional speaker, she saw the amoral potential of the 'gift of the gab' that she had handed down to her son.

Jabez was educated in France and Germany. After school his father's influence gained him a job as a parliamentary agent. When he was 22, he married Ellen Read, 2 years his junior and the daughter of a London gentleman. They settled in a comfortable house in White Post Hill, Surrey.

Climbing the Greasy Pole

Jabez Balfour's initial involvement in business emerged from his family's affiliation with the temperance movement. He inherited the political world of his parents and became a conspicuous Liberal – though, considering his behaviour, this seems as much a case of opportunism as belief.

A key platform of Liberal social reform was the idea of encouraging financial independence. Liberalism believed it was virtuous and socially healthy for working men to own their own homes. One of the institutions that emerged to facilitate this was the Building Society. In 1868, the Reverend Dawson Burns, Jabez's brother-in-law, started the Liberator Building Society specifically to help non-conformists achieve their aim of home ownership. The Liberator Building Society carried the slogan *Libera sedes, liberum facit*, meaning 'a free home makes a free man'. Its name was linked to the anti-Anglican Liberation Society, a powerful non-conformist organisation whose mission was the separation of church and state. The initial agents were mostly non-conformist ministers who had trouble existing on their stipends.

To help in this idealistic and progressive venture, Reverend Burns brought in his brothers-in-law, John and Jabez Balfour. By 1870, Jabez had usurped his older brother as company secretary. Soon after, he became managing director. The Liberator was the centrepiece of a number of companies which soon came to be known as the Balfour Group. They were mostly related to the finance, housing and construction industries and included the Lands Allotment Company, which bought land and built houses; the Housing and Investment Trust which held extant proper-ties; the London and General savings bank, which balanced the lending activities of the Liberator; a brickworks; and a number of building firms such as the controversial Hobbs and Co.

The original non-profit intentions of the Liberator founders were ruined by its sheer success. By 1879, after a mere 9 years in business, it had become the biggest building society in Britain, lending to non-conformists and Anglicans alike. For Jabez, whose social ambitions had been suddenly amplified by the unanticipated prosperity of his businesses, it must have looked like anything was possible.

By 1879, Jabez was living in the up-and-coming Surrey town of Croydon, where he had already upgraded from an unprepossessing lodge to one of its finest residences, Wellesley House, where he entertained lavishly and frequently. Much of the Balfour Group's activities were around Croydon and brought prosperity to the town. Jabez also gave generously of his own time and money and it was largely through his efforts that Croydon gained borough status in 1883. His contribution was recognised when Jabez was elected the town's inaugural mayor. By then he was already a Liberal MP for the Warwickshire seat of Tamworth in the Gladstone government. His influence was on the up and he had a reputation for being wealthy and charitable, shrewd and conscientious.

JABEZ BALFOUR'S POLITICS

While ultimately a pragmatist, Jabez was a Liberal whose often contentious policies included home rule for Ireland, the separation of church and state, the temperance cause (though he was generally quite partial to liquor and the liquor industry, and ran his Burnley campaigns from the Thorn Hotel), the abolition of hereditary peerage and voting rights for women. He ran for office five times and was successful twice, being Member of Parliament for Tamworth between 1880 and 1883 and Member of Parliament for Burnley between 1889 and 1993.

Family Business

If there was a downside to Jabez's life at the time, it was the mental disintegration of his wife, Ellen. Jabez cared for her until her condition became so bad that in 1880, the same year he was elected to parliament, she had to be put into an asylum. Still, he chose the best possible care for her in the Priory Hospital at Roehampton, a high-class clinic which today largely caters to substance abusing-celebrities, such as supermodel Kate Moss.

Yet Jabez was not always tender with those who were close to him. When his older brother, John, began to question the way the Balfour Group directors appointed themselves fees, Jabez gave him short shrift. He showed his ruthless face by falsely accusing John of embezzling money from the Tamworth brick-works. Jabez had bought the brickworks to smooth his path to a parliamentary seat in his town, and he had installed John to run it. He'd promised John an annual salary of £1000 per year but, in true Jabez style, hadn't entered it in the books. When the company went public and the accounts were audited, John was put in a difficult position from which Jabez righteously refused to rescue him. The two brothers didn't speak again for almost 10 years after this incident.

Despite his prodigious talent, Jabez had a kind of shortsightedness that often results in the downfall of high-flying tycoons – and there was also something in his character of the spoilt youngest child who knew he could get away with murder. A member of parliament, he nonetheless believed the law didn't apply to him. As an irrepressible optimist, he also believed that everything would work out in the end. Yet in 1885 the first chinks in Balfour's charmed public life began to emerge. When his seat of Tamworth was abolished in a redistribution, Jabez set out to become MP for the new borough of Croydon. Yet his opposition to a new railway for Croydon – because he had a significant interest in an already existing one – damaged his popularity. There was also a Tory campaign stating that Jabez was a direct threat to both the public and the Anglican church. Jabez lost the election to the Conservative candidate by a solid margin.

Jabez was somewhat embittered by this ungrateful treatment from a town for which he had done so much. He moved to London in 1887, where he occupied salubrious digs on Hyde Park. He also bought Burcot Estate, a grand country house on the banks of the Thames in Oxfordshire, where he entertained guests for the weekend, employed dozens of servants and had a magnificent wine collection. The standard of entertainment was lavish. There was swimming and boating and an indoor tennis court with the novelty of electric lighting, making it possible to play at night. All of this was funded by the lavish fees he awarded himself for his Balfour Group directorships.

By the time Jabez moved to London, the Balfour Group had long since abandoned the idealism of its inception, which had seen a sign outside the Liberator saying 'Speculators Need Not Apply'. Increasingly it became involved in boutique speculative property developments aimed at the wealthy. Whitehall Court, for instance, was a development which came with hydraulic lifts, lavishly dressed porters and electric lights throughout, and the smaller, more exclusive Hyde Park Court Development came with an in-house French chef and individual valets. Jabez was the first tenant of Whitehall Court, which adjoined the Balfour Group-built National Liberal Club.

The Books Were Cooked

Already rich, Jabez persisted with politics and was defeated at Doncaster in Yorkshire in an 1888 by-election before winning in Burnley, Lancashire in 1889. By the time he was back in parliament, however, his companies were in trouble, although few but the inner circle were aware of it. For a long time the Balfour Group's prosperity had been based on cooking the books. Rather than awarding themselves a share of the profits, Balfour and his cronies had long been engaged in awarding themselves whatever they wanted and then concocting the necessary balance sheet to warrant their excessive lifestyles. It wasn't exactly the kind of self-help the Liberator had been established to encourage.

The primary means by which Balfour and his associates justified the large sums they gifted themselves was by generating paper profits through selling assets (mainly land) at inflated prices between the companies they had under their control. In this way, money came into the group in the form of deposits in their bank or shareholder investments, and then were successively shifted between companies to create the false impression of financial health. For example, a block of land or development would be sold by one company to another in the Balfour Group for £10,000, then onsold to another for £15,000, and so on. Thus the apparent financial strength of the Balfour companies was the result of vastly inflated valuations of its assets. The illusion was bolstered by pliable or incompetent auditors who, like most of the shareholders, were prone to believe everything Jabez told them. On the rare occasions that they indicated their concerns in reports to the board, Jabez managed to blunt the impact with his extraordinary confidence and bluster.

A caricature of the exceedingly plump Jabez Spencer Balfour, published in the English periodical *Vanity Fair*, 1892.

It was fraud on a massive scale. However, by 1889 the press were starting to get wind of the fact that there was something rotten at the heart of Balfour's corpulent empire. The first newspaper to make noises was the *Financial Times*, which was followed by the *Economist*. Despite these attacks, Jabez continued to assure his investors their money was in the best possible hands. In a way, he had no choice. He had already gone beyond the point of return. If he owned up to his sins, then the companies would come crashing down around him. But if he continued to lie his way through, there was a chance a boom would arrive and raise prices to a level where the companies' inflated assets became marketable again. It wasn't to be. Unfortunately for Jabez, an economic downturn occurred in 1890, triggered by the the rash Argentinian investments of the English bank, Barings.

Despite the gloomy outlook, Jabez continued to tell his shareholders that everything was fine. At the end of 1891, it became clear to those with inside knowledge that Hobbs and Co., a Balfour Group building firm run by one of Jabez's Croydon cronies, was in serious trouble. The other Balfour companies rallied around it, mainly because it owed them all money. If Hobbs and Co. went under, it was likely that the whole empire would collapse like a house of cards. In early 1892, as Balfour was telling the shareholders of the need to expand the London and General

Bank, he was secretly selling his shares and squirrelling away the proceeds. He set up a trust for his ill wife, and hid the rest of the money away for himself.

In August 1892, Hobbs and Co. went under. Its debt was massive and included £2 million that was due to the London and General Bank, another Balfour Company. On 2 September that year the doors of the bank were bolted shut and a sign mounted outside that read 'Temporary Suspension of Business'.

Jabez tried to talk his way through the crisis by arguing that all the companies needed was another half million pounds to sort out their temporary financial problems. Yet by December, the official receiver had determined that the Balfour Group was collectively £7 million in debt – around £500 million or $1.2 billion dollars in today's money. From this, the receiver estimated that about £27,000 would be recoverable. Ten thousand of this was presumably money Balfour owed to the bank. By this time, however, Jabez was nowhere to be found. Rather than face the legions of angry investors, some of whom had already committed suicide, he skipped the country.

On the Run

That winter there were rumoured sightings of Jabez in all manner of places. It took until February for the British government to work out he was 11,000 kilometres away in Buenos Aires, where an extradition treaty was yet to be ratified. Even if it was, Jabez had been assured that it couldn't be applied retrospectively. He was joined there by two young women, the daughters of a deceased business colleague, one or both of whom was his mistress. Although there was no extradition treaty, once his presence in Buenos Aires became common knowledge, life began to get uncomfortable for him. There were threats by investors to kidnap him and bring him back to Britain for trial, and the press hounded him.

Because of the extra attention, Jabez moved to the provincial town of Salta, 800 miles from Buenos Aires and near the border with Chile. At the time, Argentina was entering a period of tumult, with the provinces increasingly unwilling to recognise the authority of the central government. This was to Jabez's advantage since at the end of 1893, the Argentinian government ratified the extradition treaty and in January 1894, the Argentinian President signed the order for Jabez's arrest.

The extradition, however, wouldn't prove that easy. Jabez had become a popular figure in Salta where, despite being a temperance politician, he was in negotiations to buy a brewery. Salta was in dire economic straits and Jabez's money and financial enthusiasm had led the town to welcome him. As the external situation for Jabez worsened, he acquired a loyal band of local allies nicknamed 'Balfouristas', who were determined to help prevent his extradition.

Jabez was arrested on the streets of Salta by Ronald Bridgett, the British Consul, on 28 January 1894 and jailed. The cogs of Argentinian justice moved slowly towards his extradition. Salta's judiciary slowed things down partly because they resented acting on orders from the capital and partly because they'd been bribed – something Jabez would need to do quite often to maintain his Argentinian sojourn. In April, Jabez was released from jail because of the pleas and money of his lover Miss Freeman. When the case came to court in Salta the prosecution won, but Jabez remained free for some months as he exhausted the processes of appeal.

When the supreme court pronounced against him, it seemed Jabez's Argentinian adventures were almost over. Not quite. There was a law in Argentina forbidding anyone charged with a criminal offence from leaving the country. Subsequently his Salta friends lined up to sue him for a variety of offences designed to keep him in front of the Salta judge for many years to come.

Inspector Froest

A frustrated British consul tried to bribe some of Jabez's new friends from pressing charges, but it was a slow process. A much more radical option was undertaken with the appointment of Scotland Yard's Inspector Frank Froest to help bring the fugitive home. Froest, who was a specialist in capturing absconders, arrived in Salta in March 1895 as the corrupt local courts persisted in delaying Jabez's extradition. He decided that Jabez was a flight risk and would effectively have to be kidnapped and taken back to Buenos Aires. To achieve this aim, he parked an entire train on railway sidings a few kilometres out of town. He managed to coerce the governor of Salta to sign the permission to extradite Balfour, but ran into trouble when the head warder of the prison wouldn't release him because he was due in court the next day on one of the trumped-up charges levied against him to keep him in the country.

The British had promised £50 to every Argentinian policeman who helped in the arrest and, eventually, it was agreed that they would take Jabez to the railway station where the Governor would make a final decision. However, at the station the Governor, quite sensibly, failed to turn up. Despite being surrounded by an angry mob, Inspector Froest prevailed and, before long, Jabez was in handcuffs and on the train bound for Buenos Aires.

Back in Salta, however, the judiciary wasn't impressed by this wanton usurping of their authority. They issued warrants for Balfour's recapture and for Inspector Froest's arrest. A detachment of officials and Balfouristas set out on horseback to chase the train. Having caught the train, a sherriff's officer, Chuchini, set his horse in front of the locomotive and ordered it to stop. However, when the engineer tried to slow the train down, Froest prevented him and the stoic, but too stubborn,

Chuchini was mown down. They arrived in the city of Tucuman where a warrant for the arrest of Froest on the charge of murder had been telegraphed from Salta. But Froest managed to elude the local police by changing trains. Once in Buenos Aires, Jabez was moved from the prison to a boat he shared with over 20,000 sheep. A final attempt by the Balfouristas to rescue their man by boarding the docked ship was averted by moving the ship to a different part of the harbour. When the tide grew high enough for the laden vessel to sail, there was jubilation in Britain – the wrecker of so many lives was finally coming home to face the music.

Balfour served 12 years in prison, where he was not allowed to read the newspaper, was only allowed to write one letter a month and was fed on a constant diet of mostly inedible bilge. He was released in 1906. When he emerged from Parkhurst Prison on the Isle of Wight in 1906, the portly financier was a shadow of his former self, a thin, grey-haired old gentleman with the bravado long bleached out of him. In the interim, his family had become poor, and Jabez made his first post-penitential living writing a serialised account of his time in jail for the *Weekly Dispatch* newspaper. When this ran out of steam, Jabez reinvented himself as a consultant mining engineer – despite having no qualifications other than once having owned a mine. His new profession took him to Africa, Australia, Latin America and Burma. In February 1916, while on his way to a new job in the coal mines of Wales, Jabez Spencer Balfour, aged 72, fell asleep on the train and never woke up.

On Balfour's release from jail, his son James, who had always supported his father, was waiting for him outside the prison gates. His daughter, Clara, however, moved to Canada before his release. His wife, Ellen, remained in the mental institution for the remainder of her life.

MOTIVATION

anger
charity
envy
faith
gluttony
greed
hope
lust
pride
sloth

THE WORST PRESIDENT IN AMERICAN HISTORY: WARREN G. HARDING

MAIN CULPRIT:
Warren G. Harding (1865–1923), 29th President of the United States of America (1921–23)

SCANDAL:
Was blackmailed by his mistress who threatened to go public with their affair

WHY:
A weak character, dominated by his wife and lover and manipulated by corrupt friends

I am not fit for this job and never should have been here.
– Warren G. Harding

Warren G. Harding, 29th President of the United States (1921–23); blackmailed by his lover Carrie Philips, the wife of one of his closest friends.

Warren G. Harding sat down in his Washington office to write a letter. Carefully selecting a sheet of his official United States Senate stationery, he took up his trademark snub-nosed pen and blue ink and began writing. 'Darling, Sweetheart, Adorable', he saluted his mistress. 'I am extremely in love with you this morning. I want you – in all your freshness and sweetness and charm … The "Oh, Warren! Oh, Warren!" When your body quivers with divine paroxysm and your soul hovers for flight with mine.' And on and on he wrote, page after livid page, closing with a jingly poem that began, 'I love your back, I love your breasts/ Darling to feel, where my face rests'.

In small-town Marion, Ohio, the town beauty, a statuesque, reddish-haired woman, read the letter with a mixture of passion, longing, frustration and anger at the lover who had left her behind. Carrie Fulton Phillips, wife of the local department store owner, tucked the letter into a locked strongbox, along with more than 100 other love letters from Harding that she had collected during their 15-year romance – letters that would one day play an influential role in the history of the United States, and trigger the only known successful blackmailing of a presidential candidate.

He Looks like a President

Harding met Carrie Phillips when he was 40; she was nearly 10 years younger. Like many people in Marion, he was captivated by her charm, great beauty and her sophisticated intelligence. She epitomised the high-bosomed, S-shaped Gibson Girl ideal of the time. Harding himself, editor–publisher of the *Marion Star*, had a striking appearance that would cause his later political campaign manager to say 'He looks like a President', when promoting him for that office. He was tall, deep chested and broad shouldered, with gleaming iron-grey hair and a booming voice.

Both Harding and Phillips, however, were married – to other people. The young Harding had been pursued, until he relented, by the once-divorced daughter of the town's richest man. Florence Kling DeWolfe Harding, 5 years older than her husband, was a formidable, strong-willed woman, known as the Duchess for her commanding manner. As business manager she had turned the *Star* into a profitable enterprise, at least partly by spanking newsboys who didn't measure up to her exacting standards. No-one, however, could consider the near-sighted, thick-ankled woman beautiful. Carrie Fulton, on the other hand, had married a man who worshipped her. He had met her when she was a primary school teacher in a small nearby town, then bought her a showcase home and set her up socially. Jim Phillips was a head shorter than the eyecatching Carrie, and gossip said she had simply married him because he offered the best prospects. The Hardings and

Phillipses moved in the same circles. Jim Phillips became Harding's best friend, while Carrie became Florence's soul mate and confidante. When the Phillipses were devastated after the death of their toddler son, the Hardings were there to console them and the couples became even closer. As best friends, they visited each other's homes, dined together, partied together, even travelled together – they holidayed in Florida and went on a Bermuda cruise.

Harding with his wife, Florence, known as 'the Duchess', 1923. Harding is remembered as a weak man, dominated by his wife, and many believe he would never have been president without her.

Harding and Carrie always considered Christmas 1907 their 'anniversary' – when they first secretly pledged their love for one another. But their affair actually began in 1905 when, conveniently, Florence Harding and Jim Phillips simultaneously required medical treatment. Florence had gone to a Chicago hospital for treatment of a long-standing kidney ailment and removal of a kidney. Jim suffered from depression, aggravated by his son's death. Best friend Harding persuaded him not to seek treatment at a local sanitarium, which would be too close to family and business concerns for a full recovery, and instead Phillips went off to a Michigan institution. While their spouses were absent, Harding solicitously visited Carrie. One afternoon in Carrie's bedroom they fell into each other's arms – torrid lovemaking, and letter writing, began and would continue, with a few interruptions, for another 15 years.

Virtually under the noses of their oblivious spouses the two lovers conducted a flaming affair. They scheduled their trysts almost daily – sometimes at Carrie's home or, at night, behind the shrubbery in her garden. After Harding bought one of the town's first automobiles, they were able to slip away to out-of-town hotels. Harding wrote Carrie multi-page, wildly sensual love letters from his *Star* desk, while his wife and business manager Florence sat only a few metres away. Carrie eagerly picked up the steamy mail each morning while her husband was at the department store, read it eagerly, and hid the letters away to read again later.

The Pressure's on

In 1909 Carrie began to suggest that Harding divorce Florence and marry her, as she'd had enough of stolen moments. He demurred. He couldn't let go of Florence as she was too important in his life. Carrie was infuriated. He said he loved her more than anything in the world, and yet … She broke up with him, but the stricken Harding pleaded with her to come back, and she did. Florence and Jim seemed not to know what had happened. The four continued to travel together and embarked on a grand foreign tour, sailing on the S.S. *Deutschland* with an itinerary that would take them around Europe, to Greece and to Egypt. The highlight for Florence, who had meticulously done all the planning, was the trip down the Nile, through the Valley of the Kings and past the Pyramids. For Harding, it was time with Carrie, and quick shipboard kisses and liaisons on the deserted decks while the others were sleeping. In Rome, Harding bought a nude statue of the goddess Diana and presented it to Carrie; it looked like her, he said.

Carrie fell in love with Germany. It was the time of Thomas Mann and Einstein, Wagner and Richard Strauss and the German expressionist painters – it represented the sophistication and culture the intelligent Carrie had missed in small-town Ohio. When she again implored Harding to marry her and he, amid avid protestations of undying love, again refused, she furiously told him she was determined to live in Germany 'where her heart was' and persuaded the ever-pliant Jim Phillips to pay her way to Berlin. She remained in Germany, while war clouds gathered, living just off the Unter den Linden and taking German lessons. She returned to Ohio only grudgingly, 10 days after World War I began, spouting pro-German sentiment as she came.

Meanwhile, pushed and prodded by the ambitious Florence, a reluctant Harding was pursuing a political career. He served in the State Senate, a 2-year term as Lieutenant Governor, and narrowly lost the race for Governor of Ohio. In the important election year of 1912, he attracted the Republican party's national attention by nominating fellow Ohioan William Howard Taft for a second presidential term. In 1914 he was elected to the US Senate, against Carrie's strongly expressed opposition. Letters – some of the most passionate the lonely Harding had ever written – had flown back and forth between Ohio and Germany during their separation. He coaxed her into two 'glorious' reunions. In 1912 she boarded a steamer for 5 'luminous' days in Montreal and in 1913 they met again in New York City. On her return to Marion, Harding was so happy he bought his lover a Cadillac. But he still shied away from divorce and marriage.

NO SECRETS IN A SMALL TOWN

If their spouses were unaware of their affair, others in the small town of Marion were not. Carrie's former cook, Inez McWhorter, was to later recall the day Carrie, Marion's fashion plate, walked to town in a pair of eyecatching, brightly coloured shoes. When McWhorter returned home, she found Harding with his trousers at his knees and Carrie spreadeagled on the kitchen table. McWhorter noticed she was still wearing the colourful shoes.

Confrontation and Recrimination

In 1915 Carrie took action. First she returned to Harding a packet of his love letters. Alarmed, he sent them back, pleading with her to destroy them, a step he was later to regret. Then, for the first time, she wrote him a love letter at home, knowing Florence would detect the scented stationery and open it. That would force Florence to the divorce court, surely. Confrontations and recriminations from Florence followed, but she was not about to give up her husband, whatever his transgressions. Florence cut Carrie dead and denounced her publicly.

However, that didn't end the Harding–Carrie problem, for Carrie now chose a new agenda – standing up for the Kaiser's Germany. Harding had been named to the Senate Foreign Relations Committee, and Carrie wrote him vehement letters about the German position, always with the veiled hint that she might disclose the letters if he did not do her bidding regarding foreign policy. In April 1917, President Woodrow Wilson asked Congress to declare war on Germany as a result of German unrestricted submarine warfare. Carrie's threats became more specific. Vote against war, she told him, or she would make the letters public. Harding, in a long and pleading letter, urged her to tone down her rhetoric; she was now being watched by government agents, people were saying that Carrie, who made no secret of her opinions, was a German spy. As anti-German sentiment swept the country, Harding even wrote to Jim Phillips for help, begging him to silence his wife. Harding defied Carrie nonetheless, and the war resolution passed overwhelmingly. Under pressure from Harding and Phillips, Carrie actually volunteered for a Red Cross sewing circle, but nevertheless retained her anti-war sentiments. When a group of Marion draftees was training for the military, she staged a raucous, one-woman anti-war protest at the railway station. Even after the Armistice, she vociferously attacked the Treaty of Versailles as unfair to Germany. In each missive to Harding, she gave him an earful of her sentiments. But she also reminded him that she still had a packet of incriminating letters.

I AM YOURS

'I am yours for all time, any time', Warren G. Harding wrote for his and Carrie Phillips's seventh 'anniversary'. He added that absence not only made his heart grow fonder but – using their code names for their genitals – made his 'Jerry' long for her 'Seashell'.

As the 1920 Presidential election neared, the Republican party fielded three strong candidates – General Leonard Wood, a war hero; Illinois Governor Frank Lowden; and maverick California Senator, Hiram Johnson, darling of the Progressive Party. A bitter battle for the nomination loomed. Harding's crony and political manipulator, Harry Daugherty, advanced Harding's name as a compromise candidate, citing little more than his stately appearance as credentials for the job. Harding had few other attributes – he had been an ineffective, lacklustre senator, missing two-thirds of roll-call votes, spending time writing love letters at his desk during senatorial debates. No matter. He was good looking and inoffensive.

Harding himself thought Daugherty's proposal absurd. 'You know I am unsuited for this high office even if it were possible for me to attain it', he wrote to Daugherty. Florence also opposed the idea at first. She wanted him to run for another senate term – anything to keep him from returning to Marion and the hypnotic clutches of Carrie Phillips. Carrie wrote Harding an angry letter ridiculing any presidential aspirations he may have had. She also announced that she had told Jim Phillips 'everything'. When the Phillips's daughter Isabelle married a German-born army air service private, the Hardings were conspicuously not invited to the wedding.

With impending Republican convention deadlock, Harding now emerged as a serious back-up choice. 'The best of the secondraters', one party leader caustically labelled him.

A bitter Carrie gave Harding one more try; a no-nonsense ultimatum – drop out of politics, divorce Florence and marry her or else she would go public. Alternatively, he could buy her silence for $25,000, cash on the barrelhead. It was the first time she had mentioned money. Harding, apparently considering the letter just more of her histrionics, delayed. She wrote to him again, this time more savagely, repeating the demand. He responded: 'I cannot secure you the larger competence [sic] you have so frequently mentioned' (writing in his awkward style that led the poet E. E. Cummings to call him 'the only man, woman or child who could write a simple declarative sentence with seven grammatical errors'). 'I can pay with life or reputation, but I can't command such a sum. To avoid disgrace, I will, if you demand it, return to Marion to reside … If you think I can be more helpful by having a public position and influence … I will pay you $5000 per year, in March, so long as I am in public service'. It was the last letter he ever wrote her. She never replied.

The Republican convention gave rise to the legend about a small cabal of grimfaced men convening in a 'smokefilled room' at 2 am to emerge with a candidate whom they then foisted on the voting delegates. Whether or not it happened that way, the convention, exhausted after nine fruitless ballots, stampeded for the Harding compromise on the tenth. No-one pretended he had presidential qualities in the mould of Washington or Lincoln. Harding didn't think so, either. 'Now what do you think of that!', he exclaimed. 'I've been nominated for President! I can't believe it! I've been nominated for President!'

The Cover-Up

Florence had jumped feet-first into the convention scrum, manoeuvering in a way Harding did not, meeting with delegates and party leaders, negotiating and bargaining. Reluctant at first, she now saw that he could be elected, which would keep them in Washington and give her a grand backstage role as first lady. Now the nominee, Harding launched what became known as 'the front-porch campaign', delivering his acceptance speech (much of it written by Florence) from his home on Marion's TK Street, overlooking his neat lawn and white picket fence. The small county-seat town was triumphantly decked out in red, white and blue bunting. But visiting reporters noted one exception – Jim Phillips's department store on Main Street stood bare and undecorated.

TROUBLE IN THE NEIGHBOURHOOD

One neighbour described an episode in which Carrie passed the Harding home and stopped to talk to Warren over the picket fence. Florence flew out of the house, shouting and shaking a finger at Carrie, then threw a flower pot, a garbage bin and foot stool at her retreating figure.

After his nomination, Republican leaders asked Harding the question they probably should have asked earlier: was there anything in his past that might surface and derail his campaign? After a day's thought and a heart-to-heart talk with Florence, he confessed to the Carrie affair, her possession of the incriminating love letters and her blackmailing demand for $25,000. Immediately, the party treasurer, Albert Lasker, called on Carrie in her Gospel Hill home and put it to her bluntly. The party would pay her $25,000 up front, then $2000 a month as long as Harding was in office. She and Jim would be sent on a year-long, all-expenses-paid, round-the-world trip, ostensibly for Jim the drygoods merchant to shop for raw-silk fabric in China and Japan. The only condition was that they must leave immediately and not return to the United States until after the inauguration on 4 March. Within days, Carrie's blackmail attempt successful, the Phillipses were on a transpacific steamer heading to Japan.

In 1921 Harding was elected in a landslide. And, despite the postmortem view of him as America's 'sorriest' president, the Harding administration actually chalked up some notable achievements. Harding initiated the Bureau of the Budget, putting the government on a budget footing for the first time. He held a naval disarmament conference that halted the US–UK–Japan arms race for 10 years; he browbeat the steel industry into reducing its mandatory daily work schedule from 12 hours to 8; and he spoke up strongly (in the segregated deep south) for equal rights for black citizens. But otherwise, the Harding years were a cascade of scandal. His pal, the Secretary of the Interior, Albert Fall, persuaded him to turn over control of the nation's petroleum reserves to his department then, in the so-called Teapot Dome scandal, leased drilling rights to two rich oil magnates for an under-the-table payoff of $500,000. Florence's choice as the director for the new Veterans Bureau, Charles Forbes, was to supervise construction of a vast network of veterans' hospitals. However, he was found to have taken bribes in arranging the contracts, while the hospitals remained unbuilt. Daugherty, named Attorney General, was said to have dispensed justice on a cash-and-carry basis. He claimed self-incrimination privileges and escaped jail. 'In this job, I'm not worried about my enemies', Harding said when, after 2 years of White House poker parties and all-night drinking sessions (despite Prohibition), he realised what was going on. 'It's my friends, my Goddamned friends, who are keeping me awake nights', he lamented.

I don't know much about Americanism, but it's a damn good word with which to carry an election.

– Warren G. Harding

One of those old friends also benefited from closeness to the president. Carrie Phillips persuaded her long-time lover to appoint her German-born and newly naturalised son-in-law, William Mathee, to the US consular service, and to install her brother as a federal ship inspector. She even suggested he name Jim Phillips US ambassador to Japan, and Harding agreed until baffled senators, wondering what in the world qualified a small-town clothing merchant for such an important diplomatic post, declared the idea a non-starter.

'I am not fit for this job and never should have been here', Harding said despairingly as the scandals piled up. Florence, however, gloried in her role as first lady and doyenne of Washington society, where she socialised with the fabulously wealthy Evalyn Walsh McLean, owner of the allegedly accursed Hope Diamond, and Alice Roosevelt Longworth, daughter of the late president. She was also seen as the power behind the throne; newspapers mockingly printed cartoons of 'The Chief Executive and Mr Harding'.

The End of the Affair

In 1923, Florence persuaded Harding to take an exhausting 24,000 kilometre barnstorming trip around the West and Alaska, as a prelude to a 1924 re-election campaign. A fatigued Harding was already showing telltale signs of heart disease. In Alaska he became ill from eating tainted crab. He was given drastic treatment by Florence's private physician, a homeopath whom she had persuaded Harding to apppoint as Surgeon General. Arriving in San Francisco, the weakened president was immediately put to bed. He was found dead the next morning. The death was attributed to a stroke, but Florence refused to allow an autopsy, leading to rumours that he had been poisoned. Less than a year later, after burning many of her husband's official and private papers, Florence died of her lifelong kidney disorder.

President Warren G. Harding throwing the first baseball of the season from the stands. History has not been kind to Harding and he is remembered by some only for the scandals that plagued his life.

Rumours about Harding's mistresses percolated for years afterwards. He was said to have impregnated a Marion friend of Florence's and to have had an affair with a 'tall, beautiful', blonde White House aide who supposedly slashed him during a quarrel. Nan Britton, a Marion schoolgirl who had developed a crush on him, later wrote a book, *The President's Daughter*, declaring that he had impregnated her during one of their secret meetings in his senatorial and then White House offices.

Carrie Phillips retreated into the shadows. She continued to live in Marion, becoming more reclusive and something of a town eccentric. Before World War II she joined the isolationist group, America First, and once more stridently cranked up her pro-German sentiments. She did have enough wherewithal, however, to throw the now-alcoholic Jim Phillips out of their house and to take up the hobby of raising German shepherd dogs. She was living in an increasingly littered and crumbling mansion and walked through town wearing only a fur coat with nothing on underneath. Finally, broke, senile and more than 80 years old, she was confined to a county institution, where she died in 1960. A court appointed an attorney to handle her estate. While carrying out an inventory of her possessions in preparation for sale, he followed up on a town rumour that she had sequestered away diamonds bought on her round-the-world trip. He pried open a locked cupboard and found a locked strongbox. He pried that open, too, and saw piles and piles of letters, some in envelopes, some crumpled and crumbling, yellowed, dog eared, some apparently tear stained, many of them signed 'Warren', or 'Constant' – her code name for Harding – and many written on senate stationery. Familiar with the town gossip and realising Warren's identity, the lawyer recognised the letters' historic value. But not knowing what else to do, he stored them in his office safe, where they remained for 8 years.

In 1963 the historian Francis Russell came to Marion researching a Harding biography, *The Shadow of Blooming Grove* – Harding was born in Ohio, near Blooming Grove. He learned through the local grapevine about Harding and Carrie, and about the lawyer with the trove of letters, and importuned the lawyer for a look at them.

Only solitary men know the full joys of friendship. Others have their family; but to a solitary and an exile his friends are everything.

– Warren G. Harding

He read the letters, took a few notes, and recognised, in spite of the purple, erotic, schoolboy prose and verse, how deeply and passionately Harding had loved Carrie all those years. Her tempestuous physicality had borne him through his loveless marriage to Florence, whose presence he also desperately needed, and through a political career for which he felt himself overwhelmingly unsuited. Certainly he had had affairs with other women, but the letters disclosed that, in the words of the Cole Porter song, he had 'always been true to her in his fashion'.

These letters provide a deep insight into a much-maligned president, and Russell quickly realised that they rightly belonged to history. He persuaded the lawyer to surrender them to the Ohio Historical Society. However, when news of the transfer spread through the town and Harding's and Phillips's relatives and locals found out, they were worried about the possible damage this could do to the town's reputation. They mobilised to stop the embarrassing publication and even convinced the court to put the correspondence under lock and key, which they did, until 2023 – 100 years after Harding's death. Only those letters in Russell's notes and those that had been seen by others have since crept into the public's view.

Whatever his place in the history of the United States, Harding is now Marion's proudest son and its leading attraction. The town high school is Harding High, and the leading inn is the Harding Hotel. The house from which he launched his front-porch political campaign, and the scene of angry furniture-throwing between Florence and Carrie, was purchased by the town and reverentially restored to its early 20th-century appearance. Public subscription paid for the building of a marble, colonnaded Harding Memorial on a commanding hilltop – vaguely resembling one built to a more honoured presidential predecessor, Thomas Jefferson. Here Harding and Florence are interred.

But there is no mention amid the Harding memorials of the 'darling, sweetheart, adorable' woman who attempted to influence history. Only a modest gravestone, next to Jim Phillips, marks Carrie Phillips's resting place in the town cemetery.

A PECULIAR KIND OF LOVE: EDWARD VIII AND WALLIS SIMPSON

MAIN CULPRITS:
Edward VIII (1894–1972), King of England and Bessie 'Wallis' Simpson (1896–1986), American socialite

SCANDAL:
King Edward abdicated from the throne in order to marry his previously divorced mistress, Wallis Simpson

WHY:
Edward was obsessed by Wallis, while Wallis wanted that English crown on her head

You must believe me when I tell you that I have found it impossible to discharge my duties as king as I would wish to do without the help and support of the woman I love.
– Edward VIII in his abdication speech

King Edward VIII pictured in 1936 – the year he succeeded to the throne in January then abdicated in December to marry his mistress, Wallis Simpson.

Queen Mary was about to receive some very unpleasant news. It would be news of a decisive moment in English history that would rock the nation and the British royal family and send shockwaves around the world.

For many weeks Edward VIII had been debating with himself, his cronies and the highest ministers in the British government whether he should remain King of England and, for the time being, a bachelor, or abdicate in order to marry the twice-divorced Mrs Wallis Simpson with whom he was madly in love. As he was deliberating, Edward had kept his family at arm's length, not even confiding in his fretful younger brother, George, the Duke of York – who would have to step in and become king if Edward decided to renounce the crown.

How do you think I liked taking on a rocking throne, and trying to make it steady again? It has not been a pleasant job, and it is not finished yet.

– King George VI to his brother Edward, the ex-king, 3 July 1937

Early in November 1936 Edward broke the news to Prime Minister Stanley Baldwin, that he was determined to marry Wallis Simpson. Rather than cause a constitutional crisis by attempting to compel the government, the Church of England and the people of the empire to accept his decision, the king had decided, reluctantly, to walk away from the throne.

It was a sad, even tragic meeting between Edward and Baldwin, but there was a sense of relief, too. At least the uncertainty was over; Edward had chosen the option that would cause the least damage to the monarchy and the government. There was still a host of details to be worked out, though. How was the ex-king to be addressed? By what title would Mrs Simpson be known? What income would they have? And where would they live? Please, Baldwin prayed, let it not be in England!

Yet all those issues, thorny as they may be, were inconsequential when compared to Edward's next task. He had to tell his mother, Queen Mary, that he had decided not to be king.

He Never Listened

Since the death of her husband, King George V, Queen Mary had lived in Westminster, in Marlborough House, a 17th-century mansion designed by Christopher Wren. On 16 November 1936, Edward went to dinner with his mother. It was a tiny family party, just the queen, Edward, his sister Mary, and his sister-in-law Alice, the Duchess of Gloucester. Even before Edward had broached the subject of Mrs Simpson, everyone at the table suspected why he had come. The duchess made a valiant effort to keep the dinner conversation light by introducing the subjects of racehorses and the new palate of colours chosen for the interior of Buckingham Palace. However, no-one was in the mood for chatter. When the end of the meal came at last the duchess invented some excuse to leave the dining room and hastened away.

Alone with his mother and sister, Edward unburdened himself, explaining that he could not imagine life without Wallis, that he was profoundly in love and that he must marry her. At first the queen and the princess expressed their sympathy but then, as Edward recalled later, 'The word "duty" fell between us'.

In an even voice, keeping perfect control of her emotions, Queen Mary spoke candidly about Edward's dilemma. Mrs Simpson was not a suitable choice for Queen of England and, therefore, not a suitable choice as Edward's wife. If he must have her, then let her be his mistress. Edward's personal happiness was not the point: his primary obligation was to serve his people. Queen Mary and her late husband, King George, had never let personal considerations keep them from performing their duty to the nation. And, she assured her son, there was a great deal of satisfaction, even contentment, to be derived from putting the good of the people, the empire and the monarchy ahead of one's own desires.

Should [Edward] fall in love with someone else I would cease to be as powerful or have all I have today.

– Wallis to her aunt, Bessie Merryman, 4 May 1936

Edward remained unconvinced, so Queen Mary spoke even more bluntly. If he went forward with his plans to marry Wallis Simpson, she would refuse to bless the marriage; furthermore, she would never receive that woman anywhere, under any circumstances.

As maternal ultimatums go, this one was certainly severe. Yet it soon became apparent that Edward hadn't heard a word of it. A few days after the Marlborough House dinner he sent his mother an effusive letter. 'I feel so happy and relieved to have at last been able to tell you my wonderful secret', he wrote. 'God bless you darling Mama for all your sweetness and understanding.' Sometime afterwards Queen Mary showed Edward's letter to a confidant, remarking dryly that she could not imagine how Edward could praise her 'sweetness'. 'I was extremely outspoken', she said, 'and tried to express my displeasure, but I suppose he never listened to what I said'.

Trying to Have It All

There were several reasons why marriage to Wallis Simpson was out of the question. First, the Church of England forbade divorce and remarriage – it would have been the height of arrogance for Edward, as Supreme Head of the Church of England, to make an exception for himself. Next, the royal family, the government and the king's subjects all expected him to marry a woman of spotless character; they would not accept Wallis Simpson as queen because, aside from her two failed marriages, she had made herself notorious by cheating on her last husband with the king himself. If she were permitted to marry Edward, could such a woman be trusted not to cheat on the king, too? (As it happened, after their marriage Wallis was unfaithful to Edward, with an American millionaire named Jimmy Donahue.)

Edward proposed a solution to the prime minister that he hoped would allow him to have everything he wanted: a morganatic marriage, which meant that Wallis would become Edward's wife but would not be crowned queen. Stanley Baldwin, the prime minister, along with the prime ministers of every member nation of the British Commonwealth, all rejected the idea of the king marrying Mrs Simpson under any circumstances. Furthermore, every one of the king's cabinet ministers threatened to resign if he went ahead with the marriage.

In short, Edward's intention to make Wallis Simpson his wife was opposed by his prime minister, his cabinet, the Commonwealth, the Church of England and, judging from the newspapers and the daily mail, the vast majority of the British people. If he tried to push the issue, it was possible that the country would rise up and abolish the monarchy altogether. That was the real issue – the very real threat that the royal family would be cashiered, perhaps even exiled from the country. It had happened in the aftermath of World War I when the three most powerful monarchs in Europe – the German Kaiser, the Tsar of Russia and the Emperor of Austria-Hungary – had all been overthrown.

The Duchess of Windsor Wallis Simpson, 3 December 1936, just days before Edward abdicated. The chic Simpson was generally disliked by the English people.

In the end, Edward had to choose between two options: give up his plan to marry Mrs Simpson and remain king, or marry Mrs Simpson and abdicate.

Humiliating the King

Edward did not shrink from the idea of being king. In fact, he liked the power, the glamour and the adulation that came with the crown. As for his insistence that he must have Wallis Simpson as his queen, many people at the time, from Queen Mary to the street sweepers of London, wondered why the king couldn't keep up appearances by marrying a respectable royal princess from the continent while keeping Wallis on the side as his mistress. Yet a review of the sources, including Edward's and Wallis's letters, reveals that he was determined to have her as his wife; and Wallis had her heart set on being queen. Nothing less would do. On the subject of Wallis's obsession with becoming queen, Leonard Osborne, Edward's butler, recalled how she badgered the king on the subject. 'Mrs S. had got her knife into him', Osborne said. After a night spent with Wallis, Edward was an emotional wreck, 'absolutely limp and a rag', as the king's butler put it.

Perhaps to keep Wallis happy, Edward began to give her some of the perks of royalty. He gave her a fine house in fashionable Regent's Park, sent one of the royal carriages to bring her to the races at Ascot and had news of her goings-on inserted into the official newsletter of the royal household, known as the Court

Circular. Although she was still married to Ernest Simpson, Wallis accepted all these attentions as her due, in hope of a greater honour – coronation as Edward's queen – still to come. Edward felt the same way. 'Wallis', he told one of his cabinet ministers Duff Cooper, 'is going to be queen or nothing'.

Why was the king so obsessed with Wallis Simpson? Philip Ziegler, Edward VIII's official biographer, believes that Wallis aroused in him a kind of sexual excitement unlike any he had ever experienced before. She was the dominating personality in the relationship, and there is a touch of the dominatrix (although without the whip and the leather boots) in the way she enjoyed humiliating the king. For his part, Edward appears to have derived an intense degree of sexual arousal from being humiliated.

The historical record offers eyewitness accounts from a variety of sources of Mrs Simpson treating her royal lover with contempt, even in the presence of others. Alfred Amos, a member of Edward's personal household, recalled that it was Mrs Simpson's habit, after their guests had left, to review the evening and point out every little thing she thought Edward had done wrong. She would keep berating the king and mocking his social gaffes until he wept like a little boy.

An especially notorious incident occurred while Wallis and Edward were in the middle of a dinner party. Edward asked the butler to pass along to the chauffeur his orders regarding the next day's schedule. Raising her arms high above her head, Wallis brought her hands crashing down on the table with such force that it set the china, the crystal and the silverware rattling. All the guests sat there riveted in shocked silence as between clenched teeth their hostess said, 'Never, never again will you give orders in my house!'. For the next 10 minutes Edward blubbered a string of abject apologies.

Based on these stories, Ziegler has suggested that there was something 'sado-masochistic' in Edward's passion for Wallis Simpson. 'It was perhaps a peculiar kind of love', Ziegler wrote, 'but it was love all the same'.

The Many Loves of Prince Edward

Handsome, blond and blue eyed, Edward was a prince right out of the storybooks. In his late teens and early twenties he was almost pretty. He had a slender, athletic build acquired from years of pursuing his favourite sports – swimming, tennis and riding – and he moved with a natural grace that made him an excellent dancer.

His rank, his wealth and his looks all combined to attract women, yet Edward did not lose his virginity until he was 22 years old. It was in France, 1916, during World War I. Two of the prince's older friends treated him to a splendid dinner in Amiens, plied him with fine wine, then handed him over to an experienced and patient French prostitute named Paulette. Although a professional working girl, for the duration of the war Paulette devoted herself exclusively to a certain officer of the Royal Flying Corps. Graciously, he had released her for the evening so she could deflower the future King of England. That one night fired up Edward's dormant sex drive, and soon he was pursuing any woman who caught his eye – including other men's wives.

His first post-Paulette infatuation was Marion Coke, the wife of Viscount 'Tommy' Coke, son and heir of the Earl of Leicester. His next obsession was Sylvia (he called her Portia) Cadogan, one of the Earl of Cadogan's five daughters. In rapid succession he fell in love with at least six other young women from aristocratic families, but they were all schoolboy crushes compared to his first great passion – Freda Dudley Ward, the wife of William Dudley Ward, a member of parliament. She was petite, very pretty, athletic and mad about dancing – in short, she was everything Edward found attractive in a woman. Although both parties indulged in brief flings with other lovers, the prince remained devoted to Freda from their first meeting in 1918 until 1934 when Wallis Simpson replaced her.

Queen Mary with the Duke of Windsor at Marlborough House, about 10 years after his abdication in 1936. Family relations had become strained after his abdication but Edward still visited his mother.

Wallis Meets her Prince

Mrs Simpson met the Prince of Wales in 1931 at the home of Thelma Furness, with whom Edward was having an affair. Mrs Simpson was an American from Baltimore, the daughter of a fine southern family that had a distinguished pedigree but no money. At age 20 she married Earl Winfield Spencer, a dashing aviator in the United States Navy with movie-star good looks. He may have looked like a matinée idol, but in real life Spencer was a violent, sadistic drunk. Wallis endured the abuse for 5 years before she left him.

In spite of her family's objections Wallis sought a divorce from Spencer. Just a few days after the divorce had been granted, she accepted a marriage proposal from Ernest Simpson, a stable, sober, well-to-do, well-educated British businessman. For the next 6 years Wallis lived the comfortable life of the wife of a prosperous and dependable, but dull, man.

That initial meeting in 1931 drew Wallis Simpson into the Prince of Wales's inner circle. By 1934 she had replaced both Thelma Furness and Freda Dudley Ward as the woman the Prince of Wales needed. He showered her with gifts of jewellery and even cash. She spent long evenings playing cards and dancing to the gramophone at the prince's private retreat, a mock castle known as Fort Belvedere. Ernest Simpson, like Freda and Thelma's husbands before him, did not make a fuss.

Dark haired and pale skinned, Wallis Simpson was not a renowned beauty, but she had a tremendous sense of style. Long and lean, with hips so narrow they have always been described as 'boyish', she seemed at first glance an unlikely fashion icon, yet Wallis had impeccable taste. The English society photographer, Cecil Beaton, who photographed Wallis on several occasions, said, 'Her taste in clothes shows always a preference for bold simplicity'. The finest designers of her day — Schiaparelli, Mainbocher, Molyneux and Pacquin — created clothes for her that accentuated her figure and made her appear not just glamorous, but gorgeous. No woman in the royal family dressed as well or looked as good as Wallis Simpson. In the tiny circles in which she and Edward moved, Wallis's glamour was much admired. But her fashion sense did nothing to ingratiate her with ordinary English women.

By the time his father, King George V, died in January 1936, the prince was emotionally dependent on Wallis. He had convinced himself that he could not bear the burden of monarchy without Wallis as his queen.

But Wallis and Edward were not the only illicit lovers in their circle. Her husband, Ernest, had begun an affair with Mary Raffray, on old schoolmate of Wallis's. In fact 10 years earlier, Mary had been Wallis and Ernest's matchmaker. It was the new king who approached Ernest Simpson, asking him to release Wallis. Under English law at the time, certain proof of adultery was the simplest way to secure a divorce. And so Mary and Ernest travelled to an English seaside resort, checked into a hotel and the next morning ordered breakfast served in their room so the waiters would see the couple in bed together and thus be able to testify in court that Ernest Simpson had been unfaithful to his wife, Wallis.

NAIVE BUT NOT NAZIS

Why, 4 months after their marriage and 2 years before the invasion of Poland, did the Duke and Duchess visit Nazi Germany? Some have argued that Edward and Wallis sympathised with the Nazi cause. Others have suggested that Edward and Wallis hoped the Nazis would win the war, conquer England and install them as king and queen.

The truth is much less inflammatory. They were not welcome in England. In France the aristocracy were courteous but cool. But the Nazi government were delighted to entertain the Duke and Duchess of Windsor.

Philip Ziegler believes that Edward, still hurting from the break with his family, decided to visit Germany to soothe his bruised ego and show his new wife that he was still a person of consequence.

Perhaps the worst that can be said about them is that they were politically naive; but they weren't Nazis.

From Object of Love to Object of Vitriol

For most of 1936 Edward floundered about, trying to find some way to marry Wallis, see her crowned queen, and thus keep both the crown and the woman he needed. Yet from every quarter, Edward's desire to see Wallis crowned queen was met with resounding a 'No!' The prime minister, Stanley Baldwin, said it was impossible. The prime ministers of every land in the British Commonwealth concurred with Baldwin's opinion. The Archbishop of Canterbury, the senior cleric in the Church of England, offered to try to persuade Edward to give up Wallis and embrace his obligations as king, but the good man's offer was rebuffed. The royal family refused even to shake the hand of the notorious Mrs Simpson; the idea that they would support Edward's quest to make her queen was more than absurd, it was deeply offensive. Finally, there was the British public. They loved their king, but they loathed Mrs Simpson – and how much they loathed her they would make plain very soon. With every rank of the British establishment and British society all against him, Edward was forced at last to recognise the harsh truth: if he must marry Wallis, abdication was his only option.

Wallis had wagered everything on becoming queen. By appearing almost constantly with Edward and even living with him she had compromised her reputation. By divorcing her husband she had cleared the way for what she had hoped would be her royal wedding. And she had boasted in a letter to her favourite aunt, Bessie Merryman, back in America, that she enjoyed her power as the king's mistress, to say nothing of the money, jewellery and other gifts Edward showered upon her. Now, understanding that she had gambled and lost, and foreseeing the firestorm of outrage that was sure to follow the king's renunciation of his throne, Wallis fled the country, taking refuge in France.

Meanwhile, Edward's mother, Queen Mary, made one last effort to reason with her son. When they met sometime during the first week of December, Queen Mary suggested that Edward give up Wallis Simpson 'for the sake of the country'. Her son's response shook her badly. As she later wrote to a friend, Edward 'stormed and raged and shouted like a man demented' at her suggestion. It was the final burst of temper from a man who knew that he could not have everything he wanted – the crown and Wallis Simpson as his queen. So he chose Wallis.

That emotional outburst was Edward's last as king. Once he made his decision, the bureaucrats went to work drafting a formal document by which Edward renounced the throne in favour of his brother George. The text of what was called the Instrument of Abdication was completed about midnight, 9 December 1936. It didn't seem proper to let such an awesome document linger in a filing cabinet or on some functionary's desk so, at 1 am, it was delivered to Edward's favourite residence, Fort Belvedere. The king was scheduled to sign it the next morning.

After a nearly a year of high drama, the actual abdication was strangely anticlimactic. A few minutes after 10 am, with his three younger brothers as witnesses, Edward signed the Instrument of Abdication, thereby declaring to the world his 'irrevocable determination to renounce the throne for Myself and for My descendants'. From that moment, the melodrama and the crisis were over.

A few hours later, from a radio hook-up at Windsor Castle, Edward addressed the nation. Almost pleading, the former king told his former subjects, 'You must believe me when I tell you that I have found it impossible to discharge my duties as king as I would wish to do without the help and support of the woman I love'.

It was an eloquent and touching speech. Even today, reading the complete text one cannot help but feel sympathy for Edward. The English public, however, did not see it that way. The former king was deluged with mail; hundreds of letters from angry correspondents arrived daily. Some of them attacked Wallis in the vilest language. While the household staff tried to keep the letters from Edward, he did see some of them and was stunned by what he read. He had always been coddled, pampered, cheered and adored. To be the object of such intense vitriol frightened him. But the ordeal was not yet over.

Immediately after the broadcast, Edward said goodbye to his family and sailed to France to join Wallis. But the familial bond was not broken by any means. George VI, the new king, was bombarded by telephone calls from Edward in which the ex-king went on for hours about what he needed and what was due to him, interrupting his lengthy tales of woe only to offer his brother unsolicited advice on how to be king. On one occasion George, swamped with work, declined to take a call from Edward and sent a message urging him to call back in the evening. Fruity Metcalfe, one of Edward's closest friends recalled, 'He [Edward] couldn't believe it! He's been so used to having everything done as he wishes'.

Cash and a Title

One thing Edward wished for most emphatically was a considerable annual pension either from the royal family or the English government. On the day of his abdication he had about £900,000 in cash, not to mention other assets such as income-producing properties he owned as Duke of Cornwall and Duke of Lancaster. Yet, before his abdication, Edward, perhaps reaching for as much as he could get, had represented himself to his brother George as close to flat broke. George, overwrought by his older brother's prospective abdication and his own impending coronation, made a generous pledge of an annual income of £25,000 from his own pocket. A few weeks later, when the government officials who had been reviewing the ex-king's finances showed the new king just how wealthy Edward was, George felt that he had been bamboozled.

George's first reaction was to nullify his promise, but Edward made such a fuss about it as both a moral and legal obligation – he had persuaded George to put the promise in writing and sign it – that in the end the new king gave in and agreed to honour the £25,000 income.

THE HENRY VIII PRECEDENT

In any discussion of Edward VIII and Wallis Simpson, invariably someone will bring up the case of Henry VIII, England's most married monarch. 'Henry divorced two wives and remarried', the critics say, 'and no-one made him abdicate'.

In point of fact, Henry never divorced any of his six wives. He had his marriage to his first wife, Catherine of Aragon, annulled arguing that, since she was his late brother's widow, their marriage from the very beginning had not been lawful in the eyes of God or of the state.

His fourth marriage to Anne of Cleves was also annulled on the grounds of non-consummation. Henry found the poor woman so unattractive he refused to make love to her.

As for wives numbers two and five, Anne Boleyn and Catherine Howard, it is true that Henry beheaded them, but at least he never disgraced his family by divorcing them.

On another point, however, the royal family was intractable. Edward was given the title of Duke of Windsor and upon her marriage to Edward, Wallis would become the Duchess of Windsor. But would she be referred to as 'Her Royal Highness'? Wallis wanted the title badly, saying it would give her 'extra chic'. Edward wanted Wallis to have the title because it would validate his choice. But now the entire royal family closed ranks against the couple. In a conversation with prime minister Stanley Baldwin, King George asked a rhetorical question, 'Is [Wallis Simpson] a fit and proper person to become a Royal Highness after what she has done in this country?' Then he answered his own question. 'I and my family and Queen Mary', he said, 'all feel that it would be a great mistake to acknowledge Mrs Simpson as a suitable person to become royal. The monarchy has been degraded quite enough already.'

The royal family's decision made Edward angry and bitter. Although it rankled, he kept his emotions under control for some time, but then he lashed out at his mother and his brother, the king. In a stinging letter to Queen Mary, he asserted that, thanks to his relationship with Wallis, 'for the first time in my life I am happy'. Then he went on to suggest that his mother was a hypocrite for sending him her good wishes for his marriage. In a letter to King George, Edward insisted that he was the injured party, that he was the selfless one. 'What other motive had I in abdicating except a patriotic one?' he asked his brother.

On 3 June 1937, at an enchanting French Renaissance castle, the Chateau de Candé in Touraine, Edward, the former King of England, married Wallis Simpson. No member of the British royal family attended the wedding.

MOTIVATION

anger

charity

envy

faith

gluttony

greed

hope

lust

pride

sloth

'I AM NOT A CROOK': RICHARD NIXON AND WATERGATE

MAIN CULPRIT:

Richard Milhous Nixon (1913–94), 37th President of the United States of America (1969–74)

SCANDAL:

Instructed his aides to organise a break-in and wire-tapping of the opposing Democratic Party headquarters

WHY:

He was coming up for re-election and wanted to find out what the Democrats were up to

---

I don't give a shit what happens. I want you all to stonewall it, let them plead the Fifth Amendment, cover up or anything else.
– Richard Nixon to his advisers

Richard Nixon answers questions about the Watergate scandal in the East Room of the White House, Washington DC, October 1973.

That's odd, thought Frank Wills, the night security guard at the Watergate Hotel in Washington DC. He was peering at a piece of tape pasted across the latch of the door between the parking garage and the basement stairwell in the hotel and office complex. The tape appeared to be holding the door in an unlocked position. Wills shrugged, thinking that most probably the cleaning crew put it there while bringing up supplies and then forgot to remove it. He stripped off the tape, closing the door and continued on his rounds. But when he returned an hour later, at 2 am, the tape had been replaced and the door was once more ajar. Clearly someone was in the building and wanted that door to remain open so they could easily slip in and out. That was enough for Wills. He immediately telephoned the Washington police.

That single telephone call on 17 June 1972 set off a far-reaching scandal that convulsed the US government and kept the nation in an uproar for more than 2 years. It implicated a sitting war-time president in serious crimes, and compelled the only resignation of a president in US history. Some of the president's closest advisers and staff members were convicted and jailed as a result of what the president's spokesman had initially dismissed as 'a third-rate burglary'. A pair of intrepid and indefatigable *Washington Post* investigative reporters kept the scandal aflame with continuing disclosures of White House transgressions. Their tenacity won them American journalism's highest award as well as book and film contracts. Their work ignited a Congressional investigation that stopped just short of impeachment, and making the suffix 'gate' forever synonymous with mischief at the highest reaches of society.

A Straitlaced Man

Although he had been a congressman, a senator, vice president and president, Richard Nixon had been described as 'an introvert in an extravert's job'. He kept largely to himself, confided in almost no-one, even his unhappy wife, and trusted nobody. He was uneasy in small groups and one-on-one situations; he seemed unable to relax. Trying once to show that he was a regular guy for a campaign photograph, he went for a walk on the beach – wearing a navy-blue suit, a white shirt and tie and tasselled loafers – which made him look both stiff and ludicrous, as well as afraid of getting his feet wet. One White House staff member said that in 5 years he had never seen Nixon with his jacket off, even in his private study. Another topped that: he had never seen the president with his jacket unbuttoned. Nixon was also given to angry outbursts, which his staff learned to ignore. 'I want them all fired!', he would shout. 'I mean it this time!' Then there was the legendary time Air Force One made a particularly rough landing. 'That's it!', the president raged. 'No more landing at airports!'

Yet for all the president's quirks and mistrust, the Nixon administration recorded some strong achievements, especially in foreign policy. He opened diplomatic relations with China, supported its entry to the United Nations, and was the first presi-dent to visit that once-shunned country. He also visited Moscow, negotiating the Strategic Arms Limitation Treaty, which in turn led to the Anti-Ballistic Missile Treaty and to a decade-long détente with the then Soviet Union. Although definitely a political conservative, he embraced some liberal causes, establishing the Environmental Protection Agency, the Occupational Health and Safety Administration and the nation's first federal affirmative action program.

The Department of Dirty Tricks

When police arrived in response to Wills's summons early that June morning, their torches surprised five men who had broken into the offices of the Democratic National Committee. They were in the process of wire-tapping the telephones. Nixon, America's 37th president, and the Republican Party had just launched a full-scale drive for a second, 4-year presidential term (which Nixon would win by a landslide in November, before his part in the scandal was fully known) and a vigorous campaign against the Democrats. The tapping was set up as they wanted to listen in on the Democrats' plans for the presidential race. Unfortunately for party and candidate, the five burglars were soon linked to a group called the Republicans' Campaign to Re-Elect the President, sardonically known as 'CREEP'. At first, campaign officials wrote them off as a rogue element in the campaign, overzealously operating on their own: why, after all, would a president or his staff dirty their hands with such illegalities, particularly when the president was ahead nineteen points in the polls and re-election seemed all but certain? White House staff and campaign officials simply looked blank when asked about any possible connection. And of course, the president knew nothing, nothing at all, about what his spokesman called 'a third-rate burglary'... Now about that Vietnam war …

But as disclosure followed incriminating disclosure, the president watched defiantly, stubbornly, then angrily, as the investigations edged closer and closer until the White House was engulfed in scandal and the dreaded words, 'possible impeachment', were heard.

The first chink in the presidential armour appeared when the five burglars were arraigned on burglary charges. They were obviously no ordinary burglars. A high-priced and snappily dressed attorney was on hand to represent them, even though it was Sunday morning. When arrested, all five had been wearing business suits and ties, and they were wearing blue surgical gloves that would leave no fingerprints. They were also carrying $32,000 in $100 notes. Asked their occupation, two of them said, 'anti-communist'. James McCord, one of the five, answered in a low voice that he was a retired government employee. What branch of government? he was asked. In an even lower voice, he answered, 'CIA'. Finally he acknowledged that he was currently the CREEP Chief of Security and a former CIA officer.

Inside a notebook taken from McCord, officers found the telephone number of E. Howard Hunt, along with the initials 'WH'. It was discovered that Hunt had previously worked in a White House special investigations unit. The group, headed by Hunt and G. Gordon Liddy, was known as 'the Plumbers' because their task was to stop leaks of information the administration did not want revealed. They also organised a 'department of dirty tricks', which targeted and attempted to smear Democrats and anti-war groups. Their most notorious deed was a break-in and ransacking of the office of a Los Angeles psychiatrist who had treated Daniel Ellsberg, a former employee of the Pentagon and State Department. Ellsberg had leaked the secret Pentagon Papers describing the government's Vietnam war plans. When the papers were published in the New York Times, Ellsberg was charged with espionage, theft and conspiracy. Hunt and Liddy hoped to prove that Ellsberg was mentally unstable, but found nothing useful, so they trashed the office to cover their tracks.

One of those present at the arraignment was 27-year-old rookie Washington Post reporter, Bob Woodward. When McCord acknow-ledged his CIA background and officers disclosed that the burglary target was the Democratic campaign headquarters, Woodward's ears pricked up. This was not an ordinary burglary. Soon he and a co league, Carl Bernstein, encouraged by Post editor Ben Bradlee, began digging deeper and deeper, questioning more and more sources inside the government. Finally they connected with the ultimate anonymous insider, nicknamed 'Deep Throat'.

> *Get a good night's sleep and don't bug anybody without asking me.*
>
> – Richard Nixon to his re-election campaign manager

Deep Throat

For 30 years, Deep Throat's true identity was Washington's most tantalising mystery. Whoever he was, he had vast inside knowledge about the investigation and the principals, which he furnished to the Post reporters. The White House made frantic efforts to discover the culprit. Various names were suggested and investigated; a much-mentioned candidate was General Alexander Haig, who became Nixon's chief of staff. Woodward had known the true Deep Throat for many years and made the original contact, but he resolutely kept the secret. In the book All the President's Men, he told how he and Deep Throat had met regularly at 2 am in an underground carpark. They followed all the traditions of spycraft. When Woodward wanted a rendezvous, he moved a potted plant on his apartment balcony. When Deep Throat had something to share, he left a mark on page 20 of Woodward's delivered New York Times.

Deep Throat was not unmasked until 2005, when he was 86 years old and in failing health. W. Mark Felt had been Number Two, acting associate director, at the FBI at the time of Watergate. Thus every scrap of paper relating to the Watergate investigation crossed his desk. Then in his 80s, Felt was not able to recall many details and no longer able to disclose his reasons for participating or, but it was no secret that Felt had hoped to succeed J. Edgar Hoover in the agency's top position. Instead, the White House had named L. Patrick Gray, an attorney whom Felt regarded as a naive lightweight and easily manipulated. He also resented Nixon's using the Bureau for political purposes. Anyway, Woodward said, Felt had served as an FBI counter spy during the Cold War and so he surmised that he liked the thrill and intrigue of cloak-and-dagger work. The undercover source never actually showed them FBI files or gave them specific FBI data, according to Woodward; he only confirmed what their investigations had uncovered and when they were mistaken. 'Follow the money!', he told them once, in a sentence that was to become part of the language. They later found a trail of cheques from an attorney affiliated with CREEP to the bank account of one of the burglars.

Washington Post Reporters Bob Woodward (left) and Carl Bernstein (right) walk from federal court after covering the Nixon Watergate hearings, 1974.

'Deep Throat' was the major source for the page one article Bernstein and Woodward wrote on 10 October 1972, just before the November election, which disclosed that Watergate was not an isolated event. The story stunned Washington: 'FBI agents have established that the Watergate bugging stemmed from a massive campaign of political spying and sabotage conducted on behalf of President Nixon's re-election and directly by officials of the White House and Committee for the Re-election of the President'. The activities, according to information in FBI and Department of Justice files, were aimed at all the major Democratic presidential contenders and – since 1971 – represented a basic strategy of the Nixon re-election effort.

One Year of Watergate Is Enough

Nonetheless, in November Nixon was overwhelmingly re-elected, carrying every state except Massachusetts and, on 20 January, he was inaugurated for a second term. He took that as vindication and wrongly assumed Watergate was old news. But the Watergate storm clouds were rolling over the White House. Just days after the inauguration, the Watergate burglars, plus Liddy and Hunt, went on trial. All pleaded guilty except Liddy and McCord, who were convicted by a jury. Judge John J. Sirica, known as 'Maximum John' for delivering harsh penalties, sentenced each of them to 30 years in prison, but hinted at leniency if they would come forward with a full explanation of the burglary. In a letter to the judge, McCord then confessed that he and the other burglars were under 'political pressure' to plead guilty and remain silent, that perjury had been committed at the trial and that the break-in was approved by higher-ups. That was not the news the White House wanted to hear.

In his January State of the Union speech, Nixon had called for a quick ending to the scandal: 'One year of Watergate is enough', he told the joint session of House and Senate. Even as he spoke, however, the Democratic-controlled senate was making efforts to get to the bottom of things, especially the possible role of the president in the cover-up. On 7 February 1973 the Senate voted 70 to 0 to establish a select committee to investigate Watergate. A respected folksy, but legally sharp, former judge – North Carolina Senator Sam Ervin – was named chairman of the bipartisan panel. Ervin made it clear that covering up a burglary, which after all was a felony, was a criminal offence, no matter who did the covering up.

The next months were to illuminate the worst side of Nixon's personality. 'I don't give a shit what happens', he told his advisers as the scandal was building up. 'I want you all to stonewall it, let them plead the Fifth Amendment, cover up or anything else.' And Nixon himself showed himself a master of stonewalling. He denied, dodged and dismissed everything. One of his first acts after the burglar's trial was to call in White House Counsel John Dean, who had served as a kind of point man on the legal aspects of Watergate. According to Dean's later testimony before the Senate committee, a major topic of discussion was how much money would be needed to guarantee the continued silence of the burglars. Money had already passed into their hands but, considering the sentence, probably more was needed – Dean mentioned perhaps $1 million over a period of years. If it came to that, the president said, the money could be obtained; he knew where from – in cash. The same day, $75,000 was delivered to the lawyer for E. Howard Hunt. Dean told Nixon he was worried about the White House role in the burglary and the continuing investigation. 'There is a cancer growing on this presidency', he said. Nixon praised Dean's work but a few weeks later, in another meeting, Dean told the president that he had been required to meet with federal prosecutors. As Dean was to say later, he suspected he was being set up to be the White House fall guy if any cover-up charges were brought.

They lied, and then they lied to cover their lies, and then more lies to cover those lies, so that in the end no-one knew the truth, if there was any truth.

– Bob Woodward

Two weeks later Dean was fired. He left the White House, but not until he had removed documents incriminating the president, put them in a safe-deposit box and sent the key to Judge Sirica. On the same day, Nixon announced the resignations of his most intimate advisers, Chief of Staff H. R. Haldeman, Domestic Policy Adviser John Ehrlichman and Attorney-General Richard Kleindienst, praising them, however, as dedicated public servants.

The TV Trial

The Senate Watergate Committee began televised hearings on 17 May 1973 and the next day Nixon appointed Archibald Cox, a respected Harvard Law School professor, as special prosecutor to conduct an independent investigation into Watergate. For most of the summer, Americans were glued to the television drama; 85 per cent of the country is said to have watched. People mimicked Ervin's down-home accent and admired Dean's blonde wife, who sat behind him in the hearing room. Dean was an early witness and told, in full detail, of meetings in which the president had suggested hush money and other ways that the White House and CREEP roles could be concealed.

Nixon, however, denied everything. He issued a long statement in which he claimed no advance knowledge of the burglary or the early efforts at cover-up. He said Dean was lying about the hush money conversation and about the president's role. When he learned about it, he said, he had initially ordered the FBI not to investigate the break-in, claiming that national security was involved. He also admitted that he had approved the wire-tapping of reporters and administration aides. Again, he insisted, it was a matter of national security. The White House had to know who might dangerously be leaking top-secret information.

'What did the president know, and when did he know it?', Senator Howard Baker of Tennessee famously asked in the committee hearings. Baker was a Republican stalwart, a Nixon supporter and later a Republican minority leader in the Senate, and his question indicated that senators of both parties now suspected that Nixon was deeply implicated in the cover-up. Then came the bombshell that was to bring down the Nixon White House. Alexander Butterfield, a White House aide who kept the president's schedule, was being questioned by committee staff members. One staff member asked, just in passing, if there was any kind of recording device in the Oval Office, just to record important discussions that might be held there.

'I was hoping you weren't going to ask me that', Butterfield replied. Yes, there were secret microphones in the president's desk, around the walls, in the president's hideaway study and at the presidential retreat at Camp David. They automatically put on tape every word spoken in the president's presence. Every tape was maintained in a presidential archive. That was on a Friday afternoon. On Monday, Butterfield gave the same testimony before the senators and the investigation took a sharp, new and, for Nixon, disastrous direction.

The White House stonewalled again. Other presidents had recorded Oval Office conversations too – it was important to have the precise words, both for history's sake and for the president to review. The crucial meetings during the Cuban missile crisis in 1962 had all been recorded by the Kennedy administration, for instance. And the recording had to be secret: if participants knew they were being recorded, they might speak less freely, hold back and not give the president the full benefit of their thinking. Also, it was a matter of executive privilege. When Special Prosecutor Cox asked for tapes that might reveal discussions about the burglary and cover-up, the White House adamantly refused.

The following months were a non-stop tug of war involving the Senate Committee, Special Prosecutor Cox and the presidency. Nixon was fully aware that the tapes might contain damaging information and he fought vigorously – almost viciously – to keep them under lock and key. Cox subpoenaed nine tapes that he considered relevant. Nixon turned his demand down. Judge Sirica ordered him to surrender the requested tapes. Citing executive privilege, the White House appealed. The appellate court, too, ruled that Nixon must turn the tapes over to investigators.

The events of 20 October 1973 have been dubbed 'The Saturday Night Massacre'. When Cox continued to press for the tapes, Nixon accused him of disloyalty. He ordered Elliot Richardson – who had succeeded the resigned Kleindienst as Attorney General – to fire him. Richardson refused. When Nixon repeated the order, Richardson resigned. Nixon then ordered Richardson's deputy, William Ruckelshaus, to carry out the dismissal. Ruckelshaus also refused and resigned. Finally Solicitor General Robert Bork, the third in line, issued the order.

In the midst of all the uproar and chaos, Vice President Spiro Agnew was indicted on corruption charges dating from his tenure as Governor of Maryland. Although not related to Watergate, the Agnew resignation added to the atmosphere of scandal that was now enveloping the White House.

A screen capture of the television at precisely 9.01 pm on 4 August 1974, showing the CBS news coverage of President Nixon's on-air resignation.

Leon Jaworski was named Special Prosecutor to replace Cox. But if the president thought Jaworski's appointment would defuse his legal troubles, he was mistaken. By now, the House of Representatives was openly talking of impeaching the president and, in the face of what the tapes might reveal, Nixon's own attorneys were gently suggesting he might want to consider resignation. And Jaworski was proving no pushover. He insisted he needed all relevant tapes, not just the handful already under subpoena. White House attorneys then listened to the wanted tapes and testified before the grand jury about them. It was disclosed that one crucial tape, covering Oval Office conversations between Nixon and Chief of Staff Haldeman, included 18 minutes that were not recorded. The White House lamely explained that the 18-minute gap had been an unintentional erasure. While transcribing the tapes, they said, Nixon's longtime and dedicated secretary Rose

Mary Woods had accidentally pressed the foot pedal and kept her foot there for 18 minutes while answering a telephone call. It was not an explanation many people, including the senators, believed, and photos proved that Woods would have had to be a contortionist to press the pedal and reach the telephone at the same time.

While the tape stalemate continued, the grand jury indicted Haldeman, Ehrlichman, former Attorney General and campaign chairman, John Mitchell, and four other White House aides for conspiracy to obstruct justice. A part of the indictment that was kept secret also named Nixon as an unindicted co-conspirator. Meanwhile, the House Judiciary Committee also began to subpoena tapes as it considered possible bills of impeachment against the president.

It looked like his adversaries had Nixon cornered. But Nixon, who prided himself as being 'tough', a man who stuck to his guns no matter what, yielded; but just a little. He agreed to submit edited transcripts of the tapes. The White House was turned into an enormous transcribing–typing pool and he submitted more than 1250 overwhelming pages of transcript, which were then released to the public. Gone, however, were any incriminating conversations or titbits, along with anything the White House might consider to jeopardise national security. Gone, too, were any racial slurs, four-letter words or bouts of anger. Poring over them, investigators and voters alike were staggered by the torrent of apparent foul language that permeated the discussions. The words 'expletive deleted' passed into the language and became a standing joke.

> *I brought myself down.*
> *I impeached myself by resigning.*
>
> – Richard Nixon

Edited transcripts weren't enough for Jaworski. He wanted physical possession of the tapes, to check whether anything material to his investigation had been omitted. He also reduced the number of tapes he wanted. Give them up, he told the president, and dangled a tempting bait before him – if the president yielded the smaller number of tapes, Jaworski would keep secret the unindicted co-conspirator portion of the grand jury recommendation. 'I am not a crook', Nixon had said in a televised address and he must have been torn about possibly preserving what was left of his image. But full disclosure of his role in the cover-up could have far more lasting, even disastrous, consequences. He refused Jaworski's offer. Jaworski appealed to the Supreme Court.

Nixon's attorneys had listened to the tapes and recognised how damaging they were. As delicately as they could, they suggested that the president resign, rather than face what looked like certain impeachment. Nixon was outraged. He said he would not be the first American president to step down; besides, he was not guilty of anything. As soon as he understood the nature of the offence, he had insisted on a full investigation, let the chips fall where they may. It was unjust. He was a fighter and he had never run from a fight in his life. The attorneys shook their heads; he really seemed to believe what he was saying. As a last resort the attorneys suggested he listen to the tapes himself. He was a lawyer, he would see the strength of the case against him – especially if he listened to three conversations with Haldeman on 23 June 1972, a week after the break-in. 'All right, goddammit', Nixon agreed.

He was still president, though, with important duties to perform. In the next weeks, he visited the Middle East to further negotiations with Israel and the Palestinians. He went to Moscow for a summit meeting with Leonid Brezhnev to press for the the Strategic Arms Limitation Treaty. While he was gone the US Supreme Court ruled on Jaworski's appeal. The court ruled 8 to 0 to uphold the subpoenas.

'The Smoking-Gun Tape'

It was all over then. The White House was forced to surrender the crucial tape of 23 June 1972 – what became known as 'the smoking-gun tape'. Amid the static, rasps, curses and background noise, one could clearly hear the president's voice, giving Haldeman his cover-up instructions. He was to have the CIA director tell the FBI to back off from their investigation, 'Ah, for national security reasons. It would bring up the whole Bay of Pigs thing. Just tell them that. They have to just drop it'. By the time the transcripts of the smoking-gun tape had been fully reported in the press on 5 August 1974, the House Judiciary Committee had passed three articles of impeachment against the president.

On 8 August in a televised address, Nixon announced that he was resigning the presidency as of noon the next day. According to Secretary of State Henry Kissinger, Nixon spent his last night with him, drinking, sobbing and praying; a loner brought down by his own faults.

MOTIVATION

anger
charity
envy
faith
gluttony
greed
hope
lust
pride
sloth

AN AFFAIR TO REMEMBER: JOHN PROFUMO AND THE FALL OF A GOVERNMENT

MAIN CULPRIT:
John (Jack) Dennis Profumo (1915–2006), British Secretary of State for War (1960–63)

SCANDAL:
Had an affair with a showgirl who was sleeping with a Soviet spy at the same time

WHY:
Caught up in the sleazy hi-jinks of British upper-class society and irresistibly attracted to Keeler

There was a young girl called Christine
Who shattered the party machine
It isn't too rude
To lie in the nude
But to lie in the House is obscene.
– A popular limerick from 1963

John Profumo's affair with good-time girl Christine Keeler was blamed for the Conservative government's loss at the following year's general election.

It was Saturday, 8 July 1961 and the London society osteopath Stephen Ward had invited a few friends to the cottage he rented from one of his patients, Lord Astor. The cottage was part of Cliveden, Astor's sprawling estate by the Thames in Buckinghamshire, which had for decades been a meeting place for high fliers in politics and the arts.

Ward had been given access to the swimming pool by Lord Astor and, with his guests wilting in the heat, suggested that they go for a swim. They set off for the main house, a three-storey mansion built in 1851. Ward was in his element, deep in the heart of the aristocracy, with a group of young, attractive acolytes around him. The most captivating of them all was a 19-year-old model and showgirl, Christine Keeler.

Arriving at the pool, Keeler put on one of the swimsuits provided for guests, but it was old-fashioned and didn't fit her very well. Ward said she should take it off, which she did, and dived into the pool naked.

Lord Astor and his dinner guests (which included the President of Pakistan) heard the sounds of frivolity, and some of them came out to investigate. Astor led the way with his friend John (Jack) Profumo, the Secretary of State for War in the Conservative government, beside him. They were treated to the sight of Christine splashing about in the nude. Ward greeted them, kicking Keeler's swimsuit behind a bush as he did so. Keeler, embarrassed, climbed out of the pool and tried to cover herself with a small towel.

Astor invited Ward and his friends into the house, and Profumo gave Keeler a tour. At one point he coaxed her into a suit of armour, to the amusement of other guests.

Ward, Keeler and a few more girls were back at the pool the next day, this time accompanied by their friend Yevgeny 'Eugene' Ivanov, the senior naval attaché at the Soviet embassy. Keeler was attracted to the good-looking but serious Russian, yet Profumo continued his flirtation with her. The two men vied for her attentions all day, even having a swimming race, but it was Ivanov who left with her that night. However, Profumo got Keeler's phone number from Ward. And he was a tenacious man.

Jack and Christine

Profumo was educated at Harrow and Oxford, and entered parliament as a Conservative in 1940. He had an important job, a glamorous wife – the British film star Valerie Hobson – and was respected by his colleagues. One might wonder why he would risk all that for an affair with a showgirl, but really, there was nothing that unusual about such a liaison and, if word of it did leak, he would have relied on the press to be discreet.

Christine Keeler's background couldn't have been more different. She had grown up in the Berkshire village of Wraysbury where, for several years, she lived with her mother and stepfather in a converted railway carriage. At 16, she became pregnant to a local boy. She tried, but failed, to give herself an abortion with a knitting needle. The baby was born prematurely and soon died. Shortly after this Keeler moved to London. She was working in a restaurant when a showgirl from Murray's Cabaret Club in Soho introduced her to the club's owner, who took Keeler on. She performed topless on stage, wearing a costume of gold and feathers, and between shows sat with the club's male customers, encouraging them to buy bottles of champagne. Also working at the club was a friendly girl named Mandy Rice-Davies. The two girls didn't particularly like each other and their personalities were quite different – Christine was naive and insecure, Mandy confident and calcula-ting. What they did have in common was ambition.

Keeler met Stephen Ward when he turned up at the club one night. He was captivated by her and, exercising his considerable charm, persuaded her to move into his flat. The relationship he proposed was a non-sexual one, which puzzled Keeler at first – he was virtually the only man she had met who didn't seem interested in getting her out of her clothes. She later compared their relationship to that of a brother and sister, but also claimed that he had a Svengali-like hold on her. 'He had full control of my mind', she told the court at Ward's trial. 'I used to do more or less anything he told me to.'

Keeler soon realised why she was so useful to him. Ward, the son of a Hertfordshire vicar, was 47 when he met Keeler. He was an incorrigible social climber and gossip who lived to mingle with the rich and famous, and prided himself on a list of patients that included Winston Churchill and other leading politicians. He was also a talented artist and had sketched several members of the royal family. But his services extended beyond osteopathy and art. He was continually on the lookout for beautiful, usually working-class, girls who, after being suitably groomed and coached, could entertain his illustrious friends – and attract new ones. He was never a pimp in the normal sense of the word, though. While money may have occasionally changed hands between the exotic specimens who passed through his flat in Wimpole Mews, for Ward it was never about money.

Ward had a knack for sensing people's sexual tastes, and liked to encourage them further. It was another way for him to gain power over them. Later, there would be many lurid tales told of parties at his flat, where guests could puff on marijuana cigarettes as they watched orgies through two-way mirrors. Then there was the infamous dinner party where the meal was served by a man wearing only a mask and a tiny apron, who ate from a dog bowl and asked to be whipped. At the time, he was rumoured to be a cabinet minister.

A Brief Affair

Soon after the weekend at Cliveden, Profumo began to visit Keeler at Ward's flat. It was on one such visit that their affair began. 'We had been talking and he was being charming and flirting', recalled Keeler, 'and the next thing we were kissing and he was leaping on top of me'.

Profumo, with his balding head and pudgy features, was hardly a specimen of rugged good looks. Nevertheless, as Henry Kissinger memorably declared, power is the ultimate aphrodisiac, and the affair was conducted with gusto. They had sex in the back of his car, as well as Ward's flat while he was out. One night Profumo plucked up the courage to take Keeler to his home in Regents Park. As the servants slept, he showed her through its darkened rooms, and they finished up by making love on the Profumos' marital bed.

Christine Keeler, the model and showgirl at the centre of the Profumo Affair, October 1963.

Throughout this whole time, Keeler was also seeing Ivanov. As Mandy Rice-Davies later told reporters, 'The farcical thing about it all was that, on more than one occasion, as Jack left Christine at the flat, Ivanov walked in'.

Word of Profumo's relationship with Keeler reached British intelligence almost immediately. MI5 was already interested in the friendship of Ward and Ivanov – who was known to be a Soviet spy – and had interviewed Stephen Ward. Now the head of MI5, Sir Roger Hollis, sent word to Profumo to be careful about what he said in front of Ward. While they were concerned that sensitive information might be relayed to Ivanov from Profumo via Keeler, MI5's main interest in the situation at this point was the possibility of compromising Ivanov sexually, so that they could obtain information from him or force him to defect. Profumo was asked whether he would help in such an operation, known in the trade as a 'honeytrap'. He declined.

However, the conversation made Profumo realise just how dangerous his relationship with Keeler could be for his career, and he immediately broke it off. Although they would see each other occasionally over the next few months, the affair was over. It had lasted little more than a few weeks.

Profumo must have thought that this pleasant dalliance would never be revealed and could now be consigned to memory, but rumours were already starting to spread. By mid-1962, cryptic references to the affair were appearing in the press.

If the affair had taken place only a few years earlier, the rumours might have remained just that. But this was an extraordinarily volatile time in Britain, both socially and politically. The year 1960 saw the Lady Chatterley Trial, which ended with Penguin Books being given permission to sell D. H. Lawrence's previously banned novel, thus signalling a relaxation of censorship. In 1961 a group of former Oxford students started a satirical magazine called *Private Eye*, which aimed to revive the sort of fearless, irreverent reportage not seen in the country since the early 19th century. The so-called 'satire boom' reached television the following year with *That Was the Week that Was*, hosted by David Frost, in which the government, the church, royalty and many other formerly sacred cows were lampooned mercilessly in skits and songs. The response was outrage – and huge television ratings.

THE MAN IN THE MASK

The dinner party at which the man in the mask made his appearance was at the home of Mariella Novotny and her husband, antiques dealer Horace 'Hod' Dibben. Novotny was a well-known hostess who claimed to have slept with, among others, John F. Kennedy, Robert Kennedy, Malcolm X and Brian Jones. Lord Denning, while investigating the Profumo Affair, managed to track down the man in the mask (who said he was 'grievously ashamed at what he had done') and, in his report, dismissed the rumour that he was a cabinet minister. It is now generally thought that he was Anthony Asquith, a noted film director and the son of a prime minister.

The Conservative government of Prime Minister Harold Macmillan had won a landslide victory in 1959, but the economy was bedevilled by rising inflation and industrial unrest. Macmillan's signature line, 'Most of our people have never had it so good', was looking increasingly hollow. The Labour opposition, in disarray for years, had regrouped under Harold Wilson and were looking like a viable electoral alternative.

And overshadowing all of this was the Cold War. The year 1962 was the year of the Cuban missile crisis, which brought the world closer to nuclear war than ever before. Espionage was on the front pages with the trial of William Vassall, an Admiralty official who had been caught spying for the Soviets after falling victim to a KGB honeytrap (a homosexual one in his case).

Sex, politics and espionage – the Profumo–Keeler–Ivanov entanglement had all three elements in spades. It was a big, delicious bomb of a scandal just waiting to go off. It only remained for someone to light the fuse. That someone was a young man called Johnny Edgecombe.

Shots through a Door

Edgecombe was one of two West Indian lovers that Christine Keeler was juggling in 1962, the other being Aloysius 'Lucky' Gordon. Gordon had become violent, assaulting Keeler in the street and, she claimed, holding her hostage for 2 days with an axe. Keeler bought a Luger pistol to protect herself and asked Edgecombe to be her minder. Soon afterwards, the two men met in a Soho club, and Edgecombe slit Gordon's face open with a knife.

After going into hiding, Edgecombe asked Keeler if she would help him find a solicitor to defend himself. Having found out that Edgecombe had taken another lover, Keeler refused, and said that she would instead be testifying against him in court.

An enraged Edgecombe turned up at Stephen Ward's flat. Keeler had moved out by that time, but happened to be there visiting Mandy Rice-Davies. When she wouldn't let him in, Edgecombe fired several shots into the front door with the gun Keeler had bought. The police were summoned and Edgecombe was arrested.

This had nothing to do with Profumo, Ivanov or Ward, but it was enough to break the story open. The incident gained extensive press coverage. Keeler, in the media spotlight, her name already attached to salacious rumours, started to talk about her relationship with Profumo. The Labour MP George Wigg received an anonymous telephone call. 'Forget the Vassall case', he was told. 'You want to look at Profumo.'

Just before 11 pm on 21 March 1963, Wigg stood up in the House of Commons and declared, 'There is not an honorable member in the House, nor a journalist in the press gallery, who in the past few days has not heard rumour upon rumour involving a member of the Government front bench'. He referred to 'a Miss Christine Keeler, and a Miss Davies, and a shooting by a West Indian', and demanded that the home secretary deny the truth of the rumours.

Discretion is the polite word for hypocrisy.
– Christine Keeler

His speech threw the government into a panic. Macmillan was telephoned at 1 am. A car was sent to collect Profumo from his home, where he was fast asleep after taking a sedative, and rushed him back to Westminster. Confronted by a number of senior government figures, he assured them that he had not had sex with Keeler. They worked until 4 am preparing a statement. Profumo went home to find the house surrounded by reporters.

At 11 am, Profumo made his statement to the House of Commons. He said that he had first met Keeler and Ivanov at Cliveden, and had subsequently seen Keeler on a number of occasions when visiting Ward's flat. 'Miss Keeler and I were on friendly terms', he said. 'There was no impropriety in my acquaintance with Miss Keeler.' He ended on a note of defiance, threatening to 'issue writs for libel and slander if scandalous accusations are made or repeated outside the House'.

He left parliament with the cheers of his Conservative colleagues in his ears. That afternoon he went to the races, and was photographed next to the Queen Mother.

Keelermania

Profumo's statement did nothing to stem the rumours. George Wigg went on television and talked about a threat to national security. Keeler, while negotiating to sell her story to a newspaper, handed over one of Profumo's letters to her. The satirists were having a field day.

Stephen Ward did not handle scandal well. When he saw a cartoon in *Private Eye* with a cryptic reference to 'Ward' and 'Astor', he rushed over to the magazine's offices, assuming they knew all. They didn't, but Ward proceeded to fill in some of the gaps for them. He paid a similar visit to George Wigg after seeing him on television.

Wigg made a written record of their conversation, which Labour leader Harold Wilson later called 'a nauseating document, taking a lid off the corner of the London underworld of vice'. Ward, who knew he was in deep trouble now, seemed to think that by telling the truth, or his version of the truth, to anyone who would listen, he would be able to save himself. He couldn't have been more wrong.

Events moved quickly now. The police, having received anonymous letters alleging that Ward had been living off 'immoral earnings', began a criminal investigation. They interviewed Christine Keeler and she gave them details of her relationship with Profumo, confirming what almost everyone either knew or suspected, that he had lied to parliament. The editor of the *People* told the police that the paper was planning an exposé, and the police passed this information on to the government. Profumo, who was holidaying in Venice with his wife, received a telegram from the Lord Chancellor asking him to return immediately.

Dr Stephen Ward leaving Marylebone Magistrates Court in police custody, bound for Brixton Prison, 1963.

After talking things over with his wife, Profumo returned to London and handed Macmillan a resignation letter. 'I said there had been no impropriety in this association', he wrote. 'To my very deep regret I have to admit that this was not true.' Macmillan replied, 'This is a great tragedy for you, your family and your friends'.

Christine Keeler was now the most notorious woman in the country. The press pursued her relentlessly; people wanted to meet her; men propositioned her. There was talk of a movie in which she would play herself. While the movie was never made, its producers did organise some publicity shots. The photographer was Lewis Morley, who had a studio in the same building as Peter Cook's satirical nightclub, The Establishment. Morley had used up several rolls of film when the producers demanded that Keeler strip for some nude shots, saying it was in her contract. Keeler baulked at this. The situation was getting tense when Morley suggested a compromise. He asked everyone to leave the studio, turned his back as Keeler undressed, then had her sit back to front on a chair. The resulting photograph became an icon. A few weeks later Morley shot David Frost in the same pose, and since then the photo has been endlessly reproduced and parodied.

Ward on Trial

After his resignation, Profumo went into hiding. The heat was now on Ward, and it was painfully clear that the establishment planned to make him the scapegoat for everything. Ward, deserted by the upper-class friends he had so carefully cultivated, grew increasingly desperate. On 8 June he was arrested and charged with living off the immoral earnings of prostitutes.

The trial at the Old Bailey which followed was another media sensation. Keeler and Mandy Rice-Davies had to battle their way through crowds to get into the court, where they both testified against Ward. All the sleazy stories of whippings and orgies were aired. When told by the prosecution that Lord Astor had denied having sex with her, Mandy Rice-Davies responded by saying, 'Well, he would, wouldn't he?'. The quote instantly travelled around the world, on its way neatly skewering the perceived hypocrisies of the upper classes.

The evidence against Ward was flimsy and, if anything, he had given money to the girls he was accused of living off. He poked his tongue at reporters as he arrived each day and generally put on a brave face, but it was all an act. On the day the verdict was to be handed down – guilty on two counts – he committed suicide by taking an overdose of sleeping pills.

The government commissioned Lord Denning to prepare a report on the affair. When it was released, people queued up to buy it. Denning trawled methodically through all the rumours surrounding the affair, but poured cold water on most of them and concluded that there had been no breach of national security. Nevertheless, there is no doubt that the Profumo Affair played a major part in the Conservatives' loss of the 1964 election to Harold Wilson's Labour Party.

Christine Keeler sold her story to the papers and bought a Georgian house with the proceeds. She has since become a major source for conspiracy theories about the affair. She now believes that Stephen Ward ran a spy ring which included Sir Roger Hollis, and says that the whole point of that hot summer day at Cliveden was to entrap her.

Eugene Ivanov was called back to Moscow soon after the scandal broke, possibly committed to a psychiatric hospital, and was never heard from again.

THE MAN WITHOUT A HEAD

While the British public were transfixed by the Profumo Affair, another juicy scandal was bubbling away. This was the long-running divorce case brought by Lord Argyll against his wife. Lord Argyll's legal team had named four correspondents in the case (although they allegedly could have named more). At one point, they produced a photo which purportedly showed Lady Argyll performing fellatio on a man. Only the man's body was visible in the picture, and he was dubbed 'the man without a head'. Rumours wrongly identified him as Duncan Sandys, the Commonwealth Secretary. He went to prime minister Macmillan and offered to resign. Macmillan, already with his hands full with the Profumo imbroglio, couldn't face another scandal and refused to accept the resignation. Later, in his report on the Profumo Affair, Lord Denning investigated the rumours and found there was no truth to them.

And Profumo? Forgiven by his wife, but his name now shorthand for sexual shenanigans, he devoted his life to working tirelessly and anonymously for a London east end charity, raising millions over the years. To his death he never uttered a word in public about the scandal that brought down his glittering career.

MOTIVATION

anger

charity

envy

faith

gluttony

greed

hope

lust

pride

sloth

THE PRIME MINISTER WHO GOT THE SACK: GOUGH WHITLAM

MAIN CULPRIT:
Edward Gough Whitlam (1916–), Prime Mininster of Australia (1972–75)

SCANDAL:
He was sacked by the Queen's representative

WHY:
Bad judgment led to a political and financial crisis

Well may we say 'God save the Queen' because nothing will save the governor general.
– Gough Whitlam

Australian Prime Minister Gough Whitlam addresses reporters outside the parliament building in Canberra after his dismissal by the Governor General, 1975.

November 11 was traditionally a day of reflection, a day to honour the soldiers who fought in World War I, but on Remembrance Day, 1975, in Canberra, the Australian capital, no-one could have guessed the events that were about to transpire. It would become a day that no Australian would ever forget.

Sir John Kerr, the Australian Governor General – the titular head of state – had called opposition leader Malcolm Fraser to his lodgings at Yarralumla in Canberra. Prime Minister Gough Whitlam had also been summoned to meet the Governor General that day, and had been told to arrive at exactly 1 pm. He thought that his meeting with Kerr would be a private conference. He had no idea that Fraser had been instructed to arrive at the meeting at exactly 10 minutes after 1 pm.

Whitlam was running late, and by the time he arrived, Fraser was ensconced in an anteroom quietly sipping a glass of scotch. Fraser probably had an inkling of what was about to happen. He had been secretly meeting with Kerr, gradually increasing the pressure on him to somehow intervene in the current political financial crisis that was consuming the nation. He was hoping that Kerr would 'crack' and be persuaded to take the unprecedented step – to use the latent constitutional power accorded to him to sack the elected Labor government.

Gough Whitlam was a little frazzled when he arrived at Yarralumla. Apart from his Remembrance Day activities, he had met with Malcolm Fraser earlier that morning in an attempt to resolve the current political crisis, but, just as on all the other occasions, his endeavours proved fruitless. After a few pleasantries, Kerr, with cigar in hand, asked Whitlam if he would be prepared to call a general election as a way out of the political impasse. Whitlam said no. Kerr then informed Whitlam that he had decided to exercise his power under Section 64 of the Australian Constitution, and was terminating Whitlam's commission as Australia's Prime Minister. A letter of termination was handed to Whitlam. Too shocked to do anything else, Whitlam took the letter. Kerr said, 'we will have to live with this decision'. Whitlam replied, 'You certainly will'. Minutes later, Kerr called Fraser into his office and appointed him caretaker prime minister until a general election could be held. Malcolm Fraser smiled casually as he put his right hand on the Bible and was sworn in. As news of the sacking of the Government reached the media, people began demonstrating in the streets. Violence broke out in all major cities.

Whitlam's chauffeur-driven car sped through the streets of Canberra. He was anxious to confer with his Labor Party colleagues. He returned to Parliament House and greeted his peers with the immortal words, 'The bastard's sacked us'. Having lost none of his rapier-like wit, he sat down to lunch commenting that a condemned man usually has his meal prior to execution but he was having his afterwards. A chorus of 'we want Gough' could be heard throughout the grounds of Parliament House, where more than 2000 angry people had gathered. Whitlam, not willing to waste a precious opportunity, went out to meet his enraged fans and curious spectators. He uttered the historic words: 'Well may we say "God save the Queen" because nothing will save the Governor-General'.

The fallout from Sir John Kerr's decision would haunt him for the rest of his life. If the Queen of England couldn't dismiss the British government, how could her representative in Australia have dismissed the Australian government? In political terms, a man elected by no-one had dismissed a government elected by the people. This precedent would alter the Australian political landscape forever.

Whitlam, the Flawed Leviathan

Sir John Kerr, Governor General of Australia, with Queen Elizabeth, on her visit to Australia to celebrate her Jubilee in 1977, his final year in office.

In December 1972, after 23 years of conservative Liberal Party government, Gough Whitlam was elected as the twenty-first prime minister of Australia. A stalwart of the Labor Party, he was considered a brilliant, articulate and highly focused, but somewhat arrogant individual at the peak of his powers. Whitlam believed he was destined to bring about fundamental reform in social, economic and foreign policy. His vision was of a just and more tolerant society. Herein lay his weakness. Apart from being volatile and tempestuous, he believed that the individual could, through the power of reasoning, be brought on side. It was a naive belief that would eventually cost him dearly. He was also reluctant to consult his Labor Party colleagues and, instead, relied on a small, transient group of ministers, officials and staff for advice.

Whitlam was also a poor judge of character. He even chose Sir John Kerr as Governor General, believing that he would be both malleable and grateful – an ideal agent for the government. He appointed him without even authorising a background check. Had he done so, he would have found that Kerr was an 'ideological soldier of war', a cynic with no allegiance to any political stance. He would also have discovered that Kerr had a severe drinking problem, which would eventually affect his judgment. Known as an 'ideas man', Whitlam was not renowned for his attention to detail. These failings of character would let Whitlam down, time and time again.

Nevertheless, in his first year in office Whitlam was responsible for initiating a startling number of reforms. He axed tertiary education fees, believing in free education for all Australians. Abhorring racism, he abolished the last vestiges of the 'White Australia Policy'. He encouraged the appointment of women to judicial and administrative positions. He helped establish free health insurance which was ultimately coined 'Medibank'. His government introduced a 'no fault' divorce system as well as abolishing the death penalty for all federal offences. Aboriginal people were given their own national consultative committee. The voting age was reduced from 21 years to 18 years. A supporting benefit for single-parent families was introduced. In the area of foreign policy, his reforms were equally impressive. Conscription came to an end. Australia's commitment to the Vietnam War was halted. The Peoples Republic of China was formally recognised. Cumbersome tariffs that made Australia uncompetitive were slashed. Overall, these were among the most radical and sweeping reforms in Australian history.

However, Whitlam's 'crash through' style of government was bound to make enemies. Piecemeal reforms were fine when the economy was booming, but when the world recession began to bite, the Labor Party's political enemies were given plenty of ammunition. Between 1974 and 1975, inflation rose to over 17 per cent. Unemployment figures were at a post-Depression high, numbering in excess of 270,000 jobless. Wage levels were also worrying and running over 27 per cent. In 1974, only halfway through his first term in office, Whitlam went to the polls and secured a second term, only this time with a reduced majority. The time was right for the emergence of a new breed of political animal; an opposition leader with teeth. Welcome to the fore, Malcolm Fraser.

On 31 October 2002 Whitlam stated that he never would have appointed Kerr as Governor General had he been aware of his drinking problem. 'He never told me, but while he was governor general under me he twice went to the Prince of Wales Hospital to be dried out.' Fraser appointed Kerr as ambassador to UNESCO, but he lasted only 3 weeks due to public outcry. Kerr was shunted into a permanent, injured exile, condemned like Wagner's 'Flying Dutchman' to joylessly wander the world's pleasure spots.

The deepening world recession in early 1975 played into the hands of frontbencher Malcolm Fraser. At first he declared his allegiance to Bill Snedden, the leader of the Liberal opposition. He went on record saying, 'I'm not going to challenge against you Bill, I can assure you of that'. But by March 1975, he was standing against him. Not only did he oppose Snedden in a backroom party spill, he thoroughly trounced him. Fraser began to reinterpret the function of the Senate as a political tool to thwart Prime Minister Whitlam and undermine the existing government. He concluded that by deferring supply – using his majority in the Senate to starve the government of funds it desperately needed to pay its bills – he could force the government into calling an early election. At the same time, he began leaking information to the Governor General, Kerr, in an attempt to convince him to intervene in the political and constitutional crisis.

Whitlam, rather than appealing to the conscience of swinging independent senators and attempting to get them on side, simply ignored them in the belief that the party that holds a majority in the lower house controls government. Normally this convention was considered immutable, but Fraser was not going to be bound by tradition. If it served his interest to convince the Senate not to pass crucial government bills, he would do so. His justification was that Australians were living through the 'worst of times' and had to be protected from such an incompetent government. Asked by a journalist about the question of passing the budget, Fraser answered: 'If a government is elected to power in the lower house, it can expect to be elected for a 3-year term … unless quite extraordinary events intervene'.

The Cairns–Morosi Imbroglio

Economically speaking, Australia was experiencing a new phenomenon: stagflation − a simultaneous rise in inflation combined with economic stagnation. The Australian economy needed a prudent treasurer; one that would balance the books and would give the impression of stability. Unfortunately Whitlam made the wrong choice. He selected Dr Jim Cairns as his treasurer; a position that Cairns never wanted and was manifestly unsuited to.

In 1974, Cairns had met a government personal assistant, Junie Morosi, and was immediately attracted to her. Soon they began a sexual affair. Cairns appointed Morosi as his private secretary, despite being warned by senior Labor politicians not to do so. Cairns, besotted with Morosi, made the ridiculous political blunder of allowing himself and Morosi to be interviewed by the popular tabloid newspaper *The Sun*, believing that they would be given an impartial 'fair go' simply because Morosi knew the interviewing journalist. The following day, the paper's headline read 'My Love for Junie' and a story detailed their affair. It also described that Cairns now believed that the only way to discover 'truth' was through the discovery of one's feelings. The Liberal Party immediately embarked upon a smear campaign and Cairns became the victim of ridicule.

A furious member of Cairns's staff exploded: 'Jim, you are carrying on like a lovesick kid … you've spilled your guts in *The Sun*'. Cairns continued to defend Morosi, saying that the real problem lay in the fact that she was an outspoken Asian women. Morosi and Cairns were seldom out of the newspapers in the early part of 1975. Whitlam allowed this imbroglio to be played out without intervening.

However, Cairns was finally sacked by Whitlam on 2 July 1975. He became the first deputy prime minister in Australia's history to have his position terminated. Whitlam was given little choice as Cairns had deliberately misled parliament.

As Treasurer, Cairns was involved in an attempt to borrow up to $4 billion in overseas loans and, instead of going through the proper channels and authorising the Treasury to obtain the loans, he commissioned a friend, George Harris, to be the government's agent. Cairns had agreed to provide Harris with a 2.5 per cent commission on any secured loans. During stubborn questioning by the Liberal opposition in the House of Representatives, Cairns stupidly denied the existence of the letter offering Harris the 2.5 per cent commission. Having lied before parliament, a furious Whitlam demanded that he resign. Cairns refused, believing he had done nothing wrong, so Whitlam drove to Yarralumla and asked the governor general to withdraw Cairns's commission. However, Whitlam's problems with his senior ministers were only just beginning.

The Khemlani Loans Affair

Rex Connor, Minister for Minerals and Energy, caused an even greater scandal while trying to secure the required loan monies. Connor became involved with the shadowy figure of Tirath Khemlani, a Pakistani broker. Had Connor done the necessary background checks, he would have discovered that Khemlani, a tailor by profession, had neither the contacts nor the experience to secure the $4 billion that the government needed.

A consummate politician, Malcolm Fraser ousted Billy Snedden from the Liberal Party leadership in early 1975, before controversially being sworn in as caretaker prime minister after the dismissal of the Whitlam Labor Government in November of that year.

Connor, considered by most as a dreamer, was a devout believer in 100 per cent ownership of Australian resources. His purpose in securing the overseas loan of $4 billion was to 'buy back the farm' and prevent overseas ownership. He wanted to use the monies to build a national underwater pipeline, provide Australia with a year's supply of oil and construct uranium mines and solar energy projects. In light of the value of Australia's combined primary resources, he considered the $4 billion dollar loan as 'peanuts'.

Without bothering to check Khemlani's credentials, Connor provided Khemlani with a letter of mandate to obtain the requisite loan. This was highly unusual in that it bypassed the proper channels. Such loans would normally be generated through the Treasury office, but Conner saw no reason why the monies couldn't be raised in a more 'efficient' manner. Of course, public servants within the Treasury caught wind of Conner's attemptto raise the monies and leaked the information to the press and to the Liberal Party. This provided Malcolm Fraser with atremendous opportunity to go on the attack. It enabled him to ridicule Whitlam's personal judgment, especially his choice of bumbling ministers.

For weeks on end, Khemlani kept telling Connor that the money would arrive 'in just a few days'. This led to the comical scenario of Rex Connor and his staff waiting diligently around the telex machine, only to be told, day after day, night after night, that the money was 'on its way'. Connor would leave his office at around 2 am each morning, believing that the money would surely be there the next day. The Liberals, under Fraser, began to smell a rat and increased pressure on

Whitlam by asking why was Connor being so secretive. What was he hiding? Why weren't the conventional banking channels through the Treasury being used? And, what were the monies actually to be used for?

Eventually, after considerable pressure in the House of Representatives, Whitlam informed Connor that all loan negotiations with Khemlani must cease as of 20 May 1975. When Malcolm Fraser became aware that Connor had continued to deal with Khemlani well after that date and brought it to the attention of parliament, Whitlam had no option but to ask Connor to resign. This of course created yet another media circus and further undermined the Whitlam government in the eyes of the public. The popular press presented the opinion that the government was unable to be trusted and was completely out of control. Fraser, constantly increasing the pressure on the government, maintained that Whitlam had deliberately misled parliament and insisted on the formation of a Royal Commission to investigate the matter fully.

As Michael Sexton, political observer and New South Wales Solicitor General, put it, 'Kerr was a genuine cynic, an ideological soldier of fortune ... a man who believed in nothing but himself'.

Gough Whitlam, through poor personal judgment and unwillingness to keep check on the actions of his key ministers, was in serious trouble.

Constitutional Twilight Zone

One of the fundamental tenets of the Australian political system rests on the convention that the political party with a majority in the House of Representatives is allowed to govern. Whitlam put this succinctly when he said, 'The government survives as long as I have a majority in the lower house'. Even Fraser was on record supporting this convention. Unfortunately for Whitlam, the Australian Constitution under Section 64 confers significant powers upon the Governor General, the direct representative of the Queen in Australia.

Until 1975, Section 64 was interpreted to mean that the Governor General can only act on the advice of the Prime Minister. Convention had it that the position of the Governor General was purely ceremonial. When Gough Whitlam swore in Sir John Kerr as this titular head of state, never in his wildest dreams did he contemplate the possibility that the Governor General, put into power by one man, could overthrow a government chosen by the Australian people. Once again, Whitlam had not done his homework. Had he looked into the matter, he would have discovered that Kerr, a great cynic, believed in little except his own abilities and powers. He was neither religious, nor atheistic. He supported neither the Labor Party nor the Liberal Party. He was not a liberal, nor was he a socialist. Perhaps Whitlam was relying on the personal bond between Kerr's first wife and Gough's wife, Margaret.

By mid 1975, due to a series of accidents and political manoeuvering Labor lost control of the Senate. Malcolm Fraser had successfully starved the government of the funds it needed to govern. Whitlam, never one to back away from a political stoush, fought Fraser head on. As Whitlam put it, 'This government will not be held to ransom … we will not surrender'. On 16 October 1975, in an unprecedented step, the Senate stopped the government's supply of money. The government had about 3 weeks left before it ran out of money to pay its public servants and subcontractors. Australia had entered a 'constitutional twilight zone'. Fraser was heard to say, 'If we keep our nerve we will starve him out'. Whitlam, on the other hand told Kerr that, 'They are going to crack. John, the Senate is on the brink of an historic climb down'.

The Dismissal

The primary political question of the time became: could the position of the Governor General be used as a means of breaking this political impasse? What powers and discretionary authority could be exercised by the Governor General? It was around this time, late October 1975, that Kerr began to develop a personal grudge against Whitlam, feeling that Whitlam was being condescending and treating him like his personal lackey. Encouraged by his new wife, who hated the fact that she was being snubbed by Whitlam and his wife, Margaret, Kerr began to believe that it was quite proper to exercise independent judgment. He was under no obligation to do Whitlam's bidding. Kerr began to interpret Section 64 of the constitution literally.

At around the same time, Malcolm Fraser turned to Robert Ellicott QC for legal advice. Ellicott concluded that if the government cannot obtain supply, it was within the Governor General's powers to dismiss the government and appoint a prime minister who would then call an election. Kerr, breaking convention, asked for a copy of the Ellicott document and was buoyed by its conclusions. He then turned to Ellicott's cousin, Chief Justice Sir Garfield Barwick, and asked for his interpretation, knowing full well that his opinion would not diverge from Ellicott's. Once again, he broke with convention and went behind Whitlam's back. Later, in his biography, Kerr was to say, 'Never again did I feel that I could talk to the prime minister'.

Whitlam was warned by his treasurer, Bill Hayden, that the Labor government was about to be dismissed. Whitlam, again showing poor judgment, simply laughed at the suggestion and told Hayden that he worried too much. However, Fraser's policy of 'slow strangulation' was well and truly working. Behind Whitlam's back, Kerr maintained regular contact with Fraser. They were playing Whitlam like a marionette.

On 6 November 1975 Kerr said to Fraser, 'I wonder how much longer we can gamble with this country?'. Kerr sought solace from his wife, who encouraged him to act, to somehow intervene and break the deadlock. She said that if he could not act independently, what was the point of having a Governor General?

While sipping on a glass of wine, Kerr drafted Whitlam's termination letter: In accordance with section 64 of the constitution 'I hereby terminate your appointment'. Kerr did not sign the letter in the hope that the morning of 11 November would bring about a compromise. However, after Fraser's rejection of Whitlam's suggestions in their meeting, the scene was now set for the most famous dismissal in Australian history.

After Kerr had given Whitlam the letter of termination, Malcolm Fraser returned to the House of Representatives and advised ministers of both parties of the sacking of the Whitlam government. His declaration was met with cries of 'Shame, Fraser Shame'. Labor ministers walked past Fraser's office loudly singing 'Solidarity Forever'. Chaos broke out in both houses of parliament and a general election was called for 16 December 1975. This election ultimately resulted in the political decimation of the Labor Party and conservative forces rallied behind Fraser's Liberal government.

Since that famous dismissal, no political party has ever invoked Section 64 of the Australian Constitution, and the position of the Governor General is now considered ceremonial at best.

MOTIVATION

anger
charity
envy
faith
gluttony
greed
hope
lust
pride
sloth

ALL THE PRESIDENT'S WOMEN: FERDINAND AND IMELDA MARCOS

MAIN CULPRITS:
Ferdinand Edralin Marcos (1917–89) and Imelda Romualdez Marcos (1929–), the President and the first lady of the Philippines (1965–86)

SCANDAL:
They swindled their country out of countless millions, perhaps even billions of dollars

WHY:
He had a weakness for beautiful women, and she had a weakness for beautiful shoes

I did not have three thousand pairs of shoes, I had one thousand and sixty.
— Imelda Marcos

Ferdinand Marcos, President of the Philippines, declared martial law in his country in 1972 and served as a ruthless dictator until February 1986, when he and his wife, Imelda, fled into exile in Hawaii.

The First Lady's face burned with anger and disappointment. For any other person in the world this might be a moment of triumph. Arriving in Hawaii to set up a new life of luxury with billions of dollars to cater to every whim – an impossible dream for most, but not for this lady – it was the darkest day of her life. Imelda Marcos, one of the richest and most powerful women in the world had been forced into exile with her husband, Ferdinand, the disgraced ex-president of the Philippines. The pair felt no sense of shame. They were outraged and disappointed and already plotting their comeback. Marcos considered himself to be the saviour and father to the Philippines. Imelda thought of herself as a mother to her country and a river to her people – yet all the world press could talk about was shoes.

When she and her husband were ousted from power in 1986, Imelda's wardrobe closets in the Malacañang Presidential Palace yielded more than 3000 pairs of size 8 shoes. The press had a field day. Every day there was a new story about shoes. Brown shoes. Black shoes. Alligator shoes. Plastic disco shoes with heels that lit up. Stiletto heels. Sandals. Pumps. T-straps. Ferragamo shoes. Andrew Geller shoes ...

The papers also revelled in accounts of her vast collection of lingerie, including a bulletproof bra, and mocked her for her ostentation. But there was nothing about her achievements. Where did water, power, food and shelter come from and who had provided this as governor of metro Manila for 11 years? And who reclaimed hundreds of hectares and built homes for the people and gave them pieces of land? Who built the housing projects for the poor? Who brought food to centres and mobile stores to bring cheap food to the people? Imelda Marcos – protector of her people in every aspect, from womb to tomb.

She was incensed that the press was portraying her as a frivolous woman. So what if she had a large wardrobe? She was the First Lady of a great emerging nation – its star and its servant; the people expected her to present herself well as their representative to the world. Surely some money should be budgeted for that?

When she went into exile she considered herself penniless. She took with her 'only' thirty-two articles of luggage. But in that luggage was an estimated $9 million in gems, cash and bonds. Eleven priceless gems were stashed in a Kleenex box carried through customs by her granddaughter. Indictments handed down in the Philippines and the United States stated that Ferdinand and Imelda raided the country for a minimum of $684 million – but a closer figure would probably be several billion.

Although one American ambassador described Imelda as a woman of very limited resources – 'having a shrewd native intelligence, a certain physical charm, but a limited education' – she managed to become not only one of the best-shod women in the world but also one of the richest. Her secret? The love of a man. Ferdinand Marcos's weakness for beautiful women gave Imelda an immense power over him. At first the power lay in her youth and beauty but, after 25 years of marriage, when he took a mistress, Imelda settled for blackmail.

The Golden Years

It began in blazing sunshine. In April 1954 the 36-year-old Ferdinand Marcos was serving his third term in congress as chairman of the Import Control Committee and, even though his name had been mentioned in allegations of bribery and pay-offs, he was seen as a rising political star. He had just announced his engagement to his live-in lover, beauty queen Carmen Ortega. However, after he met another beauty queen – the girl they called the Muse of Manila – Imelda Romualdez, Ferdinand was so stunned by her beauty that he dumped Carmen and immediately proposed marriage to Imelda. The next day he reinforced his proposal with a symbolic love message of two roses. One of the roses was a closed bud to symbolise his young love for her, the other was in full bloom to represent the love that was to blossom between them. Eleven days after they met they were married. She was 24 years old.

Former Philippine First Lady and beauty queen, Imelda Marcos, known as the 'Steel Butterfly', pictured in 1976.

In December 1965 Ferdinand Marcos was swept into power by a wave of popular support and judicious vote buying. He and his beautiful young wife were the darlings of the poor and down-trodden of the nation. Their presidential campaign was founded on the liberal disbursement of peso-stuffed envelopes and his slogan, 'This nation can be great again'. In support of her husband, Imelda formed important alliances with the society matrons of Manila and quickly bloomed into a wily and persuasive lobbyist. They were a formidable double act on the hustings, promising new roads, schools and the uprooting of corruption. He earned the endorsement of the Civil Liberties Union with his unshakeable opposition to Philippines' involvement in the war in Vietnam.

The early years were golden. The United States, through the CIA, was keeping close tabs on Philippine politics. The islands had become an important strategic staging point for the US military in Vietnam and they needed a cooperative government in place to ease the way. Ferdinand quickly became a willing partner. One of his first acts as president was to break his campaign promise and commit troops to Vietnam. The United States awarded him $125 million in aid packages and the money was used to modernise the Philippine army.

Marcos put the rejuvenated army to work on road projects and utility upgrades. A rice production program took just over a year to turn a rice shortage into a surplus and the country became a rice-exporter before the end of his first term.

This was the time when Ferdinand saw Imelda as his greatest asset and he appointed her to top government posts. She became an ex officio member of the cabinet, governor of metro Manila and director of human settlements. As director of cultural affairs, she built arts centres and remodelled the face of Manila. She cast herself as an international cultural diva and even imported the Beatles to perform.

But by 1969 the golden years were beginning to tarnish. Imelda had come to think of the Philippines nation, its treasury and all its assets as her own personal fortune.

THE KENNEDYS OF SOUTHEAST ASIA

At every meeting Ferdinand would finish with the same popular promise: 'I will give you everything you want – except my wife!'. Ferdinand and Imelda sang duets for the crowds and were a big hit – they were the JFK and Jackie Kennedy of Southeast Asia.

Alone, or with her husband, Imelda eventually owned all or part of the national airlines and banks. She also owned a resort on Long Island. The pesos flowed in a torrent while she hobnobbed with the Shah of Iran. She threw sumptuous parties surrounding herself with celebrities, such as the pianist Van Cliburn and the actor George Hamilton. Upon all of her newfound celebrity friends she lavished fabulous gifts. She once flew a sixty-guest entourage in four government jets to the coronation of the King of Nepal. Her shopping sprees in New York, Paris and London became legendary. She owned a mind-boggling jewellery collection and her luxury apartments and mansions were stuffed with Michelangelos, Botticellis and Canalettos. She flaunted this unbridled excess in a country where the average wage was less than $2 a day. Ferdinand's greatest asset was fast becoming a liability and that was when Ferdinand made what was possibly the greatest mistake of his career. He found another woman.

The seeds of the downfall were sown when the president decided that his image needed a facelift. He was well known for telling highly embroidered tales of his exploits during World War II. He liked to depict himself as a fearless guerilla hero, but the facts were otherwise. US military records later raised serious questions about his wartime conduct – among those documents was an arrest order accusing him of wartime racketeering. But none of this deterred Ferdinand. His imaginary gallantry had been a winning factor in the first election and he hoped to regenerate support by making a movie that would turn his mythical fantasies into history. It would be called *Maharlika*. The part of Marcos was to be played by the handsome American actor Paul Burke and there would be a co-star to play the role of 'Evelyn', Marcos's girlfriend – a busty, leggy, American, blonde bombshell. The part was awarded to an actress named Dovie Beams.

The President and the Starlet

Dovie Beams styled herself a Hollywood actress, but her film credits were limited to a few B-grade movies. She was a tall, curvaceous and worldly blonde who claimed to be 23 years old (and looked it) but was actually 38. She'd been in

Manila only a few hours when she was escorted to a cocktail reception to meet the backers of the film. She noticed that one of the men who was introduced simply as 'Fred' was obviously someone important. When they ate he sat at the head of the table and the others were quick to defer to him. Later in the evening he contrived to be alone with her and offered a clumsy compliment: 'You have the best looking legs I have ever seen'. Then Fred revealed himself to be Ferdinand Marcos, President of the Philippines. He kissed Dovie on the back of the neck and exercised the same whirlwind romantic style with which he'd wooed Imelda so many years ago. 'I'm in love with you', he said.

He called Dovie the very next night – and the next. In a few days Dovie was taken to the presidential mansion in the resort town of Baguio. Here she was smuggled through platoons of sentries and security guards to the ground floor of the mansion house where Marcos greeted her. He escorted her upstairs and through three doors which he carefully locked behind them until they were at last alone in the presidential bedroom suite. There Marcos confessed his love for her and claimed to be impotent with his wife – that they'd been sexual strangers for some time. And the affair began.

The fact that we know so many details about the affair is due to a crucial error on Marcos's part. Despite his obsession with security, his lust had blinded him to one fact: the beautiful Dovie was no wide-eyed innocent. She carried with her a tape recorder. When the lovemaking began, so did the recording.

The passionate love affair continued for 2 years while the film was in production. Dovie would spend her days in the arms of the tall American actor playing Ferdinand Marcos and her nights in the arms of Ferdinand Marcos trying his best to emulate a handsome American. Both performances were recorded for posterity. Dovie's little tape recorder was tucked under the bed during each tryst, where it captured the unmistakable voice of Marcos crooning love songs to Dovie, romping in the shower, commenting on her body parts, urging her to perform oral sex – every moan, whimper, rustle and thump of their vigorous sexual relations. Ferdinand begged Dovie to have his baby and she eventually agreed, although her assurances seemed to be as reliable as a Marcos campaign promise. When he discovered birth-control pills in the presidential mansion he angrily confronted her, but Dovie soon talked him round. Tape-recorded conversations revealed them making plans for a child and an obsessive Marcos keeping track of her menstrual cycles for months ahead.

Dovie maintained the recordings for 2 years. When film production was over and still no baby was due, Ferdinand's interest began to fade. He suggested a cooling off period and Dovie agreed. Before she returned to California for the film's post-production, Ferdinand arrived with a Polaroid camera to record a set of souvenirs. He took a series of nude snapshots of Dovie. They exchanged snippets of pubic hair, and assured each other of their mutual love and parted.

Seven months later, after having no word from Marcos nor receiving final payment for the movie, Dovie realised that the cooling off period was actually a termination. When her calls were not returned and the movie company refused to pay her any more money, the little tape recorder came into its own. Dovie insisted on a final payment of $100,000 or she would embarrass the president. The company coughed up another $10,000 but refused to pay more. Dovie was issued with barely veiled threats that her health might be in danger if she persisted. Dovie was

Imelda Marcos examines her famous shoe collection at the Marikina Shoe Museum in Manilla, 2001. The first shoe museum in the country houses part of Imelda's collection of several thousand pairs of shoes which she left behind when she fled to Hawaii.

either a very brave woman or she didn't know the capabilities of her erstwhile lover. It was a common saying in Manila that Ferdinand's political campaigns were won by the three Gs – 'gold, guns and goons'. Violence and intimidation had been a part of his life since he was a boy.

Convicted of Murder

When Ferdinand was only 18 his father, Mariano, was defeated in a congressional election for the second district of Ilocos Norte. The successful candidate was a close neighbour, Julio Nalundasan.

Nalundasan held his victory party at home – just a few hundred metres from the Marcos's front door. Ferdinand was home from law school in Manila where he was distinguishing himself as both a scholar, and a sharpshooter on the University of the Philippines pistol team. Late that night, revellers from Nalundasan's victory party poured out onto the street carrying a coffin and held a mock funeral for the political career of Marcos senior. It was an insult, an extreme humiliation and it was also a big mistake.

The very next night Nalundasan was killed – by one shot in the back. The murder weapon had been a competition pistol. Ferdinand Marcos was convicted of the murder and given a prison term of 10–15 years. By the time the supreme court met to consider his appeal, however, Ferdinand had graduated from law school with honours. His first case was his own defence.

The conviction hinged on the evidence of an eyewitness who claimed to be one of three conspirators; the other two were Ferdinand Marcos and Marcos's uncle. The witness claimed that Ferdinand had insisted on carrying out the killing personally because his uncle might miss. On appeal, this evidence was rejected, the case was overturned and Marcos's reputation as a man to be reckoned with was assured.

Going Public

In Manila on 11 November 1970, Dovie Beams called a press conference and produced a tape recorder. The battery of journalists was amazed to hear the voice of their president singing his off-key love songs and desperately begging for oral sex. For her own protection Dovie was whisked away from the conference straight to the airport where she was placed on a flight to Hong Kong. On the flight she found out how long the reach of Marcos really was. The seating arrangements had been changed and she found herself sitting beside Delfin Fred Cueto, a thug and reputed hitman who claimed to be Marcos's half brother. In Hong Kong Dovie eluded Cueto but when she tried to board her Pan Am flight to the United States the Philippines consul-general turned up and tried to block her departure. He made such a fuss that the Hong Kong police stepped in and placed Dovie in the protective custody of the British intelligence agency MI5. British and American agents finally escorted her safely home. Cueto was detained and deported back to Manila.

If you know how rich you are, you are not rich. But me, I am not aware of the extent of my wealth. That's how rich we are.

– Imelda Marcos

Now Marcos relied on the time-honoured politician's defence of denial, counter attack and more denial. He dredged up psychiatric reports from Dovie's past and branded her a 'psychiatry case'. He released the nude Polaroid photographs to a Marcos-controlled newspaper accompanied by a series of salacious stories in an attempt to debunk her, but it only served to keep the scandal alive. Dovie responded by releasing more tapes as well as the clippings of pubic hair. The president's image was in tatters.

This was to be a defining moment for Imelda. Her cheating husband had delivered himself into her hands. If she chose to play the injured wife his future would be lost. If she chose to stand beside him there might still be some chance to retain power. Imelda made her choice, but Ferdinand would be forced to make major concessions. For the first time it was mooted that she might stand for president herself. Constitutionally, Ferdinand couldn't stand again so it might be better to keep it in the family. Imelda was dispatched on a diplomatic world tour. She met with Pope Paul VI in Rome and Richard Nixon and Henry Kissinger in Washington. Queen Elizabeth entertained her at Buckingham Palace. To keep the Americans interested she also met with Brezhnev, Qaddafi and Jiang Qing, the widow of Mao Tse-Tung. Internationally, Imelda had become the acceptable face of the Philippines. Now firmly in control of her husband it was time to take control of the country.

In one bold stroke Ferdinand made his move. He raised the spectre of a communist takeover and imposed martial law. He then suspended the constitution and swore himself in as both president and prime minister. He was in control of the country and Imelda was in control of him. Thus began the 16 years of rule known as the Conjugal Dictatorship. While Ferdinand ruthlessly suppressed all political opposition at home, Imelda's extravagance went into overdrive. In one real-estate shopping expedition in New York she considered purchasing the Empire State Building but turned it down. At $750 million it wasn't out of her price range but she thought it 'too ostentatious'. Instead she bought the $51-million Crown Building, the $60-million Herald Centre and two more prime chunks of Manhattan.

By the end of 1983 Imelda's excesses and Ferdinand's political machinations could no longer be sustained. When Benigno (Ninoy) Aquino, returned from exile in the United States to lead the opposition, he was shot in the head as he stepped off the plane. This was the final straw. The country was in an uproar. A further 3 years of struggle took its toll on Ferdinand's health and on 25 February 1986, the pair fled aboard a US military helicopter into ignominious exile in Hawaii.

On 28 September 1989, Ferdinand Marcos died in Hawaii. Imelda brought his body back to the Philippines in expectation of a state funeral but Ferdinand was denied his place in Manila's Pantheon of Heroes. His embalmed body remains in a glass viewing case in his home province of Ilocos Norte.

Dovie Beams returned to the United States and married a nightclub owner. The couple were convicted of fraud in connection with $18 million in illegally obtained loans. She is said to be working on her memoirs.

Imelda Marcos remains a popular figure in the Philippines.

MOTIVATION

anger
charity
envy
faith
gluttony
greed
hope
lust
pride
sloth

THE LIBERAL AND THE UNSTABLE STABLE BOY: JEREMY THORPE

MAIN CULPRIT:
Jeremy Thorpe (1929–), leader of the British Liberal Party (1967–76)

SCANDAL:
Charged with conspiracy to murder his homosexual ex-lover

WHY:
Desperate to cover up the affair as homosexuality was illegal at the time

He is a fraud. He is a sponger. He is a whiner. He is a parasite. But of course he could still be telling the truth.
– Justice Cantley on Norman Scott

British Liberal politician Jeremy Thorpe leaving the Old Bailey courthouse with his wife Marion, 22 June 1979, after being acquitted of conspiracy to murder his former lover, Norman Scott.

The newspapers called it 'the trial of the century'. Jeremy Thorpe, the flamboyant former leader of the British Liberal Party was charged with conspiracy to murder his homosexual ex-lover, a male model named Norman Scott. According to the prosecution, Thorpe and three other men had hired an airline pilot Andrew Newton to kill Scott. The hit was planned for one rainy night on the English Devon moors. However, Newton had bungled the job and, only succeeded in shooting Scott's dog, a Great Dane called Rinka.

On 22 June 1979, the jury delivered their verdict. Thorpe and his co-defendants were not guilty of all charges. Thorpe emerged from the Old Bailey with his arms raised in triumph. He was a free man, but his political career was well and truly over.

A Conservative Upbringing

Thorpe had been destined for politics from the beginning. The son and grandson of Conservative members of parliament, he was educated at Eton and Oxford, where he studied law, and his fierce ambition became obvious to all. He was known as a great wit and raconteur and a brilliant mimic, and cultivated a dandified image by wearing frock coats, fancy waistcoats and buckled shoes. Beneath the glittering surface, however, his colleagues detected a somewhat lightweight intellect, but all agreed he was going places.

With his background, he might have been expected to join the Conservative Party, but instead threw in his lot with the Liberals. By the early 1950s the once-mighty Liberal Party had been reduced to a handful of seats, and the Conservatives would have provided him with a much easier path to electoral success. But Thorpe dreamed of restoring the Liberals to their former glory, and becoming prime minister along the way. He became candidate for the seat of North Devon, and set about charming the voters. To increase his public profile, he worked briefly as a television interviewer. His efforts paid off. In the 1955 election he halved the Conservative majority and came second. In 1959, he won.

Thorpe, who was quite radical for a member of the Liberal Party, was soon making his mark in Parliament. He was passionate about human rights, opposed to capital punishment and an outspoken critic of apartheid.

The Stable Boy

Some time in 1960 or 1961, Thorpe visited his friend Brecht Van der Vater, who owned Kingham Stables in Oxfordshire. He noticed a good-looking young man

THE 'SOUTH AFRICAN CONNECTION'

In 1971, Norman Scott told his story to Gordon Winter, a South African journalist working in London. Although Winter wrote anti-Apartheid articles, he was actually an agent of the South African government. Scott allowed Winter to copy his dossier on Thorpe, and Winter, in the cause of duty, slept with him. Winter tried to pass the story to the newspapers to damage Thorpe, and was surprised when they declined it.

When Thorpe found out about this, he presented the story to Prime Minister Harold Wilson as evidence that the Scott affair was a South African plot. Wilson, who also suspected the South Africans were conspiring against him, accepted this and threw his support behind Thorpe. The journalists Penrose and Courtier, briefed by Wilson, wasted a huge amount of time searching for non-existent South African involvement. The result was that the waters were terribly muddied for anyone trying to get to the truth about Thorpe and Norman Scott.

leaning over a stable door and struck up a conversation. Norman Josiffe, 20 years old at the time, was mentally fragile and confused about his sexuality. On the whole, he preferred the company of animals to people. The meeting ended with Thorpe giving Josiffe his telephone number.

Shortly after this, Josiffe fell out with Vater and left Kingham Stables. He had a breakdown, tried to commit suicide by taking an overdose of pills and was briefly hospitalised. He had left his national insurance card with Vater so he couldn't work in Britain. He then remembered Jeremy Thorpe, who had written inviting him to dinner in London.

He set off to see Thorpe, accompanied by his Jack Russell terrier, Mrs Tish. Arriving at the House of Commons he sent a message to Thorpe, who came out and greeted him warmly. That night, Thorpe drove Josiffe to his mother's house in Surrey. Thorpe instructed him to tell Mrs Thorpe he was a member of a television crew who would be accompanying him overseas the next day. That night, according to Josiffe's account (later strenuously denied by Thorpe), the MP entered his room with a towel and a jar of Vaseline and had sex with him, causing him to, as he was later to famously put it, 'bite the pillow'.

Thorpe bought Josiffe clothes and shoes, took him on trips to the country, introduced him to his friends and arranged a job for him with the Liberal Party. He tried to organise a new national insurance card, but for various reasons Josiffe never received this. (He would later become convinced that Thorpe, whom he saw as his employer, was deliberately and maliciously withholding the card.) For a while, he lived in Thorpe's tiny London flat.

Josiffe valued Thorpe's friendship but, being Catholic, was terribly ashamed of what he called 'the inevitable sex thing'. In December 1962 he told a friend that he was planning to shoot Thorpe, then kill himself. The friend was sufficiently worried to contact the police.

British politician Jeremy Thorpe, electioneering in his constituency of North Devon, 1979, prior to his appearance at the Old Bailey, London.

The police interviewed Josiffe. He told them all about his affair with Thorpe, and gave them some of his letters. The police made a few inquiries with their colleagues in North Devon, but no-one was keen to embark on such an investigation involving a member of parliament. They decided there was insufficient evidence of a homosexual affair. Josiffe's statement, along with the letters, were sent to MI5, where they were deposited in Thorpe's file – MI5, Britain's counter-intelligence agency, routinely kept files on politicians.

After the interview, Norman Josiffe returned to Thorpe's flat and said nothing about having spoken to the police.

Josiffe spent the next 3 years working on and off as a riding instructor in Ireland, making half-hearted suicide attempts, and telling people that a wicked man named Thorpe had ruined his life. He believed that Thorpe had infected him with the 'disease' of homosexuality, and hoped that doctors would one day be able to cure him. Nevertheless, he kept going back to Thorpe for more.

In March 1965, he wrote a seventeen-page letter to Thorpe's mother, which began, 'For the last five years, as you probably know, Jeremy and I have had a "homo-sexual" relationship'. He complained of his shabby treatment at Thorpe's hands and his dire financial situation.

When confronted, Thorpe told his mother the letter was all lies, and asked his friend and fellow Liberal MP Peter Bessell for help. Bessell was another politician whose overactive sex life posed a threat to his career (though in his case, he was heterosexual). He flew to Dublin to meet Josiffe, told him that Thorpe regarded the letter as blackmail and threatened him with extradition. Josiffe thought that would be marvellous. 'I can come back to England and get the whole matter sorted out', he said. He told Bessell how he had given the police Thorpe's letters, and said that he had lost a suitcase with a further fifty letters while on a trip to Switzerland. Bessell said he would help get the suitcase back and also do something about the national insurance card.

Thorpe then delegated the job of handling Josiffe to Bessell, and for a while Bessell paid Josiffe a weekly 'retainer' of £5. He retrieved the suitcase from Switzerland but the letters in it were removed before it was sent on to Josiffe. He also spoke to the Home Secretary, Sir Norman Soskice, explained the trouble Thorpe was having and tried to persuade him to have the correspondence held by MI5 destroyed.

The New Leader

In January 1967, Thorpe was elected leader of the Liberals. Not everyone in the party was happy about this. Many were uncomfortable with his flashy style, and the mainly left-wing Young Liberals considered him a closet Conservative. The media, however, welcomed the ascension of the headline-grabbing MP. He was further honoured when the Labour Prime Minister, Harold Wilson, a great admirer of Thorpe, made him a Privy Counsellor, giving him access to classified documents relating to national security.

In 1968 Thorpe married Caroline Alpass. While he was on his honeymoon, his Liberal Party enemies moved to have him overthrown. Thorpe returned early, seething with righteous indignation, and forced a confidence vote which he won easily.

Norman Josiffe also tasted success in 1968. He had transformed himself into Norman Scott, male model, and was living in London in style. Despite the fact that he was having an affair with a man, he married a girl named Susan Myers and they had a son. Bessell hoped that Scott would now forget the past, but Thorpe was more pessimistic. He was right to be. Scott's modelling career was largely fantasy. He continued to pester Bessell for money, and the absurd business of the national insurance card had still not been settled. When he continued to sleep with men, Susan left him. Scott blamed the breakdown of his marriage on Thorpe, who he said had 'made him' a homosexual and prevented him from earning a living. He threatened to go to the press with the story.

Thorpe should have simply ignored Scott's threats. The alleged affair was years in the past, Scott no longer had any of Thorpe's letters and no newspaper would have believed his stories. It seems, however, that Thorpe had become as obsessed with Scott as Scott was with him. According to Bessell's account of events, Thorpe began to talk about having Scott killed. There was some discussion of how this would be achieved, with one suggestion being that Scott be poisoned and his body dropped down a disused mineshaft in Cornwall.

Thorpe had found a benefactor for the Liberals in Jack Hayward, a multi-millionaire who lived in the Bahamas. With the help of Hayward's money, Thorpe mounted an extravagant campaign during the 1970 election. When the results came in, however, the Conservatives under Edward Heath had won in a landslide. Thorpe escaped any recriminations when just over a week later his wife, Caroline, was killed in a car crash.

In 1971, Norman Scott took his story to the Liberals, and showed them letters from Bessell which confirmed the weekly payments. Thorpe admitted that he had known Scott but denied the affair, and pointed out that the letters suggested it was Bessell who was being blackmailed. The Liberals held an internal inquiry. Scott was subjected to a blistering interrogation by Lord Byers, leader of the Liberals in the House of Lords, who didn't believe a word Scott said.

Scott was shattered by this experience but continued to tell anyone who would listen about Thorpe, including his doctor, a man named Gleadle. In 1974 Gleadle approached Thorpe's attorney, saying his patient had letters which he would sell for £25,000. David Holmes, the deputy secretary of the Liberal Party and Thorpe's best friend, took over negotiations and knocked him down to £2500. He wrote out a cheque and Gleadle handed over the letters. Whether Scott, who now spent most of his days in a drug-induced stupor, actually gave permission to Gleadle to do this is unclear, but he was happy to take the money. It was a bad move for Thorpe, though. The letters, mainly the ones from Bessell, proved nothing against him, and he could now be connected to a payment to Scott via his attorney and best friend.

Death of a Great Dane

On the night of 23 October 1975, Norman Scott was being driven across Exmoor in Devon by a man he knew as Peter Keene. A few days earlier Keene, whose real

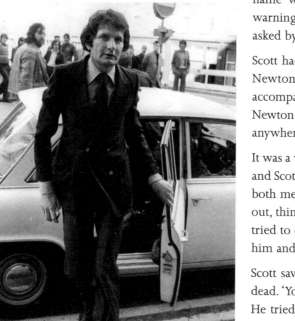

name was Andrew Newton, had introduced himself to Scott, warning him there was a plot to assassinate him, and he had been asked by a friend to protect him.

Scott had met Newton in a hotel in Combe Martin that evening. Newton had been unnerved by the fact that Scott was accompanied by his dog, a huge Great Dane bitch called Rinka. Newton was terrified of all dogs, but Scott had refused to go anywhere without her.

It was a wet and windy night. Newton seemed to be growing tired and Scott offered to drive for a while. Newton stopped the car and both men got out. Rinka, who was on the back seat, also sprang out, thinking she was going for a run. Scott grabbed her leash and tried to control her, but Newton thought she was going to attack him and shot her in the head.

Scott saw Rinka collapse and, bending over her, realised she was dead. 'You shot my dog!', he screamed. 'You can't involve Rinka!' He tried to give the dog mouth-to-mouth resuscitation. Newton put his gun to the back of Scott's head, then swore. The gun had jammed, or he pretended it had. As Scott sobbed over the body of the Great Dane, Newton got into his car and drove off.

Norman Scott (previously known as Norman Josiffe), the former male model who accused Liberal Party leader Jeremy Thorpe of conspiracy to murder him, May 1979.

Scott flagged down a passing motorist and was taken to a hospital in Minehead where he was treated for shock and told doctors that Jeremy Thorpe had ordered him to be killed. Local police learned of the incident with sinking hearts – they knew only too well about Norman Scott and his ravings.

Andrew Newtown was quickly tracked down and arrested. He told police that he was being blackmailed by Scott, and had only intended to frighten him. He was convicted and sentenced to 2 years in prison.

Peter Bessell, who had lost his seat in parliament and now lived in California, had been persuaded to write a letter stating that he had been blackmailed by Scott. This briefly took the heat off Thorpe but, when Bessell realised that he was being made the scapegoat for the whole affair, he told reporters that he had lied to protect Jeremy Thorpe. Word of the £2500 payment to Scott leaked out, which was closely followed by the publication of the letters Scott had handed over to the police back in 1962. Most of Thorpe's colleagues were now convinced that he had lied about his relationship with Scott, and he was forced to resign as the Liberal Party leader.

That might well have been the end of the saga for Thorpe had it not been for the intervention of his friend Harold Wilson. In May 1976, a couple of weeks after he had resigned as prime minister, Wilson summoned two BBC journalists, Barrie Penrose and Roger Courtiour, to a meeting. He told them that he had long suspected his government was being destabilised by right-wing elements in MI5, and by the South African intelligence agency BOSS. Wilson said that BOSS was behind the campaign against Thorpe, and Norman Scott was a South African agent. He told the journalists that this was the British Watergate, and said he would assist their investigations in any way he could.

Penrose and Courtiour left the meeting with their heads spinning. They began to follow up the leads Wilson had given them. They met with Norman Scott, but he didn't seem like a South African agent to them. In fact, the further they dug, the more convinced they became that Thorpe had conspired to kill Scott. They flew to California and interviewed Bessell.

In October 1977, shortly after his release from prison, Andrew Newton told reporters that he had been hired to kill Scott. The director of public prosecutions ordered an investigation into his claims.

The 'Trial of the Century'

In desperation, the police now sought help from Penrose and Courtiour, whose lengthy investigations into the Thorpe affair were well known. The journalists shared what they knew. According to the scenario they had pieced together, Thorpe had asked David Holmes to have Scott eliminated. Holmes had turned to his friend John Le Mesurier, a Welsh carpet salesman, who had then brought a slot machine salesman named George Keene into the plot. It was Keene who had engaged Andrew Newton, a 29-year-old commercial pilot who would 'do anything for a laugh'. To pay for the hit, £20,000 from a Liberal Party benefactor was diverted to David Holmes.

On 4 August 1978, Thorpe, Holmes, Le Mesurier and Deakin (a nightclub owner who was also involved) were arrested. The committal hearing took place in Minehead, a small coastal resort town, which had never seen such excitement before. Reporters poured in to cover the latest chapter in what had become a national soap opera. Bessell, who had flown back from California, and Newton had been given immunity from prosecution and testified against Thorpe and the others, as of course did Norman Scott. The hearing ended with a ruling that there was enough evidence for the case to go to trial.

Thorpe managed to have the trial postponed for 8 days to allow him to contest the next election, which he lost. The trial finally opened at the Old Bailey on 8 May 1979. The prosecution believed they had a strong case, but were hampered by the fact that two of their witnesses, Bessell and Newton, were self-confessed liars, while Scott had been an object of derision for years. Bessell was further damned as a witness when it was revealed that he had a deal with the *Sunday Telegraph* to sell a book he had written, and would receive twice as much money if Thorpe was found guilty. The Judge, Mr Justice Cantley, made no secret of his contempt for all three men.

All the journalists looked forward to what they expected to be the highlight of the case – Thorpe in the witness box. They were crestfallen when it became apparent that none of the accused was going to give evidence.

At the end of the trial, Justice Cantley gave a summing up that was so ridiculously biased that it immediately entered legal history. He began by saying that this was 'a bizarre and surprising case', which was undeniable, and that the four accused were 'men of hitherto unblemished reputation', which was more dubious. Mr Thorpe was, in case the jury had forgotten, 'a national figure with a very distinguished public record'. Then, after demolishing Bessell as a witness, he moved on to his pet subject, Norman Scott. 'You will remember him well', he said, 'a hysterical, warped personality, accomplished sponger and very skilful at exciting and exploiting sympathy'. He later expanded on this theme. 'He is a fraud. He is a sponger. He is a whiner. He is a parasite. But of course he could still be telling the truth … You must not think that because I am not concealing my opinion of Mr Scott I am suggesting that you should not believe him. That is not for me. I am not expressing any opinion.'

THE 'ROYAL POSTCARD'

When Norman Scott left the employment of Brecht Van der Vater, he took a postcard Thorpe had written to Vater on the occasion of Princess Margaret's engagement to Anthony Armstrong-Jones (a friend of Thorpe's). 'What a pity about HRH', Thorpe had written. 'I rather hoped to marry the one and seduce the other!' Scott gave the postcard to the police when he was interviewed in 1962.

Years later, at the time of the trial, much was made of this by journalists eager to find a 'royal connection' in the Thorpe affair. They were disappointed when both defence and prosecution refused to bring it up in the trial. The suggestion was that there was a relationship between Thorpe and Armstrong-Jones (now Lord Snowdon), but this was entirely untrue. The 'royal connection', like the 'South African connection', did not exist.

Justice Cantley did express an opinion about the £20,000 which, wherever it went, had not gone to the Liberal Party as its donor had intended. Even if Thorpe had been deceitful about this, he said, that did not prove a criminal conspiracy. The jury took 52 hours to reach their verdict of 'not guilty'. Thorpe and his second wife, Marion, left the court and returned to their London mansion. Later, along with Thorpe's mother, they could be seen on the balcony, waving to bemused passers-by.

Journalists were astonished by the verdict. Numerous articles about Thorpe's secret life which were ready for the printing presses were hastily shelved, as were two television documentaries.

Thorpe's triumph was brief. The establishment, which had given him the benefit of the doubt for so long, now closed ranks against him and the Liberal Party didn't want to know him. In the early 1980s Thorpe contracted Parkinson's disease, which ended his hopes for a return to public life.

Today, Norman Scott lives in an 11th-century house in Devon, surrounded by dogs, cats, geese and ducks. He was never too bothered by Thorpe's acquittal. He was content to know that the man who he felt had ruined his life had himself been destroyed.

MOTIVATION

anger
charity
envy
faith
gluttony
greed
hope
lust
pride
sloth

'I DID NOT HAVE SEXUAL RELATIONS WITH THAT WOMAN!': BILL CLINTON

MAIN CULPRIT:

William Jefferson 'Bill' Clinton (1946–), 42nd President of the United States of America (1993–2001)

SCANDAL:

Had a series of sexual escapades with White House intern Monica Lewinsky then lied about it

WHY:

He was an arrogant womaniser and Lewinsky was naive and confided in the wrong person

President Bill Clinton in 1999 – the signs of strain clearly showing from his recently-exposed extramarital sexual liaisons with Monica Lewinsky.

I did have a relationship with Miss Lewinsky that was not appropriate ... In fact, it was wrong. It constituted a critical lapse in judgment and a personal failure on my part for which I am solely and completely responsible.
– President Bill Clinton

Linda Tripp sat in her upstairs study in Columbia, Maryland one evening in early January 1998 and stared at the telephone. Should she pick it up and place a call that would undoubtedly uproot her existence and perhaps bring down the US government? Or should she maintain her secret, one that went to the highest reaches of government – a secret whose details she had been nurturing, expanding and developing for well over a year?

She had many motives for disclosing the secret. Tripp, a 50-ish divorced mother, was a long-time (and well-paid) government employee. She had worked in the White House of President George H. W. Bush and President Bill Clinton and later in the Pentagon. She had long felt, however, that her abrupt transfer from the Clinton White House had been unfair, even though it included a substantial salary raise. She had a severe case of 'Whitehouseitis', the malady of having been on the inside near the levers of power and wanting desperately to hold on to that éclat. Moreover, she had witnessed, in the proximity of the Oval Office, some untoward – and, to her mind, disgraceful, indeed scandalous – behaviour. Now a court action was edging dreadfully close to exposing those incidents. Tripp feared that she might be compelled to reveal what she had seen and what it portended. Being called to testify, she thought, might jeopardise her job and her reputation.

Former intern Monica Lewinsky meeting President Bill Clinton at a White House function. This picture was submitted as evidence in documents by the Starr investigation into 'Monicagate' in 1998.

But she also had an ace up her sleeve. At the Pentagon she had befriended a young co-worker who, like her, had been pushed out of the White House and was distraught about it. The young woman, Monica Lewinsky, had told Tripp that she suspected she had been transferred because of her relationship with an older, married man – the President of the United States and the most powerful leader in the free world. All ears and all sympathy, Tripp encouraged Lewinsky to tell her more and more. Lewinsky opened up, describing in detail the intimate and lurid encounters with the president extending back over many months. The two held long and regular telephone conversations; the younger woman confiding, and the older counselling.

This is historic, this is important, Tripp thought. Not to mention outrageous. She bought a tape recorder. Without telling Lewinsky she began to tape the calls and to prod the eager Lewinsky with leading, probing questions. She had gathered more than 20 hours of Lewinsky's confidences about the man Lewinsky called, in moments of lover's anger, 'the big creep'. Taping was really for self-protection, Tripp told herself; a weapon to use if she had to testify and was then attacked for her testimony. But there was another, less idealistic motive.

Washington was always hot for a tell-all, scandalous book focused on the illicit carryings on by people in high places. There were already plenty of racy stories about Clinton's appetite for young women, but Tripp had spoken to a literary agent about what was sure to be a blockbuster bestseller. The agent, a conservative with an abiding dislike for Clinton, urged her to keep taping.

Linda Tripp picked up the telephone and dialled the number of the Office of Independent Counsel Kenneth Starr – those few minutes of conversation set off the most frenzied scandal in US history, one that brought the government and much of the country to a virtual standstill for more than a year.

Just What the Opposition Needed

President Bill Clinton was riding high when the uproar began. He had been sworn in for a second term a year earlier. His approval ratings were over 70 per cent. The Democratic president had waged a bitter fight with the Republican Congressional majority over the government budget and many government offices had actually been shut down for lack of operating funds. Republicans, determined to shrink what they saw as a bloated, wasteful government, were sure the shutdown was a winning issue. But when the public realised the national parks were closed, they couldn't apply for social security and welfare cheques might be delayed, a huge clamour went up. The Republicans admitted defeat, and the government reopened, giving Clinton a clear triumph. He was succeeding on the diplomatic front, too, intervening in the Bosnian conflicts, the struggles in Haiti, the violence in Northern Ireland and engineering new talks between Palestinians and Israelis.

But there were some untidy items. As Governor of Arkansas, he had carried on – or so it was alleged – a long, illicit relationship with a woman named Gennifer Flowers. It was only when Clinton and his wife Hillary faced television cameras and discussed their strong marriage that his successful 1992 Presidential campaign took hold.

There was also another lawsuit from Arkansas, filed by a young woman named Paula Corbin Jones, who accused him of grasping, fondling and propositioning her. The case had dragged out several years amid talk of a settlement, but now a group of attorneys, who made no secret of their political enmity towards Clinton, had taken over the case and was pushing it aggressively. His attorneys had protested that the President of the United States could not be sued while in office, but the Supreme Court had ruled unanimously that the legal protection granted him as president did not extend to private matters. On 17 January Clinton was to give a legal deposition and be questioned about Jones's charges – a distasteful idea that he hardly looked forward to. There were allegations about seven other women, too, and Jones's attorneys indicated they might subpoena all of them.

Independent Counsel Starr, a former circuit court judge, Washington insider and staunch conservative, had spent nearly 3 years investigating various charges against the Clintons, mostly about a failed real-estate transaction known as Whitewater, with a few detours into supposed transgressions by the White House travel office and the sudden death of a White House lawyer who was a colleague and friend of Hillary Clinton. Linda Tripp's telephone call was just what he was looking for to give his obsession new life. Just 2 hours after Tripp set the telephone down, six members of the Starr staff and an FBI agent were in her living room. The next morning Starr applied for, and was granted, legal authority to expand his investigation to cover the sexual peccadilloes of the President of the United States.

One Thing Led to Another

Ironically, the relationship that now threatened the Clinton presidency began during one of his most triumphant moments. During the 1995 government shut-down, the administration ostentatiously temporarily laid off much of the paid White House staff. Unpaid interns, Lewinsky among them, continued to work. Thus, one evening the 21-year-old Lewinsky ferried papers to the president in the lonely Oval Office. The two, she was to say later, 'made eye contact'. The next evening they 'made eye contact' again. After some smiles and conversation she daringly flipped up her skirt to show off her thong underwear. One thing led to another, to use the old expression, and soon they retreated to a secluded doorway where they kissed and the young woman performed oral sex.

Over the next 19 months, Lewinsky told Tripp and her tape recorder, there were at least ten such episodes. Lewinsky would surreptitiously come to the nearly empty White House late at night or on weekends. Once, Lewinsky related, she was performing oral sex while the President spoke on the telephone to a Congressional leader. Another time, while the White House kitchen was closed, he nibbled take-out pizza during the act. Some evenings he would telephone her from the Oval Office or a hotel room during campaign trips, and they would carry on steamy, sex-laden conversations. They exchanged gifts. His to her was Walt Whitman's *Leaves of Grass*.

Oddly, even in the tightly controlled White House, little of this was known, or at least acknowledged. A few sharp-eyed observers suspected – Clinton had a reputa-tion for what one staffer called 'bimbo eruptions'. Before the 1996 elections, the White House personnel office engineered Lewinsky's transfer to the Pentagon. Ostensibly it was a well-deserved promotion. The inside story was that the young intern spent entirely too much time loitering round the presidential office. Sex was never specifically mentioned, but who could resist talking about such a dynamite subject? Lewinsky told her mother and ten friends about the relationship. Tripp repeated all the latest, luscious details each week to her bridge partners.

Now, thanks to Linda Tripp and a gung-ho team of prosecutors, the libidinous liaison was definitely out in the open – way out in the open. As soon as they received the go-ahead for an expanded investigation, the prosecutors asked Tripp to schedule a luncheon with Lewinsky, then outfitted her with a hidden 'body wire' to record the conversation. They schooled her in what questions to ask. Particularly, they wanted to know if Clinton had directed her to lie in her Jones case testimony. Asking someone to lie under oath could constitute subordination of perjury or obstruction of justice, both of which are criminal offences.

A LITTLE HELP FROM HER FRIENDS

Tripp certainly tried to help Monica. A transcript of one Tripp-Lewinsky conversation went like this:

Tripp: *He knows you're going to lie. You've told him, haven't you?*

Lewinsky: *No.*

Tripp: *I thought that night when he called you established that much?*

Lewinsky: *Well, I mean, I don't know.*

Tripp: *Jesus. Well, does he think you're going to tell the truth?*

Lewinsky: *No ... Oh, Jesus.*

Tripp: *So, he's at least feeling somewhat safe that this is not going to go any further right now, right?*

Lewinsky: *Yeah.*

Tripp was exuberant in her 15 minutes of fame. It took little persuasion for her to turn over her twenty secret tapes, parts of which quickly leaked out.

That the Office of Independent Counsel had been empowered to investigate a president's alleged affair with a woman half his age was news – big news – and the media went wild. Tripp and Lewinsky found their pictures on every front page, and reporters stalked their every move. The major television news anchorpeople had flown to Havana to report the papal visit of Pope John Paul XXIII. They immediately dropped the Pope and flew home to report on the more juicy Washington scandal. The footage about the Pope was relegated to the last part of the newscast.

In the midst of the uproar, the Palestinian leader Yasir Arafat visited Clinton. A few US and Palestinian reporters and cameramen were offered a photo opportunity of the two leaders seated side by side before an Oval Office fireplace. Under photo-opportunity rules, a few questions were allowed afterwards. The first two reporters politely dealt with the Middle East, and possible efforts to restart the Israeli–Palestinian peace talks. The next question, directed to Clinton by an American reporter, went, 'Could you clarify for us, sir, exactly what your relationship was with Ms Lewinsky, and whether the two of you talked by telephone, including any messages you may have left?'. The foreign reporters who were present were baffled by the exchange. Why would a 'private matter' – which in their countries would simply have been ignored or covered up – be allowed to deflect from something as important as peace in the Middle East?

On 22 January Clinton had scheduled a 1-hour interview on the prestigious PBS *NewsHour* with Jim Lehrer. Lehrer was certainly one of the most gentlemanly, yet knowledgeable and persistent, of interviewers. The theme was to be the upcoming State of the Union address. Instead Lehrer opened the interview with a polite question about Lewinsky and a 'possible sexual relationship'. Clinton looked at the camera directly and said, 'There is no sexual relationship'. He also declared that he never asked anyone to lie. Critics immediately noted that he had said 'is', the present tense, not 'was'. He didn't deny a relationship in the past. The media scrum continued.

Earlier that day Clinton had told his senior staff that, 'There is no basis, no basis whatever', for the allegations. It was simply another unprincipled attack by his political enemies. One of those who accepted that denial was his wife, Hillary. On the morning of 21 January, she recalled in her book *Living History*, 'Bill woke me up early. He sat on the edge of the bed and said, "There's something in today's paper you should know about". Hillary asked him what he was talking about. Clinton told her that the news reports would say he had been having an affair with a young intern and had instructed her to lie in her Jones deposition. Both charges were untrue, he swore to his wife. She believed him and told others so.

In his staff talk, Clinton had insisted that the Presidential business should go on regardless. His State of the Union message, high-light of the presidential year, was scheduled for 27 January, after a week of turmoil. Speculation about the speech abounded. Would he mention the scandal? Confess? Apologise? Resign? To everyone's surprise, he never mentioned it, and even his enemies praised the speech, which dealt instead with the economic boom times, the shrinking budget deficit and proposed legislation in health care, education and the environment. Monica Lewinsky? Who's she?

BIG NEWS

In his book, *One Scandalous Story*, Marvin Kalb tabulated the number of stories and words printed about the Monica Lewinsky scandal in the nation's leading newspapers. In 2 days the New *York Times* published thirty-two stories, which amounted to 15,000 words; the *Washington Post* published forty-one stories, which totalled 17,248 words.

However, Starr's team had by no means forgotten Lewinsky. They asked Tripp to set up a new lunch date. But this time Lewinsky was met by a phalanx of prosecutors and FBI agents who took her, under threat of arrest, to a hotel room for 12 hours. There they suggest-ed she arrange a meeting with Clinton and 'wear a wire' as Tripp had done. If she did not cooperate, she might face jail herself. Alternately weeping and stonewalling, Lewinsky pleaded to be allowed to telephone her mother. According to her authorised biography, the prosecutors ridiculed the idea that a 23-year-old adult needed hermother's presence, but finally relented. When mother Marcia arrived, she immediately arranged for a lawyer to represent her daughter and, at the lawyer's insistence, the interview ended there.

Over the next weeks, lawyer William Ginsburg negotiated an agreement under which Lewinsky received immunity from prosecution in exchange for grand jury testimony. She testified for 6 hours, being pushed insistently by prosecutors to recount in graphic terms the physical details of their encounters.

Lewinsky had confided to Tripp that she had kept a blue dress carrying the stains of Clinton's semen. This was the kind of secret Tripp could not keep to herself for long, and soon her agent was leaking it to the media, with resulting banner tabloid headlines. But a search of Lewinsky's apartment failed to locate the dress. In her grand jury testimony, however, she confessed that she had given it to her mother 'for safekeeping'. The Starr team immediately obtained the dress and had the stain tested for DNA. They then requested a blood sample from the president which, having little choice, he reluctantly yielded. The test showed an incontestable match; there was only one chance in 7 million, DNA experts said, that the semen was not the president's. ('Thank God it's not 100 percent', one Clinton loyalist said.) To the prosecutors, this was the smoking gun. Everything Lewinsky had confided to Tripp was true.

A few months after 'Monicagate', the Clintons greet bystanders while attending the Cologne Philarmonic Orchestra in June 1999 with other G8 world leaders.

Clinton had been artfully dodging questions for months. But by August 1998 he could evade no longer. Under a deal with Starr, he would be questioned in the White House, not the grand jury room at federal courthouse, with the grand jurors viewing it by videotape. Testimony was to be kept limited to a strict 4 hours; the president of the United States had more important matters to attend to. The questioning was sharp, stern, even hostile, and the president was cool and even tempered. The first exchange set the tone. 'Mr President', prosecutor Robert Bittman asked, 'were you physically intimate with Monica Lewinsky?'. Clinton read from a written statement, acknowledging 'inappropriate intimate contact' with Lewinsky. But that 'did not consist of sexual intercourse' and 'did not constitute sexual relations' under the definition given him during the Jones trial – a long and convoluted definition about improper fondling and touching of specific body parts 'with intent to arouse' – but he never mentioned oral sex. Aides said later that polls showed most Americans believed sexual relations meant acutal intercourse, not oral sex, and Clinton merely reflected that widespread opinion.

Never losing his cool as the questioning became more combative, Clinton gave long and legal hairsplitting answers. He denounced his political opponents, pointing out that the Jones case had nothing to do with Lewinsky and was simply an effort 'to take a wrecking ball to me and see if they could do some damage'. Confronted by White House logs that showed telephone calls and visits from Lewinsky, he said he couldn't remember times and dates and didn't consider them important. At one point, when asked why he had concealed the relationship so assiduously, he replied frankly, 'I did what people do when they do the wrong thing. I tried to do it when nobody else was looking.'

Then came the moment that was to define the whole Clinton appearance. Prosecutor Bittman recalled that in the Jones deposition Clinton's attorney had stated that, 'There is no sex of any kind in any manner, shape or form'. 'Wouldn't you agree', Bittman asked, 'that that was an utterly false statement?'. Clinton famously and smilingly replied, 'It depends on what the meaning of 'is' is. If 'is' means is and never has been, that is one thing. If it means there is none, that was a completely true statement.' The 'is, is' answer found its way into Bartlett's *Familiar Quotations*.

That morning, Clinton had finally broken the truth to Hillary. She was shocked, outraged and steely cold thereafter, condemning him, Clinton said in his memoir, *My Life*, to sleep on the sofa for the next 6 weeks. That evening she participated in a high-level meeting about what he would say to the public in a televised address. He and his advisers wavered between a frank appeal for forgiveness and an outright denunciation of the vengeful prosecutors. He turned to Hillary imploringly for guidance. 'It's your speech, Bill', she said, 'Say what you want'.

In his 4½-minute speech, Clinton was first contrite and explanatory, then turned angrily on the Starr team, denouncing what he called their pursuit of personal destruction.

Those were the first tiny inklings that the tide was turning. Democratic pollster Mark Penn showed that a clear majority of viewers had accepted Clinton's apologies. After 8 months of non-stop 'Monicagate', they wanted to move on. The country had problems other than semen stains on a blue dress. And, as the television idol Oprah Winfrey was to show again and again, they believed in the healing importance of redemption and the forgiveness of sins.

PRAY FOR ME

The day after Clinton made his televised 4½-minute speech, addressing the Lewinsky scandal, he held a prayer breakfast at the White House in which he prayed for forgiveness. At an African-American church, he again sought forgiveness and asked the congregation to pray with him. He said he was seeking solace in the Bible and from a counsellor. Some of the worshippers wept and comforted him.

Then Independent Counsel Starr released his 445-page report to Congress, followed up 10 days later with the release of Clinton's videotaped testimony. The Starr Report described in strong terms what it said 'may constitute grounds for impeachment', including such indictable offenses as perjury and obstruction of justice. Then, to support its case (it said), the Report went into lurid and almost pornographic detail about the Clinton-Lewinsky sexual activities, even including graphic descriptions of Clinton using a cigar to stimulate sex play and describing when, and how often, he ejaculated. To ensure that the Report got the widest exposure possible, it was released on the Internet even before Congressmen had received their copies.

Clinton opponents were jubilant – at first. Leading Democrats, led by Senator Joseph Lieberman, who would become a vice presidential candidate 2 years later, raised their voices with calls for Clinton's resignation. Others pleaded with Congress to pass a resolution of censure, which would denounce Clinton's behaviour but neither impeach him nor push him out of office. No such thing had ever been done in US history and Congressional Republicans, who smelled blood, rebuffed the idea. They were looking forward to the November election, where voters, repulsed by the Monicagate scandal, would surely increase their majority.

Then a funny thing happened. Poll after poll showed that voters were disappointed in Clinton but equally disgusted with the Starr investigation. Voters who had lived through the sexual resolution of the 1960s and 1970s did not find themselves shocked by revelations of Bill-and-Monica behaviour. They seemed to consider Starr and his group nothing but prim scolds, out to humiliate Clinton on political grounds. Others were outraged by the report's X-rated detail, which, it was pointed out, could be easily read by impressionable children on computer screens. Some libraries set up a minimum age for those who could read the report.

And then, in the November elections, came the even bigger surprise. Far from the Clinton scandal bringing about their defeat, the Democrats actually gained four seats in the House of Representatives.

The opposition was not beaten, but it was obviously losing steam. The Republican House quickly drew up articles of impeachment, its responsibility under the Constitution, and rushed them to the Senate, which would hold the impeachment trial before the new Democratic House members might affect the outcome. The Senate then dutifully voted for the impeachment to proceed.

The verdict was by then virtually a foregone conclusion, containing some elements of farce. Chief Justice William Rehnquist, charged by the constitution with presiding, turned up in a specially designed robe with crimson sleeve stripes, that reminded some people of a costume from a Gilbert and Sullivan operetta. Clinton said he was too busy with presidential duties to watch much of the proceedings, which devolved into a series of predictable and desultory speeches on both sides, perhaps highlighted best by the closing speech by former Arkansas Senator Dale Bumpers in Clinton's defence. Deriding the opponents' righteous insistence that the issue was not the president's behaviour, but his character and violation of con-stitutional principles, Bumpers paraphrased the old saw about money: 'When they say it's not about the sex', Bumpers said, 'it's about the sex'.

Under the Constitution, a two-thirds vote of 100 Senators was required to convict Clinton and remove him from office. The vote fell far short. The Senate voted 45 to 55 against the perjury charge, and 50 to 50 on obstruction of justice.

Almost a year to the day after her telephone call, Linda Tripp was almost just a footnote. She had received nearly $600,000 cash settlement because the Pentagon had illegally leaked her personnel file. She left government service, had her face lifted, her hair cut, married an old sweetheart and went into the antiques business. But it remained for her once-talkative young friend to have the last word. 'I hate Linda Tripp', Monica Lewinsky said.

MURDER AND MYSTERY

Above: Fatty Arbuckle (seated centre) at his trial, charged with sexual assault and manslaughter of a Hollywood starlet. Although acquitted, the case's negative publicity caused Arbuckle's early retirement.

MOTIVATION

anger

charity

envy

faith

gluttony

greed

hope

lust

pride

sloth

THE ENLIGHTENED DESPOT: CATHERINE THE GREAT

MAIN CULPRIT:
Catherine the Great (1729–96), Empress of Russia (1762–96)

SCANDAL:
Possibly ordered the murder of her husband, Peter III

WHY:
He was a huge embarrassment to wife and country

For to tempt and to be tempted are things very nearly allied ... whenever feeling has anything to do in the matter, no sooner is it excited than we have already gone vastly farther than we are aware of.
— Catherine the Great

Catherine the Great was renowned for her equestrian skills and love of horses which led to many rumours of a sexual nature, including the story that she died while having sex with a horse.

On 28 June 1762, Catherine the Great set in motion the coup d'état that would topple her husband, Peter III of Russia, from the throne. Within a week Peter was dead and Catherine was Empress of Russia. It was an incredible act of political manipulation but rumours of sexual excess, perversity and murder were to haunt her all her days.

On Friday 21 August 1745, the wedding day of Sophia Augusta Frederika, Princess of Anhalt-Zerbst, who would become known as Catherine the Great, was married to Grand Duke Peter Fedorovich, heir to the Russian throne. It was the most glittering public celebration ever seen in St Petersburg. Elaborate fountains flowed with wine, a multitude of banquet tables groaned under mountains of food and squadrons of yachts and galleys crowded the river in front of the Winter Palace. The cavalcade consisted of a seemingly endless line of 120 coaches, each accompanied by flocks of retainers and escorted front and back by detachments of horse guards, cuirassiers, hussars and dragoons. Troops lined the way from the palace along Nevskii Prospect to the Church of Our Lady of Kazan. Thousands gathered to cheer the royal couple as they rode in a coach the size of a small castle. The procession was so long it took 3 hours for the consorts to travel the few blocks to the church.

For the 16-year-old bride, the future could not have looked brighter. Nobody present could possibly have guessed what the young duchess's future life at the Russian court would hold for her.

A Boisterous Young Woman

Catherine was born on 12 April 1729 in Stettin, Pomerania (now in Poland). Her father, a minor prince, was a high-ranking officer in the Prussian army. Her mother was the Princess Johanna of Holstein-Gottorp, a family line that could lay direct claim to the crown of Sweden.

The sole aim in Catherine's mother's life was to produce marriageable heirs, to ensure continuity of the family line and retain the rights to their ancestral land holdings. Sons, of course, were favoured, so most of the mother's attention was given to Catherine's two sickly younger brothers. The princess grew up independent, outspoken and unrestrained. She adored rough-and-tumble games with boys and displayed a precocious interest in sex, often shocking her Lutheran tutors with unseemly questions about sexual matters.

Some things she found out for herself. At around the age of 10 she discovered the joys of masturbation. Her diaries record the occasion: 'I was very boisterous in those days ... As soon as I was alone I climbed astride my pillows and galloped in my bed until I was quite worn out ... I was never caught in the act nor did anyone ever know that I travelled post haste in my bed on my pillows.' Later she would learn to regret these frank admissions.

The Education of a Princess

For a woman whose reputation was to include allegations of bestiality and nymphomania, Catherine's early experiences were remarkably sedate. One youthful relationship throws light on her awakening sexuality. The man was Prince Georg Ludwig, her uncle who was 10 years her senior. The besotted older man made frequent visits to the house, spending hours on end entertaining his 13-year-old niece. Her tutors complained of the interruptions but the girl, Lolita-like, was enjoying this new power and the attention it brought.

Peter III was prone to tantrums or long periods of sulky silence. He loved practical jokes and was generally an embarrassment to the Russian court.

Ludwig begged Catherine to marry him. She thought he was joking – she was still too young to know anything of love. Then she warmed to the idea and the relationship moved on to the stage of stolen kisses. That's when her mother put a stop to it.

However, what Catherine didn't realise was that the entire affair had been carried out at her mother's connivance. In fact, she was being coached in the art of seduction because, behind the scenes, her mother had been painstakingly arranging a better marriage for Catherine – to her cousin Grand Duke Peter Feodorovich. Peter was the nephew of the Empress Elizabeth of Russia and heir to the throne.

Catherine may have learned how to attract a man with seductive smiles and meaningful glances, but she would go to her wedding bed entirely ignorant of how sex with a man was actually achieved. Prior to the wedding, she assembled her ladies and maids at a slumber party to quiz them about marital relations, but nobody proffered any clear ideas. Those who weren't as naive as the duchess-to-be were wary of passing on knowledge which was more properly provided by her mother. When Catherine approached her mother she was severely scolded.

It's little surprise then that Catherine's wedding night ended up being fraught with tension. After midnight her ladies put her to bed where she spent several expectant and excited, but lonely, hours. Eventually the drunk and giggling Peter joined her. Catherine later recalled her disappointment that nothing happened that night.

The Russian Embarrassment

Peter was even less experienced than Catherine was. She discovered what most people in the court already knew – that Peter the Grand Duke, at the age of 27, was still a spoilt little boy.

Peter had been raised by the ladies of the court, and they indulged his every whim. The result was a young man of startling immaturity whose personality expressed itself in violent tantrums or long-lasting sulks. He was addicted to practical jokes and drilling peepholes in the palace walls to spy on people. His boorish behaviour was such an embarrassment to the diplomats of the Russian court that they issued a memorandum to the Empress Elizabeth: 'His Imperial Highness must be taught not to make ugly faces at people, not to hold indecorous conversations with his inferiors, and not to empty his wine-glass over the heads of the footmen who wait at table'.

Peter's favourite pastime was playing with toy soldiers. He was an avid admirer of the Prussian military and had battalions of toy soldiers, fortresses and miniature cannons so that he could play at war. Instead of a place for conjugal pleasure, the marital bed became a playground battlefield covered in dolls, toys and wooden soldiers. Peter marched up and down, shouting commands and making cannon sound effects with his mouth.

Catherine was aghast when she thought that some day in the future this backward child would become the commander-in-chief of the great Russian war machine. She threw herself into study, assembling a library of the most advanced books on statecraft, philosophy and politics. The future looked uncertain and she wanted to prepare herself to be a strong support for a husband who clearly wasn't fit for the duty of a ruler.

Gossip and Rumour

To ease her sexual frustration, Catherine took to physical activity and horse riding, shocking the court with her joy in riding astride – unheard of at that time. The royal court was a hotbed of gossip and soon rumours began to circulate that the only sexual pleasure Catherine had was when she had a horse between her legs. It wasn't long before enemies of the monarchy reversed the order and whispered that it was the horse that was astride the duchess. This scandal soon reached the ears of the Empress Elizabeth.

The empress, aware of her nephew's unsuitability for leadership, was determined to groom another successor – hopefully Peter's son – but the years rolled by and no sign of a pregnancy came. The empress began to nag at Catherine that horse riding was the reason she couldn't conceive. She exhorted her to make herself more agreeable to her husband, 'to display affection and even passion; and, in short, to employ all means in her power to win his tender regard, and accomplish her conjugal duty'.

RECENT RUMOURS

The latest rumour is the story of Catherine's secret pleasure palace, supposedly discovered 250 years after her death by German troops in the winter of 1941 at St Petersburg. This story tells of four incredible rooms that were said to be stocked with chairs, sofas, paintings, tables, carpets and chandeliers, all designed with the most graphic sexual motifs. Apparently, everywhere one looked there were frescoes of satyrs, nymphs and fauns in every imaginable sexual position. Underfoot were carpets of writhing, lustful bodies. It was a room that had obviously been conceived to try and excite the most jaded sexual appetite. However, legitimate historians have little interest in these claims.

Catherine, resentful of the attitude that the brattish grand duke could never be at fault, began to harden her heart. If the game was about a public image disguising private pleasures, she would learn to play it better than anyone.

At the age of 23, after 6 years of suppressing her natural urges, Catherine allowed her sexuality full rein. She took her first lover. Serge Saltykov was a chamberlain at the court and the first in a long line of young paramours. She never tried to hide the fact, reasoning that gossip about handsome and cultured young men was better than gossip about horses.

This added fuel to the legend of Catherine being lusty and insatiable. Although it was common for male royals to take mistresses, it wasn't acceptable for women – and this woman was completely candid about her carnal desires. She once confessed, 'I have a mind like a cat in heat'.

Hearing about Catherine's love affairs, the empress could no longer deny that the lack of offspring might be Peter's fault. But getting him to submit to an examination was fraught with problems. He was obsessively shy about his body and never allowed anyone to see him naked. The empress tried to trick him into an examination, decreeing that he must take a bath. But Peter threw a fit. He'd never taken a bath in his life, he screamed, and he didn't intend to have one now. A bath might endanger his health – it might kill him. He was not a baby, he raged, and would not be treated like one. Eventually the tantrum passed and the examination was done. It was found that he had a minor disability – probably a constriction of the foreskin – which was easily remedied.

On 20 September 1754, Catherine gave birth to a son, whom the Empress Elizabeth named Paul. However, after the birth, the baby was immediately spirited away to the empress's apartments and Catherine was rarely allowed to see him.

Nobody in the court thought for a minute that Peter had fathered the child, least of all the Empress Elizabeth. It was said that Saltykov was the most likely candidate. When an ambassador commented on the child's dark colouring in contrast to Peter's paleness, Elizabeth allegedly shouted that if he was a bastard, he wouldn't be the first in her family. The old empress had an heir and that was enough.

Marriage on the Rocks

By this time, the marriage had turned completely sour. Peter took every opportunity to abuse Catherine verbally and physically. He threatened that he'd dispose of her the moment he became tsar. He also took a mistress – Elizeveta Vorontsova. With a face ravaged by smallpox scars, Vorontsova was reputed to be the ugliest woman in the realm, and had a personality to match. She was a loud, vulgar and abusive drunkard. Catherine's friends believed that Peter had chosen her specifically to spite his wife, but Catherine consoled herself with the thought that Vorontsova was the only person in the court to whom Peter did not feel inferior.

In any case, Catherine had no feelings left for Peter. She had come to realise that the greatest risk to her future happiness was her own husband, and so she quietly set about protecting herself.

Where Peter was ignorant of the tides of popular opinion, Catherine was very sensitive to them. In January 1762, when the Empress Elizabeth died, Catherine endeared herself to the population. She made a great show of respect by openly weeping for Elizabeth. In stark contrast, her husband, the new tsar, behaved like a clown. He refused to stand vigil over the body and seemed to be making a deliberate mockery of the occasion. He pulled faces, made jokes and interrupted the funeral service several times with loud laughter.

Heads began to shake and Catherine realised that she had two choices – to go down with Peter, or to rise against him.

Rumours and Manoeuvres

Though Catherine was aware that Peter would be his own worst enemy she left nothing to chance. If he was going to make a move against her she would be ready. She began to cultivate powerful friendships in the court's three major spheres of influence. Her contact in the military was her new lover, Grigorii Orlov. Orlov was a war hero and one of five brothers who held sway in the guards regiments. Though only a few thousand men strong, the guards were the key to the armed forces – not only through military power but also social prestige and political knowledge.

EMPRESS OF THE ENLIGHTENMENT

Although only 2 per cent of the Russian population was literate in the 18th century, Catherine was a voracious reader and made every effort to improve her mind. She befriended the French writer Voltaire and employed the French writer and philosopher Diderot to improve the national library, thus gaining a reputation as a patron of the Enlightenment. She kept abreast of literary and intellectual movements in Western countries and wrote polemics and librettos. She wrote plays in French and Russian, a book titled *Notes on Russian History* as well as twelve volumes of her own memoirs.

Catherine's apparent predilection for young military men provided even more fuel for the rumour mongers. Lewd cartoons appeared showing the sex-mad duchess inspecting the guards with a view to choosing a mate. They conjured up visions of a long line of troops, trousers down, huge penises erect and the debauched lady inspecting each for size, weight and length. But Catherine's real interest lay elsewhere – she was after their hearts and minds.

Her ally in the diplomatic community was Nikita Panin, a senior diplomat and a wily politician. Catherine assured Panin of a senior position in the court and in return his political knowledge and clout were at her disposal. He lobbied behind the scenes and kept her abreast of the tides of public opinion. This covered two major areas but how could she keep tabs on the machinations of her husband? Catherine's masterstroke was to befriend the Princess Ekaterina Dashkova. She was the sister of Elizeveta Vorontsova, Peter's mistress. With Dashkova reporting to Catherine he could never make a move without her knowledge.

Catherine was aware she was playing a dangerous game. It was one thing to make allies but now she was actively involved in conspiracy against the crown. If Peter heard one breath of it she would face imprisonment and death.

Meanwhile, Peter took to his new role as commander-in-chief of the military in the manner of playing with them as if they were his box of toy soldiers. He insulted them by imposing uniforms and discipline in the style of the enemy, Prussia. He ordered the firing of cannons in St Petersburg day and night. The constant din of mock warfare plagued the city. Peter wanted to know what the sound of 100 simultaneous cannons would be like and ordered it to be tried. He was only dissuaded from this folly when he was advised it would shake the city to pieces.

On 24 April 1762, Peter made his biggest mistake. He signed a treaty with the King of Prussia, restoring all Prussia's occupied territories. The Russian army was outraged. They had suffered great losses during the Seven Years War (1756–63) but had endured it all in the name of Mother Russia. Peter had wiped their efforts out with a single stroke. The army was ripe for revolt.

Bloodless Revolution

The first Russian Revolution began with a domestic argument. At a formal dinner, the emperor humiliated Catherine by calling her a fool when she refused to rise for a toast. That very night Dashkova reported that Peter had ordered Catherine's arrest. At the same time, Captain Passek, a senior member in the conspiracy, was arrested. Catherine feared he would talk. It was time to make her move. At the time she was 33 years old.

Catherine the Great ruled Russia for 37 years until her death in 1796. She was highly literate, intelligent and was known as 'Great' due to her many reforms aimed at modernising Russia.

The administrative brilliance that was to characterise the reign of Catherine the Great was first seen in the early morning of 28 June 1762. She was awakened early by Alexei Orlov, the brother of Grigorii, who told her that everything she had planned was ready. She was carried by coach to the outer suburbs of St Petersburg to the quarters of Grigorii's own regiment, the Izmailovski Guards. Cheering soldiers rushed to receive her and she addressed them with a dramatic three-sentence speech: 'I have come to you for protection. The Emperor has given orders to arrest me. I fear he intends to kill me.'

She said nothing more. The soldiers rushed to kiss the hem of her dress. Allegiance was sworn. The meticulously choreographed revolution had begun. Catherine immediately had herself sworn in as empress, then, flanked by a joyous crowd, she moved on to other military headquarters in the city and was rapturously received by all. By the end of the day the city was hers.

Aware of the great power of symbolism she dressed herself in the green uniform of a colonel in the Preobrazhenskii Guards – this had been the rank of Peter the Great. She mounted a white stallion and, sabre in hand, assumed the role of commander-in-chief. The troops cheered as she led them to confront Peter.

And what of Peter? The only real military action he ever saw was against his own wife. His troops deserted him and he was forced to hand himself over to ignominious arrest. A week later he was dead.

Fearing another round of dangerous rumours Catherine ordered an autopsy and issued news of the result – Peter had died of haemorrhoidal colic. Nobody believed it – and they were right, as years later a letter surfaced that put the blame squarely on the empress: 'Alexi Orlov [younger brother of Catherine's lover and involved in the coup] then went in and seized him exhausted as he was by the throat, squeezed it with all his extraordinary force, and the unhappy Prince dropped down dead as if he was shot'.

Catherine was quick to cope with the scandal. She ordered a state funeral for Peter with full honours. The body lay on public display for 2 days with a cravat discreetly covering his throat and a large hat hiding most of the blackened face.

Lingering Rumours

Catherine saved face – and the throne – but the rumours never left her. She ruled for another 37 years, until her death, with gossip and scandal dogging her every day. When she died, at the age of 67, tales persisted that she'd been crushed by a horse while attempting to have sex.

Today's Russia's leaders, like the Soviets before them, remain ambivalent about Catherine's place in their pantheon of great rulers, not because she usurped a throne or the sexually perverse rumours but because of the question of murder.

MOTIVATION

anger

charity

envy

faith

gluttony

greed

hope

lust

pride

sloth

'THE INTERVIEW': AARON BURR JR AND THE DEATH OF A FOUNDING FATHER

MAIN CULPRIT:

Aaron Burr (1756–1836), 3rd Vice President of the United States of America (under Jefferson)

SCANDAL:

Killed Hamilton in a duel and charged with treason

WHY:

Political and personal rivalry

The President has undertaken to prejudge my client by declaring 'of his guilt there can be no doubt'. He has assumed the knowledge of the Supreme Being himself, and pretended to search the heart of my highly respected friend. He has proclaimed him a traitor ... He has let slip the dogs of war, the hell-hounds of prosecution, to hunt down my friend.

— Chief Justice Marshall in defence of Aaron Burr

Vice president under Thomas Jefferson and formative member of the Democratic Republican Party, Burr killed his political rival Alexander Hamilton in a duel.

Before dawn on 11 July 1804, Vice President Aaron Burr, asleep on the couch of his country house, was woken by a servant. It was already a hot and muggy New York summer's day. Burr dressed himself in dark clothes and a coat. He received a small group of friends who had gathered to wish him luck. He then set out with his friend William Van Ness for the nearby banks of the Hudson River where they hired a boat and oarsmen. They crossed to the New Jersey shoreline and pulled into shore at a secluded place not far from the village of Weehawken. The place looked to have been deserted for some time and the two men set about clearing the ground of leaves and twigs. While they were engaged on this task, another row-boat turned up containing four men: the oarsman; Nathaniel Pendleton; Dr David Hosack; and Alexander Hamilton, a founding father of the United States of America. Hamilton and Burr had agreed to meet for 'an interview' – the euphemism of the day for what we would call a duel.

Hamilton and his second, Pendelton, climbed the bank to where Burr and his second, Van Ness, were clearing the ground. Even though the two parties were about to shoot at each other, they exchanged courteous greetings with little apparent enmity – the idea of duelling was all about defending gentlemanly honour, rather than being about vengeful violence. While the spectre of politics and ambition lurked strongly in the background as motivation for this duel, it remained a graceful display of machismo from two of America's biggest egos.

I have resolved, if our interview [duel] is conducted in the usual manner, and it pleases God to give me the opportunity, to reserve and throw away my first fire, and I have thoughts even of reserving my second fire.

– Alexander Hamilton

They agreed to use the pistols Hamilton had provided. While he and Burr stood apart, the two seconds tossed for the right to choose which side of the duelling grounds they preferred and who would give the order to fire. It was now almost 7 am and the sun was up. Its light gave a reflective glare off the first wind-driven ripples in the river. Pendleton put Burr against this glare in the belief it would make him easier to see. Yet it also meant Hamilton would be staring into the sun.

The duellists were given their pistols and took the ten required paces to their shooting positions. The guns had a regular trigger and a hair trigger. Van Ness set the triggers on Burr's gun and handed it to him. When Pendleton asked Hamilton if he would like the hair trigger set, he replied, 'Not this time'. Hamilton was intent on a kind of bravado not unknown to the 'code duello', the elaborate set of rules for resolving matters of honour in this way. He had decided not to shoot at Burr on the first exchange. It was bravery bordering on lunacy, but perhaps not as much as it seemed. The duelling pistols of the time were deliberately constructed to make it difficult for the contestants to hit each other. The barrels were not allowed to be longer than 11 inches (28 centimetres). Accuracy was further restricted by the requirement that the inside of the barrel be smooth, as opposed to the grooves found in a rifled barrel. The shot ball was also smooth which meant it tended to bounce around inside the barrel, further restricting its range and accuracy. As few as one in fourteen contestants were fatally wounded in a duel while the majority were able to walk away without the need of medical assistance.

Pendleton asked the two duellists if they were ready. Hamilton raised his pistol into the air and called a halt to the proceedings while he reached into his pocket and pulled out a pair of glasses, which he put on to help him see against the glare of the sun. The two duellists now adopted their formal duelling stances, right foot in front of the left, stomach sucked in to further minimise the target, the pistol arm drawn across the body as a further defence. They tried to steady themselves against their quickening pulses and waited for Pendleton to call 'Present!', the cue for the duellists to fire at will.

The two guns went off in close succession. When the smoke cleared, Hamilton had fallen to the ground. Burr had fired first and hit him. It was a lucky shot since Burr had slipped on a stone in firing. As he was hit, Hamilton's gun had gone off and lodged in the boughs of a tree some 3.5 metres above Burr's head. Burr looked at his fallen foe and felt considerable remorse while Pendleton called for the doctor who was waiting in the rowboat on the water. When Burr went to see how Hamilton was, Van Ness drew him away fearing the doctor might identify him. He got back in his boat and was rowed home.

Alexander Hamilton, one of America's foremost constitutional lawyers, had an illustrious political career and founded the Federalist Party.

When Dr Hosak found Hamilton he was being held up in a sitting position by Pendleton. The bullet had entered just above his right hip and had passed through his liver and diaphragm before lodging in one of his vertebrae. Hosak pronounced the solemn diagnosis that Hamilton had received a mortal wound.

They rowed Hamilton back across the river during which he lingered on the point of death a couple of times. By the time they had brought him home he had recovered enough to be able to speak. In bed he received his wife and children who wept, as did many of his friends who came to say goodbye. The following afternoon, one of America's founding fathers and a hero of the American Revolution was dead.

From Geniality to Hatred

A brief look at the lives of Hamilton and Burr tells us they had quite a lot in common. They were both New York trial lawyers and successful veterans of the American War of Independence, although Hamilton was a Federalist and Burr a

Republican. Burr in particular was a moderate, and friendly with many in the Federalist Party. They shared some political views, such as the abolition of slavery. As trial lawyers who frequently crossed each other's paths in court, their relations had been cordial for a long time, even if they were political opponents. When Hamilton challenged James Monroe – another future president of the United States – to a duel over his part in releasing evidence of Hamilton's affair with Maria Reynolds, whose husband was blackmailing Hamilton, Burr, as Monroe's second, had actively intervened to preserve the peace between the two men. It could even be said that although Burr killed Hamilton, he had once before saved his life.

So what took them to the duelling grounds that morning? While the superficial answer is that Hamilton impugned Burr's honour by calling him despicable and refused to adequately apologise, what was really at stake was both men's vainglorious ambition to reach the pinnacle of public fame – which each thought he deserved. In short, Hamilton began slandering Burr for political advantage, while Burr's reaction to this slander was to challenge him to a duel – it was also issued strategically with his own political future in mind.

Another thing the two men had in common was that their careers had been nose-diving in the direction opposite to their images of self-importance and, by playing out the duel, both hoped to spur the revival of their public careers.

A Prickly and Arrogant Man

Alexander Hamilton's rise to first secretary of the United States Treasury had been a spectacular one. He was born illegitimately to a Scottish businessman and a French mother on the West Indian Island of Nevis. He impressed Nevis with a newspaper letter about a cyclone – so much so that the people of Nevis funded his passage to New York where he went to King's College, now Columbia University. When the War of Independence began, he organised his fellow students into an artillery company and was rewarded with the rank of captain before he was promoted to lieutenant colonel and joined the personal staff of George Washington.

Hamilton's subsequent success had as much to do with Washington's patronage as his undoubted abilities. When the war ended, Hamilton founded the Bank of America in 1784, was a defender of the constitution in 1787 against the likes of Thomas Jefferson, and then went on to serve as the treasury secretary in the Washington cabinet between 1789 and 1795, where he was largely responsible for giving the new nation a solid financial system, and for creating the US Navy.

Hamilton's insecurity of origins, scepticism of democracy and fondness for the high moral ground made him a prickly and arrogant man with a penchant for upsetting people.

Once Washington retired, Hamilton lost political influence. His attempts to control from behind the scenes the cabinet of Washington's successor, John Adams, resulted in Adams having to sack many cabinet members. Adams had resisted but ultimately acceded to Washington's request to make Hamilton his second in command during the quasi-war of 1798–1800, which saw Hamilton rise to the rank of general. The split in the Federalists, to which Hamilton's ambition greatly contributed, enabled a landslide victory by their radical Republican political opponent, Thomas Jefferson. This also also saw Burr elected vice president in the elections of 1800.

Hamilton had returned to private life as a lawyer, where he dreamed of military glory in anticipated wars against the French or Spanish, and tried as much

as possible to manipulate the destiny of Federalist politics from New York. However, by the time he fought his duel with Burr, his influence as an elder statesman was also waning. This is the major reason he came to dislike Burr – the origins of which go back to the presidential election of 1800, where Hamilton had chosen Jefferson over Burr. Despite many of the high ideals being discussed in American politics at the time, the machinations of the founding fathers were frequently very dirty and, while they were prone to avenging their honour in duels, they also loved nothing better than sticking knives into each other's backs.

Alexander Hamilton and Aaron Burr take aim in the duel that would end Hamilton's life, 1804.

A Burr in His Side

If Hamilton was a bastard, Burr was from pedigree Puritan stock. His father, the Reverend Aaron Burr, was the second President of Princeton University, while his maternal grandfather was the celebrated Calvinist theologian Jonathon Edwards. Burr never really knew either of them as his maternal grandparents and parents all died within a year of each other, leaving him an orphan at the age of 2. He was raised by his strict Puritan uncle, from whom he often ran away.

Like Hamilton, Burr was something of a child prodigy. He gained entrance to Princeton aged 13 and graduated by the time he was 16 years old. His religious vocation ended when he abandoned Calvin's theology, with its idea of an 'elect' few, for the democratic notion that heaven was open to all.

A natural rebelliousness accompanied Burr throughout his life. He was a sensualist, kept many mistresses and his politics were pragmatic. Yet underlying this devil-may-care approach was a certain Puritan dread which meant that he often unconsciously sabotaged himself at his moments of greatest opportunity.

Having quit theology, Burr took up law. He was active during the War of Independence and earned a reputation for being a brave fighter, rising to the rank of lieutenant colonel. Yet he earned the ire of George Washington, and John Adams's acceptance of Burr as a brigadier general in the quasi-war was vetoed by Washington on the grounds that Burr was too prone to intrigue. Or, perhaps it was because Burr had said 'he despised Washington as a man of no talents, and one who could not spell a sentence of common English'. Like Adams, Washington's second officer, General Hamilton, had been in favour of giving Burr the job.

In 1800, Burr almost became president due to an unforeseen peculiarity of the electoral system. Instead of voting separately for president and vice president, each member of the presidential electoral colleges, whose members were elected by the states, had two votes. It was presumed the presidential candidate would outvote the vice presidential. However, in 1801 it came down to seventy-three votes each for Jefferson and Burr and the decision devolved to the House of Representatives where it took 3 days and thirty-six ballots before Jefferson was made president. If Burr had played his cards right he probably could have mobilised the Federalists to vote for him. But he dithered. Although he gained a reputation as a brilliant and impartial leader of the senate, he had lost the trust of his party and earned the life-long enmity of Jefferson who, from that moment on, determined to destroy him. One of the key Federalists who voted for Jefferson – even though Burr was closer to his own politics – was Alexander Hamilton.

Hamilton was not the first in his family to die at Weehawken. In 1801 his son Phillip had been killed while duelling with a Jefferson supporter, Thomas Eaker. Phillip had been described by one contemporary as 'a sad rake' and called Eaker a rascal. Like his father, he had refused to apologise.

When he killed Hamilton, Burr was still the incumbent vice president. Yet Burr had fallen out with Jefferson and Jefferson had named Burr's political arch enemy, George Clinton, as vice presidential candidate for his intended second term. To compensate, Burr had decided to campaign for Governor of New York against the Clinton candidate, Morgan Lewis. But Jefferson gave support to Lewis, and tacit support to the Clinton mouthpiece, James Cheetham, to embark upon a campaign of serious, and often seriously inaccurate, slanders against Burr in his scandal sheet newspaper, the American Citizen.

One of Burr's reasons for standing for governor was that he had considerable Federalist support. A radical faction of the Federalists, irritated by the Virginian hegemony epitomised by Jefferson and his cronies, believed in mounting a New England secession from the United States and Burr was in no mood to argue against them. Of course Hamilton, the great Federalist, was opposed to this. As many of his Federalist colleagues indicated their willingness to support Burr, Hamilton increased his campaign of calumny against Burr which had started in 1801 with Hamilton's support for Jefferson.

For a while Burr looked like a sure thing for governor but, in the end, the Republican candidate, Morgan Lewis, prevailed comfortably, leaving Burr with egg on his face and his enemies circling to finish off his political career.

Badmouthing Burr

By the time Burr challenged Hamilton, he must have already known Hamilton had been badmouthing him about town for some years. In fact, a letter allegedly written by Hamilton in 1801 had been quoted by Cheetham in the *American Citizen*. In the document, Hamilton claimed that history had never before seen such 'an enormous complication of fraud, dissimulation and perfidy assembled in the same individual'. The letter also accused Burr of something 'so atrocious, no human language can furnish a term sufficient of its baseness', a sentiment which has led some people to surmise Burr was being accused of incest with his daughter, with whom he was known to be close. Throughout his gubernatorial campaign, Burr countered the mudslinging, through the *Morning Chronicle* newspaper, which adopted his cause. But he did not engage to the same extent in smearing his enemies as did the Jefferson–Clinton camp and Hamilton. This situation changed with his bitter defeat to Morgan Lewis. To some extent, Burr must have felt the lust for revenge against his detractors, though if this was his sole motivation, then it would have been better to challenge George Clinton, Cheetham or even Jefferson, who were the chief architects of the slander, even more so than Hamilton.

Like Hamilton, Burr's ambitions had turned from political to military glory. It was a turbulent time with the nation's borders yet to be fixed and alliances with the European powers in constant flux. War seemed likely. And what better way to announce your preparedness for military glory than by bringing your courage to national attention in a high-profile duel.

Burr had been hearing about Hamilton's slurs on his character since 1800. At a dinner party held by his political ally, Judge Tayler, in 1804, Hamilton disparaged Burr again. This was noted by Tayler's son-in-law, Dr Charles Cooper, in two letters he wrote in April 1804. Both letters were leaked to the *Albany Register*, which quoted Cooper as saying that 'General Hamilton and Judge Kent have declared in substance, that they looked upon Mr Burr to be a dangerous man ... [and] I could detail to you a still more despicable opinion which General Hamilton has expressed of Mr Burr'.

It wasn't until June that Burr saw this second letter but, when he did, he wrote to Hamilton requesting an acknowledgement or denial of the despicable opinion. Hamilton's response was lawyerly. He argued that he could not disavow anything so imprecisely defined. The letter also included an essay on the meaning of the word 'despicable'. Burr bristled at this reply, deeming it arrogant and evasive. Hamilton, however, would not budge. While the two men and their seconds argued over the semantics in subsequent letters and conveyed messages, the die was already cast. For Burr, Hamilton had failed to address the charge of dishonour, while Hamilton perceived that to back down would damaged his chances of subsequent military appointments. The date of the duel was set for 11 July. By the afternoon of the following day, Hamilton was dead.

Coda

It's doubtful that Burr wanted to kill Hamilton and, if he did, his strategy backfired when there was a massive outpouring of public grief over Hamilton's death. Burr became *persona non grata* with many of the people whose support he needed and his opponents were quick to milk this for all it was worth. Although Burr had behaved honourably throughout the duel, and although the duel had been fought in New Jersey where the practice was legal, his enemies did their best to have him arrested for murder. Warrants were issued for Burr's arrest in New York, and then New Jersey. Neither warrants was prosecuted, however, perhaps reflecting the insincere motivations of those behind them. Despite being a wanted man, Burr returned to Washington to complete his vice-presidential term, during which his fair-minded behaviour as leader of the senate was crucial to protecting the independence of the judiciary while Jefferson and his allies pursued the impeachment of Supreme Court Justice Samuel Chase.

This would be Burr's last major political achievement, but it wasn't the end of his talent for scandal. When his vice presidency ended, attentions were directed west. With co-members General James Wilkinson, the commander of the US military patrolling the Louisiana border with Spain; and Jonathon Dayton, an Anglo-Irish aristocrat who owned an island on the Ohio River (as well as the tacit support of future president Andrew Jackson and the British Government), the conspiracy aimed to seize parts of Louisiana and Mexico and establish a new nation in the south-west of the North American continent. The plan came undone, however, when Wilkinson got cold feet. Already in the pay of the Spanish government as an agent, he decided that his ends would be best served by shopping Burr to Jefferson and Burr was charged with treason. Against Jefferson's wishes, he was found not guilty, but the trial put an end to his dreams of glory. He lived in England for some years then returned to New York where he practised law in relative obscurity. He did, however, live to see the 1835 Texan War of Independence at which he drily observed that what was once considered treason had by then become heroism. And perhaps it was the story of Aaron Burr's life that he never quite got the timing right.

During Burr's trial for treason, Thomas Jefferson seemed desperate to secure Burr's conviction. He had circulars printed and sent out throughout the West of the country asking 'every good citizen to step forward, and communicate to the government any information he may possess'.

MOTIVATION

anger

charity

envy

faith

gluttony

greed

hope

lust

pride

sloth

THE STAR-SPANGLED KILLER: HOW DANIEL SICKLES GOT AWAY WITH MURDER

MAIN CULPRIT:
Daniel Sickles (1819–1914), politician, diplomat and American Civil War Union General

SCANDAL:
Murdered Barton Key in cold blood and got away with it

WHY:
Key slept with Sickles's wife

My reconciliation with my wife was my own act done without consultation with any relative, connection, friend or adviser ... If I ever failed to comprehend the utterly desolate position of the offending though penitent woman – the hopeless future, with its dark possibilities of danger, to which she is doomed when proscribed as an outcast, I can now see plainly enough in the almost universal howl of denunciation with which she is followed to my threshhold, the misery and perils from which I have rescued the mother of my child.

— Sickles, letter to the editor, *New York Herald*, 20 July 1859

Daniel Sickles served as a Union general during the American Civil War and was seriously wounded by a cannonball at the Battle of Gettysburg in 1863.

On the afternoon of 27 February 1859 in Lafayette Square, near the White House, Barton Key, United States Attorney for the District of Columbia was talking to New York lawyer Sam Butterworth, when Congressman Dan Sickles approached in a hurry. Dressed in an overcoat, despite the warmish weather, his eyes had the cold, sinister gleam of a man who has surrendered to his rage.

'Key', he shouted, 'you have dishonoured my bed – you must die'. Sickles pulled a derringer pistol from his overcoat and fired, but the bullet only grazed Key's hand. He made to shoot again, but Key grabbed Sickles and pulled him into a clinch, blocking him from pulling the trigger. Sickles dropped his gun to the pavement and the two men wrestled. Eventually Sickles broke free. He pulled another gun from his overcoat. Key backed away, crying, 'Don't murder me!'. He threw a set of opera glasses to the ground to prove that he was unarmed. Sickles shot again. This time he hit Key in the thigh. Key stumbled back and found a tree to lean against, but his leg wouldn't support him and he slid to the ground. 'Don't shoot me', he cried. But Sickles came closer to the prone Key and shot again. Again the gun misfired. He pulled out a third pistol, another derringer, and came even closer. He leant over Key and cocked the gun. From a range of centimetres, he put a bullet into his enemy's heart. Even then he'd not quite finished. He cocked the pistol yet again and put it to Key's head to deliver the *coup de grâce*, but this gun misfired as well. Within minutes, Barton Key was dead.

It was a cowardly murder. At a time when men still resolved issues of honour by fighting duels, Key, armed only with his opera glasses, never stood a chance. What's more Sickles got away with it. He was acquitted in America's first ever successful temporary insanity defence. But who remembers to pack three guns when setting off for an impulsive killing in a fit of blind rage?

AN EXCITABLE BOY

At one point, Sickles's father attempted to set his restless son up as a gentleman farmer. But Sickles found the country-side boring. Instead, he moved into the house of Lorenzo Da Ponte, the 80-year-old Professor of Italian at Columbia University. Da Ponte had written librettos for Mozart, had been a friend of the fabled Casanova and had amassed a formidable amount of notches in his peripatetic bedpost. Da Ponte and his son, also Lorenzo (a professor at New York University), offered to prepare Sickles for university. Sickles followed the elder Da Ponte's example by enthusiastically educating himself in the brothels of Manhattan, becoming what was known as 'a sporting man'.

Knickerbocker Sickles

Dan Sickles was no stranger to scandal. A sixth generation Knickerbocker (a powerful and prestigious New York family), whose father had become wealthy on Wall Sreet, he was a classic New Yorker, full of charm and bustle, and with an exquisite nose for the main chance.

An innate political animal, Sickles gave his first speech at a rally when he was 17. He gravitated to the Democrats of Tammany Hall, who would dominate the New York political scene for much of the 19th century and who were famous for their blind loyalty to each other – as well as their outrageous corruption and nepotism.

By the time he married, aged 33, Sickles was a successful Democrat attorney, New York state assembly man and a rising son of the political scene who had cultivated many powerful friends.

Despite this success, Sickles always lived beyond his means. His luxuries included an expensive, exclusive arrangement with his favourite prostitute, Fanny White. He was censured by the state assembly for bringing her into the dining room of the hotel where he and his fellow members stayed. Forever juggling debts, he was vulnerable to financial chicanery. At one point he was charged with larceny, but his Tammany connections helped the case 'disappear'.

Love and Marriage

At 15 Teresa Bagioli was a voluptuous, bona fide stunner. Educated at the best Catholic school in New York and a speaker of five languages, she was a heady brew of beauty, cultivation and innocence. For a man whose instincts were competitive,

The renowned beauty Teresa Bagioli, whom Sickles seduced when she was 15 and later married, only to go on to neglect her and their daughter, Laura.

she would make a fine envy-inciting asset. She was the daughter of Maria Bagioli, the adopted (and natural) daughter of Lorenzo Da Ponte, Columbia's first Italian professor and Sickles's tutor. When Sickles first met Teresa she was 3 years old. By the time she was 15, Teresa had a powerful adolescent crush on the dashing young politician. It was a situation Sickles couldn't resist. He seduced her, slept with her, got her pregnant, then married her – displaying just enough morality not to ruin the life of a young girl whose family had been so good to him.

If he loved Teresa, however, it was never exclusively. Politics would always come first with Sickles. And there were other women, too. Soon after their marriage in 1852, Sickles was offered a posting to London as assistant to James Buchanan, a veteran Democrat from Pennsylvania and a long-time presidential aspirant. While the salary was much less than he earned as an attorney, he took the job, mainly because of the political advantages it offered. Teresa, who had just given birth to their daughter, Laura, was unable to join him immediately. It was considered too dangerous for mother and child to travel so soon.

In lieu of his wife, Sickles invited his old friend Fanny White to London. He made the New York papers when he took her to a royal reception held by Queen Victoria, where Fanny was introduced as Miss Julia Bennett of New York. She curtseyed and shook the puritanical monarch's hand. Egalitarian scallywaggery, perhaps, but you wonder what Sickles's old friends and new in-laws must have thought when they read the story. Teresa, luckily, was already on her way to London via ship.

In London, Teresa proved an excellent political asset. Her language skills put her a peg above the average American diplomat's wife, and she impressed her husband's crotchety old bachelor boss, James Buchanan. She impressed him so much, in fact that, when his niece was in America, he appointed Teresa as official legation hostess. Indeed, Buchanan appeared so enamoured of Teresa that there were rumours of an affair – doubtful, given the more persistent rumour that Buchanan, who had never married, was a closet homosexual. It showed, nonetheless, that Teresa knew how to attract and maintain the attention of older, powerful men.

After 2 years in London, Sickles returned to America – to the dismay of his British creditors. James Buchanan had decided to make a last run for president and Sickles, now part of his inner circle, returned to prepare the ground. On the instigation of his Tammany friends, Sickles decided to run for congress himself. Both Buchanan and Sickles were victorious, and the winter of 1856 was spent in Washington.

Sickles rented Stockton Mansion, a four-levelled, white stucco home in view of the White House. It cost him his entire congressional salary – evidence that Sickles had to have been on the take. Teresa and his daughter, Laura, joined him and again Teresa proved an asset for her husband. She was ranked one of the three most beautiful women in Washington and held receptions one afternoon a week, while the weekly Sickles dinners became a much sought-after Washington invitation.

A Star-Spangled Lover

Barton Key, the Washington DC district attorney, had helped his new friend, Dan Sickles secure the lease on Stockton House. Key was from a prominent Maryland family. His father had composed the *Star-Spangled Banner*, while one of his uncles was a supreme court judge. He owed Sickles a favour. Key had lost a court case he shouldn't have and Sickles had interceded with Buchanan to confirm his continuing appointment as district attorney. More of a lover than a lawyer, Key was a 39-year-old widower, a good-looking blond with sad eyes and an easy southern charm. The court of female opinion rated him very highly and he in turn courted female attention, frequently skiving off work to spread his charm at the afternoon receptions of the Washington wives.

AN IDEAS MAN

Sickles was influential in the establishment of a horse-drawn omnibus network in Manhattan and, without his advocacy for the establishment of Central Park (including sneaking a favourably inclined judge onto the bench of the New York Superior Court), it would have been left to the whims of private developers.

Sickles, on the contrary, was more of a man's man. Full of restless energy and ambition, he preferred the vigour of masculine politicking to the more refined modes of discourse required for charming society ladies. He had already made himself indispensable to President Buchanan and was spending less and less time at home. While enjoying the sparkle of Washington social life, her husband's frequent absences left Teresa lonely and anxious. Because of their age difference and the era, she felt she had little control over her marriage. Her anxiety was justified. Much of Sickles's 'business' in Baltimore was conducted in a hotel with a married woman.

Sickles's dalliances and neglect made Teresa susceptible to the advances of Barton Key. She wasn't mature enough for the world she mixed in, and had become intoxicated by the social atmosphere, with its gossip and the attentions of powerful men. With her own powerful man ignoring her, was it a case of nature abhorring a vacuum that led her into the arms of Barton Key? Or maybe she even mistakenly thought that, by having an affair, she could somehow bring balance to her marriage by inflaming her husband's jealous desire, and in that way bring him closer to her?

Whatever the reasons, Teresa and Key were soon enjoying assignations. At Stockton Mansion, in carriages and at the congressional cemetery in New York. They soon

became the subjects of gossip and were so indiscreet that some people assumed Sickles must have given his blessing. But he was too immersed in the political conundrums of trying to heal the Union to notice the treachery of his wife. When the gossip finally did reach him, via one of his aides, he organised a meeting with Key who denied the affair and offered to challenge the sources to a duel. Sickles was mollified.

If Key was smart, he would have called it quits then and there. Unlike Sickles, however, Key had fallen in love with Teresa. He rented a house in a mixed neighbourhood so he and Teresa could continue to meet undetected. But it wasn't to be. Weeks later, Sickles received an anonymous letter, probably from a jealous southern woman who covetted Barton Key, revealing the whereabouts of the love nest. Sickles sent his secretary, Woolridge, to confirm it. That day, Sickles, whose cold streak was paired with a melodramatic one, wept in congress. That night he confronted Teresa who, after initially denying the affair, confessed. Far from being made insane by the situation, however, Sickles made her write her confession down and sign that it had been written without duress.

Barton Key, the Washington DC district attorney who fell in love with Daniel Sickles's wife, Teresa Bagioli, and paid the price with his life.

The next day Sickles conferred with some of his Tammany colleagues about what should be done. He was concerned his political enemies would be able to use his status as a cuckold against him. While he alternated between grief, anger and strategy, Key, unaware of any of this, and having dandified himself at the barbers, showed his fatal love for Teresa by lurking in the square outside her house, hoping for a response to the waved white handkerchief which was their special sign.

Woolridge, Sickle's secretary, spotted him and Sickles was outraged. Sickles's colleague Sam Butterworth proposed that Sickles challenge Key to a duel. But

Sickles had decided that Key, who had already lied to him, deserved to die like a dog. Butterworth left the house and engaged Key in conversation. Sickles followed soon after, then ... bang, bang, bang ... the rest is history.

The Trial

Following the murder, Sickles gave himself up and was jailed. The warden gave him his office in which to wait out the time until his trial. His meals were brought from home, and his dog was there to keep him company whenever he wasn't being visited by a long list of family and influential friends.

If Barton Key had been still alive he would have prosecuted Sickles himself. In his absence, however, President Buchanan appointed Robert Ould as prosecutor. The Key family protested, demanding a special prosecutor, as Ould had only ever acted in one murder trial. Buchanan refused. Ould was in debt to Buchanan for his career and pliable. Any doubt concerning Buchanan's bias is dispelled by the fact that a presidential page had witnessed the murder and come to tell Buchanan directly afterwards. The president had told him to get out of Washington straight away. In Buchanan's schema, and Sickles's too, Ould's inexperience was an asset.

Bridle your virtue,
Tether the tongue;
Pity the fair vine
Blighted so Young!
Why not the tomb?
Sad, shattered life;
Think her doom =
Widow yet wife.

– From 'Judge Not' verse about Teresa Sickles's predicament, 1859

Against Ould were six of the best lawyers in America, including Edwin Stanton – who Buchanan appointed attorney general not long after – and Sickles's friend James Topham Brady, one of New York's most successful murder trial lawyers. They entered a novel plea of temporary insanity, arguing that the mental anguish of discovering he was a cuckold prevented Sickles from being responsible for his actions. Butterworth lied in evidence, claiming he thought Key was armed, but it was the moral disdain of the Sickles's Irish servant Bridget Reilly, calling her mistress 'disgust incarnate', that won the jury over. With temporary insanity not actually provable, the trial came down to the sympathy of the jury for the defendant. It helped that in those days juries were all men. During the trial, the defence leaked Teresa's confession to the press. The jury's natural sympathy for the cuckolded man was also helped by Ould's surprising omission of any reference to Sickles's own extra-marital romps – possibly at the behest of Buchanan.

The jury found Sickles not guilty. Unlike today, where an insanity plea usually ends with the defendant being confined in a mental institution, Sickles was immediately released. His political reputation, however, especially as a go-between for the north and south was in a mess, even though public opinion was with him. He lost much of this support when the newspapers gave him a shellacking upon revelation he had not only been corresponding with his wife, but had forgiven her. The public were appalled at this weakness and he was forced to write to the editor in a New York newspaper explaining why.

If Sickles forgave his wife, he was made quickly aware that she was now a political liability. He installed Teresa and Laura on the rural outskirts of Manhattan and, while the marriage remained intact, he was less and less at home. Teresa's destiny was a kind of living limbo, almost the ultimate form of revenge.

The Civil War and Beyond

Barton Key left a nasty taste in Sickles's mouth and he was no longer as enamoured of southern gentlemen as before. Moreover, he was *persona non grata* with them, which made his political task of healing the rift between northern and southern Democrats impossible. This scandal would have ended in Sickles becoming yesterday's man, but for the fact that the Civil War broke out. It was a fantastic chance for Sickles to remake himself. An opportunist if ever there was one, he became committed to the war, the abolition of slavery and the Republican president Abraham Lincoln. He started his own New York army brigade, and eventually became a general in the Union army.

One of his legs was blown off in battle, and he played an important role in the Battle of Gettysburg — though whether it helped the Union victory or nearly brought about defeat is still in dispute. Once the war was over Sickles, the northern war hero, was able to re-establish his political career and he went on to a number of important postings, including military governor of North and South Carolina and ambassador to Spain, where he had an affair with Queen Isabella.

OPINION OF THE DAY

In the first place this Key
he was a false friend,
Sickles he thought that
on him he'd depend,
But the false-hearted villain,
his honor betrayed,
He took his wife away,
and Sickles him he slayed.

– Lyrics from a popular song of the time sum up the majority public opinion of the day

As for Teresa, he left her with his daughter and the chickens on the outskirts of New York. While the wives of generals were crucial to army morale in the Civil War, Sickles never brought Teresa out to support him in public again. She contracted tuberculosis and died at the age of 31. After her death, Sickles also went on to abandon their daughter, Laura, who died drunk and destitute aged only 38. Sickles didn't attend her funeral.

Sickles lived 20 years longer than both his wife and daughter combined. He married again and meddled in politics right up to his death aged 93; he was a man full of activity but without a moral core. The year before his death, he was arrested for embezzling $28,000 from the New York State Monuments Commission. The man who had once got away with murder escaped again without being sentenced to jail, though this time the death was his own.

End Note: Teresa's Confession

Following is the confession about the affair with Barton Key, that Sickles forced his wife, Teresa to write:

I have been in a house in Fifteenth Street, with Mr Key ... Usually stayed an hour or more. There was a bed in the second story. I did what is usual for a wicked woman to do. The intimacy commenced this winter, when I came from New York, in that house — an intimacy of an improper kind. Have met half a dozen times or more, at different hours of the day. On Monday of this week, and Wednesday also. Would arrange meetings when we met in the street and at parties. Never would speak to him when Mr Sickles was at home, because I knew he did not like me to speak to him; did not see Mr Key for some days after I got here. He then told me he had hired the house as a place where he and I could meet. I agreed to it ...

Mr Key had kissed me in this house a number of times. I do not deny that we have had connection in this house [Stockton Mansion], last Spring, a year ago, in the parlor, on the sofa. Mr Sickles was sometimes out of town, and sometimes in the Capitol. I think the intimacy commenced in April or May, 1858. I did not think it safe to meet him in this house, because there are servants who might suspect something. As a general thing, have worn a black and white woolen plaid dress, and a beaver hat trimmed with black velvet. Have worn a black silk dress there also, also a a plaid silk dress, black velvet cloak trimmed with lace, and black velvet shawl trimmed with fringe. On Wednesday I either had on my brown dress or black and white woolen dress, beaver hat and velvet shawl. I arranged with Mr Key to go in the back way, after leaving Laura at Mrs Hoover's ... I went in the front door, it was open, occupied the same room, undressed myself, and he also; went to bed together. Mr Key has ridden in Mr Sickles' carriage, and has called at his house without Mr Sickles' knowledge, and after my being told not to invite him to do so, and against Mr Sickles' repeated request.

This is a true statement, written by myself, without any inducement held out by Mr Sickles of forgiveness or reward, and without any menace from him. This I have written with my bed-room door open, and my maid and child in the adjoining room, at half past eight o'clock in the evening. Miss Ridgely is in the house, within call.

Teresa Bagioli, Lafayette Square, Washington, D.C., 26 February 1859.

MOTIVATION

anger

charity

envy

faith

gluttony

greed

hope

lust

pride

sloth

THE MAESTRO'S MELANCHOLIA: PYOTR TCHAIKOVSKY'S STORMY LIFE

MAIN CULPRIT:
Pyotr Ilyich Tchaikovsky (1840–93), Russian composer

SCANDAL:
Possibly committed suicide by drinking a glass of unboiled water in order to develop a fatal illness

WHY:
Suffered unbearable guilt about being homosexual and may have been manic depressive

I shall do everything possible to marry this very year, but if I should lack the courage for this, I am in any event abandoning forever my habits and shall strive to be counted no longer among the company of homosexuals.
– Pyotr Ilyich Tchaikovsky

Tchaikovsky was one of the first Russian composers to be widely listened to in the west. His life, however, was plagued with bouts of depression and despair and it is thought that he may have committed suicide.

The annals of great composers are peppered with tales of tormented genius, but none can measure up to the legendary agonies of Pyotr Ilyich Tchaikovsky, music's martyr to inner turmoil. Even his most reverential early biographers expressed their pity for his pathological terror of society, and that was well before any dared suggest he was gay. The more we learn about the private life of the composer of the 'Sugarplum Fairy', the more shocked we become at how tempestuous and even dangerous it was, even to the point of possibly being suicidal. Rumours of the composer's attempts to take his own life were widely spread, even during Tchaikovsky's own time, and his biographers are ambiguous about whether his death was self inflicted.

The Terrible Wound

A trill is a rapid alternation between two notes. Tchaikovsky's whole life was a trill between stardom and secrecy, celebrity and escape, harmony and wrenching hallucinations, soaring beauty and self-destructive despair. If one melodramatic scene can be excerpted from the operatic conflicts of Tchaikovsky's life, it would be the rapid flurry of wild emotional escapades that led to his disastrous marriage in 1876. It began when he was on the rebound from, not one, but two doomed romances. Tchaikovsky was confused after he had been dumped by a famous soprano (who went off to Poland to marry a baritone). In rapid succession, he was also jolted by yet another romantic setback of the homosexual variety. His emotions spun out of control. He realised that his younger brother, Modest, a playwright and educator – who later furnished the libretti for Tchaikovsky's operas – was having an affair with a young deaf boy that he himself desired. Either out of jealousy or guilt, Tchaikovsky penned an impassioned and high-minded letter on ethics to his brother. Modest must have been baffled, since just a few months earlier Pyotr had written from Paris, 'What the hell, having fun's the thing'. This new letter was a sermon on the virtues of marriage, which would enable both of them to conquer the 'unnatural' passions that had derailed their careers and exposed the whole family to threats of blackmail. The older brother decided that the best way to end the crisis for both of them, was for him to set an example by getting married. It was no matter that he didn't have a clue as to where to find a woman to marry. This was all an exit strategy. He wrote, 'I shall do everything possible to marry this very year, but if I should lack the courage for this, I am in any event abandoning forever my habits and shall strive to be counted no longer among the company of homosexuals'.

With that, Tchaikovsky hopped into a carriage and sped away from Moscow to the country house of his friend Bek-Bulatov, where for the next 4 days he took part in one of the most notorious gay orgies of 19th-century Russia. The particular target of Tchaikovsky's passions that wild weekend was his own coachman.

When it did happen a few months later, Tchaikovsky's marriage was an utter fiasco. Antonina Milyukova was a 28-year-old former student from Moscow. Like most professors, he barely remembered her 4 years after she had been in his class. Reeling from heartbreak and sexual confusion, he was easy prey to her aggressive advances. He received the first of a battery of her love letters in March 1877. Suddenly, right on cue, there was a candidate for the wedding he had hoped for. For her part, she had just inherited her dowry and was on the prowl for a husband. By the time Antonina and Tchaikovsky were reunited in St Petersburg on 20 May, the whole wedding scene was written – and its tempo might as well have been marked presto.

They married on 6 July, spent all of 20 days together under one roof, and (no surprise) failed to consummate the union. In a panic over what he had done, at the earliest opportunity Tchaikovsky used his delicate mental state as an excuse and fled. He hid at his sister's country villa from the prying eyes of Muscovite society for the next 2 months. Upon his return he sheepishly admitted to his wife that it had all been a dreadful mistake and optimistically expressed his hope that they could remain 'friends'. As always, he had no idea what he was getting into. He erroneously assumed that she would simply agree to annul the marriage as readily as she had acceded to being part of it in the first place. Antonina dug her heels in, for years refusing his repeated requests for a divorce.

Throughout his life Tchaikovsky would suffer panic attacks and paranoia whenever it occurred to him that Antonia might expose his fondness for young boys, so he paid her hush money of 100 rubles a month until 1881. She outlived him, spending her last decades in a mental hospital, paid for by Tchaikovsky's pension, until her death in 1917. In his diaries he referred to her as 'a terrible wound'.

RISKY BUSINESS

While there were long-standing rules against homosexuality in the Russian military (instituted by Peter the Great), and there was even a law against gay sex that was introduced by Czar Nicholas I, the ban was rarely enforced, partly because so many aristocrats swung that way. In fact, it was the trial of Oscar Wilde, 2 years after Tchaikovsky's death in 1893, that turned up the heat on anti-gay feeling across Europe. Until that time, Tchaikovsky's main risk as a gay man was blackmail and embarrassment – it was unlikely he would ever go to jail.

A Formidable Influence

If Tchaikovsky's marriage was bizarre, then his relationship with Nadezhda von Meck is even stranger. She has become the prototype for generations of generous benefactors since her time, the mysterious 'beloved friend' to whom the composer dedicated so many of his works.

Mrs von Meck was the immensely wealthy widow of a railway tycoon. Thanks to the deep pocketbook left by her husband and the knowledge of an accomplished amateur, she was a formidable influence upon the musical world of Moscow. One of her artists-in-residence was a longtime boyfriend of Tchaikovsky's, the violinist Iosif Koteck. Koteck probably told von Meck about Tchaikovsky's great talent and financial difficulties and, in 1876, she began commissioning him. Von Meck was 9 years older than Tchaikovsky and had eleven children as well as a tremendous financial empire to govern. On first impression, there was nothing remarkable about the arrangement. Across Europe, there was a trend towards women as patrons of the arts that was beginning to redefine the way music and art was commissioned. The Vatican and royal families became less important as patrons and private citizens, many of them wealthy bourgeoisie such as Mrs von Meck, stepped up to write the cheques.

The relationship between Tchaikovsky and Mrs von Meck went much further than just the classic scenario involving a benefactress and impoverished artist. It resulted in the creation of hundreds of works, many of them masterpieces. More than 1200 letters passed between them for 14 years, full of erotic tension and culminating in a nasty break-up. And then there was the strange condition imposed by Tchaikovsky on the relationship: they must never meet.

The 13-year period of von Meck's support was not only the most productive time in his career, it was also a comedy of pursuit and flight as she smothered him with romantic praise while he ran away to hotels and country houses all over Europe to avoid her. Inevitably, twice they met by accident at parties. On both occasions, Tchaikovsky slipped away, without a word to the woman who had paid him the equivalent in today's money of millions of dollars and guaranteed him the financial peace of mind that made his work possible.

Mrs von Meck probably knew Tchaikovsky was homosexual. For her part, in an early letter to Tchaikovsky she was frank about her own butch demeanor: 'I am very unsympathetic in my personal relations because I do not possess any femininity whatever; second, I do not know how to be tender, and this characteristic has passed on to my entire family. All of us are afraid to be affected or sentimental, and therefore the general nature of our family relationships is comradely, or masculine.' Eventually, von Meck realised the advisability of the pact that prohibited contact between the two. In a much later letter she wrote, 'You make up for my disappointment, mistakes and yearning; yes, if I had happiness in my hands I should give it to you. But now I fear acquaintance with you for quite a different reason and because of a different feeling.'

Early Life

That was just the sort of confession of love that would send Tchaikovsky packing. As desperately as he craved the attention, he was repelled by intimacy. The roots of this dual nature went deep. He grew up in what one biographer called a 'feminised' environment. Coddled by his beloved French governess, Fanny Durbach, and his piano teachers, by the age of 7, Tchaikovsky was recognised as a musical prodigy. He was a hybrid of Russian stoicism and European sentimentality – his father was a Russian mining engineer and his mother was from a French émigré family. Tchaikovsky had an older brother, Nikolay, a younger sister, Aleksandra (Sasha) and younger brothers Ippolit, Anatoly and Modest, the playwright to whom Pyotr remained closest all his life. He barely knew his father, a descendant of Cossacks and the manager of the ironworks, which was the principal industry in the provincial town of Votinsk, about 965 kilometres east of Moscow.

Tchaikovsky's father was a big fish in a small pond. He made the mistake of moving to St Petersburg when Pyotr was 10, hoping to take up a business opportunity that never materialised. The family slipped into financial and social distress. Pyotr was packed off to an all-boys boarding school, where his homosexual tendencies were noticed at once by the many older boys, whose considerable homosexual experience on their parental estates was the subject of dormitory boasting. Pyotr's first, and perhaps greatest, passion was for Sergei Kireev, the first of many young objects of his adoration. His other schoolmates included middle-class boys whose families aspired to social climbing, as well as aristocrats, such as Prince Vladimir Meschersky – who would remain a presence in Pyotr's life well after their graduation. The prince, who was a particularly active homosexual, is the perfect example of the morality of the time. Russia already had a well-established tradition of sexploitation. The serfs were essentially at the beck and call of their owners, just as the younger and poorer boys at school were at the disposal of their elders and betters.

Pyotr was still at school when tragedy struck. He was only 15 when his mother died of cholera. His older sister, Sasha, became head of the family, which was struggling with debts as well as disappointment. Their father was all but completely absent from their lives, and it became painfully obvious that the artistic Pyotr was going to have to become more pragmatic and find a way to provide for them. The legal profession was the first choice. Tchaikovsky left school in 1859 to take a clerkship in the ministry of justice. The job was mind-numbing drudgery. What little is known of Tchaikovsky's 4 years in the law is mainly rendered by the bold contrast of his daily desk duty and the fast company he kept in the St Petersburg gay underworld. Late nights of cards, laced with vodka and culminating in fumbled erotic encounters gave way to the cold reality of returning to the office to answer the bell each morning.

It wasn't long before Tchaikovsky's ambivalence towards his career and the guilt over his hedonism caught up with him. The masquerade of the decent, regimented civil servant was not for him. Creative tensions were also bubbling within and, when in 1861 he made his first trip abroad (visiting Berlin, Hamburg, Antwerp, Brussels, London and Paris), it became harder than ever to sit still and copy contracts.

The Troubled Composer

On 11 April 1863 Tchaikovsky abruptly quit his job. He began attending classes full time at the St Petersburg Conservatory, which was run by the brilliant composer Anton Rubinstein. What a difference the musical world offered! In the summer, he was invited to stay at the dacha of Prince Alexei Goltsyn where he started incorporating folk melodies into his compositions. The intoxicatingly exciting first orchestral performance of one of his works came in August 1865 – he had set Schiller's ode to joy for choir and orchestra (the same text that Beethoven used for his Ninth Symphony). He conducted for the first time that November and was well on his way to a hugely successful career in music when he was recruited to teach in Moscow by Anton's brother Nikolai Rubenstein. He was immediately welcomed by Russia's Kutcka or 'Mighty Handful' of five famous composers – Cesar Antonovich Cui, Mily Balakeriv, Nicolai Rimsky-Korsakov, Alexander Borodin and Modeste Mussorgsky. However, Tchaikovsky mixed their nationalistic sound with a pan-European style.

But even as he found his voice in music, Tchaikovsky was plagued by depression, insomnia, headaches and bizarre hallucinations. His love life was also messy. He kept a 14-year-old student, Vladimir Shilovsky, as a muse, and to whom he dediated several works. But his sexual orientation was unsteady. He also enjoyed a brief infatuation with Desirée Artot, an up and coming mezzo-soprano who he met in the spring of 1868. She performed on stage in Moscow that autumn and, by December, Tchaikovsky was writing letters to his father and brother that hinted at marriage. However, in January Artot ran off to Warsaw and married a Spanish baritone. That was the start of the crisis that led to Tchaikovsky's own unhappy marriage.

Pyotr Ilyich Tchaikovsky's works include six symphonies and three piano concertos – only two of which are finished – plus a violin concerto and eleven operas.

Meanwhile, the masterpieces just kept on coming. Some of the greatest ballet and orchestral music of all time poured from his fantastically prolific pen. From *Romeo and Juliet* in 1869 he went on to create *Swan Lake* in 1875, the same year as his great piano concerto in B flat minor. That year he visited Bayreuth in Bavaria, the Mecca of opera, where he met Franz Liszt and heard Wagner's music. This prompted a series of operas from Tchaikovsky. His recognition as a genius spread as quickly abroad as it did at home – in the 1870s his works were the toast of London, Boston and New York, where they often made their debut. For all his mercurial ways when it came to personal attachments, Tchaikovsky was an unfailingly disciplined craftsman who maintained a regimen of composing and 2-hour afternoon walks that never failed him. Mrs von Meck kept writing the letters and cheques until suddenly her funds ran out, much to Tchaikovsky's resentment.

By that time, Tchaikovsky was an established power of his own on the world stage. As his fame grew, he toured the musical capitals of Europe as well as briefly visiting the United States; the opportunities to enjoy anonymous sex with a long roster of willing and always younger men were plentiful. Tchaikovsky was promiscuous, especially when he was on the road, but not incapable of strong feelings. When one of his longtime lovers (and former servant), Alyosha, was drafted into the army, the composer tried hard through official contacts to get him a safe assignment.

No matter how much adulation or fun he enjoyed, Tchaikovsky could never stave off for long the mood swings and feelings of guilt. The physical embodiment of this duality in Tchaikovsky's life was the constant shuttle between the gay underground of the city and the rural innocence of his house in the countryside, the courtier's popularity in the imperial household and the lonely nights at hotels and friends' estates across Europe where he would take refuge and compose. The double nature of his messy personal life is also reflected in his music. Posterity still delights in the sweet pastels of *Swan Lake* and the 'Sugarplum Fairy' from *The Nutcracker Suite*, but there is a darker side. The thunderous bass chords pounded out by the virtuoso performer in the almost too-famous second piano concerto, or the chaotic battlefield music of the *1812 Overture*, reveal the inner agonies.

Depression and Death

The double life of Tchaikovsky is, at least in one significant way, completely understandable. The composer of the *Pathetique* had a pathological tendency towards the extremes of euphoria and dark tragic foreboding that one hears in the wild swings of his music. Now called bipolar condition, the most recent terminological revision of what used to be manic depression or, in much earlier times, melancholy, the diagnosis accounts for the volatility of so many artists. Tchaikovsky's condition has long raised questions about the circumstances of his death. One early story, which most biographers dismiss as apocryphal, had him trying to kill himself as a young man by jumping into a river, desperate over a romantic breakup. More serious issues are presented by the story of his death at age 63. Although it is well known that he died of cholera in the early hours of 25 October 1893, having suffered from a stomach ache and the symptoms of cholera for about 5 days, there was a story that shortly circulated that, already sick, he deliberately downed a glass of unboiled water at a late-night supper at Leiner's, a St Petersburg restaurant. His brother recalled that the company was aghast at the risk, but Tchaikovsky waved off their fears and told them not to worry. The dispute over the cause of his death has kept biographers busy ever since. Whether or not he killed himself are just the final two notes in that long trill of his double life.

THE FAT MAN IN THE BATHROOM: FATTY ARBUCKLE

MAIN CULPRIT:
Roscoe Conklin 'Fatty' Arbuckle (1887–1933), Hollywood comedian, actor and director

SCANDAL:
Arbuckle was accused of the rape and murder of party girl and actress Virginia Rappe, though it is widely viewed as a fraudulent claim

WHY:
An ambitious district attorney was determined to get a guilty verdict and use the gutter press to his advantage

We are not trying Roscoe Arbuckle alone ... in a large sense we are trying ourselves. We are trying our present-day morals ... The issue here is really and truly greater than the guilt or innocence of this poor, unfortunate man ...
– Judge Lazarus

Roscoe 'Fatty' Arbuckle was at the peak of his career when he was accused of murder in 1921. After two trials that resulted in hung juries, a third resulted in an acquittal and a written apology from the jury, unprecedented in US legal history.

The roaring twenties had just begun and so had Prohibition. The scandal that rocked the fledgling movie industry and brought down its biggest, brightest star began with a private booze party in an upmarket hotel room.

The 'big' star had every reason to feel good. He'd just finished three feature films at a hectic pace. All three had been made at the same time – and in the time normally allotted for one. Fatty Arbuckle was at the top of his field. The 120-kilogram man had amazed everyone on set with his extraordinary energy and conscientious work ethic. Arbuckle knew these latest films were the funniest he'd ever made and now the hard work was done. It was Labor Day weekend – time for a little hard-earned rest and recreation.

Arbuckle and two buddies, director Fred Fischbach and actor Lowell Sherman, had driven from Los Angeles up to San Francisco and booked themselves into the city's very best hotel, the St Francis. On the twelfth floor Arbuckle and Fischbach shared room 1219, Sherman took room 1221 and the corner-room, 1220, was fitted out as a reception lounge. The perfect set-up for a party.

During prohibition, San Francisco was known as an open town, liquor was as freely available as ever. For someone like Arbuckle it was delivered. Crates of bootleg whisky and gin were stacked in readiness. There was no guest list but there was a telephone and besides, wherever the Hollywood stars went it was inevitable a party would start.

This party would start at noon when Virginia Rappe, a model and sometime movie actress, knocked on the door. Virginia was known as a party girl and was there at the invitation of Fischbach. She asked if she could bring some uninvited guests – her manager, Al Semnacher, and his friend Maude Delmont. Soon more people turned up, including showgirls Zey Prevon and Alice Blake. Late-riser Arbuckle was still in his pyjamas and bathrobe but this was a casual weekend get-together and nobody minded. Breakfast was ordered and drinks were poured. The ladies drank gin and orange juice and the men whisky – a victrola was ordered to provide the music. More guests arrived and the party warmed up, catered for by a steady stream of waiters and bellboys. Within a week, Arbuckle would stand accused of the vicious rape and murder of Virginia Rappe on that night.

An Unconceited Man

Before the day of the party, you'd be hard pressed to find anyone to say a bad word about Arbuckle. Actress and co-star Minta Durfee described him as the most unconceited man who ever lived, and later gave him her hand in marriage.

Added to Arbuckle's charm was his astonishing talent; he could tumble like an acrobat and sing like an angel. When the great tenor Enrico Caruso heard Arbuckle sing he urged him to '… give up this nonsense you do for a living … With training you could become the second greatest singer in the world'.

But Arbuckle was already on his way to becoming the greatest comedian in the world. From his start in vaudeville he'd found his way to the Keystone Studios of Mack Sennett. It was at Keystone that Arbuckle helped the young rookie English actor Charlie Chaplin, who joined the company in 1914, when Arbunckle was the star. Chaplin's most famous character, 'the Tramp' was created when Charlie borrowed Arbuckle's balloon pants, boots and trademark tiny hat. Chaplin would rise to become the biggest star in movies, but at that time the mantle was Arbuckle's.

In 1916 Arbuckle was one of the few director–stars in the movie business, but he was tiring of the simple slapstick formulas of the Keystone Studio. Paramount Pictures stepped in and offered him an unprecedented deal – $1000 a day, 25 per cent of the profits and – for Arbuckle, the best part – complete artistic control. After 2 successful years Paramount realised what a goldmine they had found in Arbuckle. In 1918, Paramount executives Adolph Zukor, Jesse Lasky and Joseph Schenck moved to ensure their hold over the star. They offered him $3 million over a 3-year period – an astronomical amount for that time. It was the biggest contract ever seen in Hollywood, but Arbuckle would earn his money.

However, the films were never shown. Once they were in the can Arbuckle, Fischbach and Sherman jumped into a Pierce Arrow and headed for San Francisco and the fateful party at the St Francis Hotel.

The Accusation

On Monday 12 September 1921, Bambina Maude Delmont swore out a complaint against Roscoe Arbuckle, accusing him of the murder of Virginia Rappe. The case would go on for 8 months in front of six different judicial hearings.

In her statement to the police, Delmont claimed that, on the night of the party, around 3 am, Arbuckle had grabbed Virginia outside his bedroom door and said, 'I've waited 5 years to get you'. Virginia struggled, but was no match for the big man, who allegedly dragged her into his bedroom and locked the door. Delmont could hear sounds of a struggle and Virginia's cries for

The silent screen comedic actor Fatty Arbuckle wearing his trademark tiny hat and balloon-style pants.

help. Delmont banged on the door with her fists and her shoes but to no avail. After an hour Arbuckle, wet with perspiration, opened the door. Delmont rushed into the room to see Virginia naked and dying on the bed. Arbuckle had ripped off the girl's clothes. Her underwear and shirtwaist dress were torn to pieces and scattered around the room. Virginia screamed, 'I'm dying. I'm dying. Roscoe killed me!'. She was covered in bruises and there were two 'monkey bites' on her neck. Six days later she died.

San Francisco district attorney, Mathew Brady prosecuted the case. Brady was determined to secure a murder verdict and had no compunction about using the gutter press to help his case. He issued public statements treating the accusations as proven facts before one word of evidence was heard. The headlines screamed: 'Fatty Arbuckle sought in orgy death! Brady says evidence shows murder'.

The Grand Jury

A grand jury hearing is held in secret with no defence representation, since it is only convened to establish grounds for an indictment. To them Delmont told the same lurid story of bestial lust but, even without a defence opponent, Brady was having trouble finding corroborating evidence. Showgirl Zey Prevon, who saw Rappe after the alleged rape, told a completely different story.

According to Prevon, Virginia was lying on the bed fully clothed and complaining of pains. It was then that she started to tear at her own clothes in a kind of frenzy. She said, 'I'm dying. I'm dying'. Brady's assistants badgered Prevon for hours to try and get her to testify to the three magic words sworn to by Delmont – 'Roscoe killed me' – but Prevon denied it. They suggested that she had been bought off and threatened her with perjury charges but Prevon was adamant that she never heard Virginia say those words. Eventually, after hours of grilling, she cracked and agreed to sign a statement that she heard Virginia say, 'He hurt me'.

The jury voted for a manslaughter indictment.

At the coroner's inquest Delmont told a different story from the account she'd told the police and the grand jury. To the police, the newspapers and the grand jury she said that Arbuckle had grabbed Virginia saying, 'I've been waiting to get you for 5 years'. At the inquest this was never mentioned. She had described Virginia's screams but now she said there wasn't a sound. She had claimed that Virginia was naked with her shredded clothing littered around, but now she said that she was fully dressed. This time there were no bruises or 'monkey bites'.

Evidence was provided by the two doctors who had treated Virginia and Dr Ophuls who carried out the post mortem. They all agreed that there were no signs of violence – no bruises, no haemorrhaging of blood – examination of the vagina also failed to reveal any abnormality. Death was caused by peritonitis caused by a rupture of the bladder. As to what caused the rupture of the bladder, they could not say.

Brady had no intention of allowing Zey Prevon to testify. Even though the coroner's jury said they could not come to a conclusion without her evidence, Brady would not budge. He insisted that they consider a verdict. And they did. Since a rupture of the bladder caused death – which could have been caused by pressure from Arbuckle – the jury decided he should be charged with manslaughter.

The Police Court Hearing

Brady was determined to get a murder charge. If he could convict Arbuckle for murder he could run a campaign for the governorship of California, as he would be seen as the man who 'cleaned up' the movies. He had one more card up his sleeve – a police court hearing. This time there would be a defence.

Hours before the hearing began, Rappe's manager, Al Semnacher, caused a sensation by announcing to the press that Arbuckle had in fact pushed a piece of ice into Miss Rappe's vagina. The papers screamed the hysterical headlines that most people even today associate with the case (though somehow the ice has become a bottle): 'Torture of Virginia Rappe Charged!!!'.

Semnacher now became Brady's star witness. But his story changed on the witness stand, and he described Arbuckle's conduct towards the women at the party as 'gentlemanly'. Apparently he hadn't actually seen the ice incident (three witnesses had already testified that Arbuckle had placed ice on Rappe's stomach because they all thought she was suffering a stomach ache). Within hours the prosecution deemed Semnacher a 'hostile witness'.

Virginia Rappe, the model and silent movie actress who claimed she was raped by Fatty Arbuckle at a wild party in 1921, and died a few days afterwards.

When the defence attorney, Frank Dominguez, got Semnacher to the stand he accused him of blackmail. Pointing at Semnacher he said, 'We intend to prove that this man, acting upon the suggestion and instigation of Mrs Delmont and a third person, conceived of the idea and carried out the plot of taking Miss Rappe's torn clothing to Los Angeles, and later with these articles in their possession, of extorting money from Roscoe Arbuckle'.

There was an uproar of objections from the prosecution and the judge ruled the evidence inadmissible. Dominguez was not allowed to follow this line. But he still had in his possession telegrams sent by Delmont saying, 'We have Roscoe Arbuckle in a hole here. Chance to make some money out of him'. Delmont had a long rap sheet with charges for racketeering, bigamy, fraud and extortion. Dominguez had affidavits from some of her victims. He could wait until she took the stand.

But Delmont was never called, as Brady knew she would torpedo his case. Ever since she made the accusation, she never told the same story twice. He couldn't afford to call her. The judge was appalled that such an important witness would not appear. He warned Brady, 'I must advise you gentlemen of the prosecution that you are taking a chance on a motion to dismiss; you are travelling very close to the line that may lead me to dismiss the charge'. Brady toughed it out and insisted that the judge make a decision.

In his summation, Judge Lazarus harangued the prosecution for presenting the flimsiest possible case and demolished every piece of prosecution evidence. The clothes were torn by the deceased herself; the piece of ice was hearsay; there were no bruises. 'I do not find any evidence that Mr Arbuckle either committed or attempted to commit rape'.

The defence team was overjoyed but their joy was short-lived as the judge continued, 'We are not trying Roscoe Arbuckle alone … in a large sense we are trying ourselves. We are trying our present-day morals … The issue here is really and truly greater than the guilt or innocence of this poor, unfortunate man'. The judge decided that Roscoe Arbuckle would be tried for manslaughter.

The First Trial

A tremendous man skipped up the steps as lightly as Fred Astaire. He was tremendous, obese – just plain fat. 'Name's Arbuckle', he said, 'Roscoe Arbuckle. Call me Fatty. I'm a funnyman and acrobat. Bet I could do good in pictures. Watcha think?' With no warning he went into a feather-light step, clapped his hands and did a backward somersault as gracefully as a girl tumbler. And that was how the famous and later infamous Fatty Arbuckle introduced himself to motion pictures.

– Mack Sennett, Keystone Studios

The prosecution led with the medical evidence attempting to establish that Arbuckle may have caused Rappe's bladder rupture, but the doctors could provide nothing conclusive. It was revealed that Rappe, who the prosecution had always claimed was a virgin, actually had gonorrhoea.

The statements of Prevon and Blake were entered but it was now obvious they'd been made under duress.

A fingerprint expert was called. He was so incompetent that defence attorney Gavin McNab debunked his claims to the hooting laughter of the courtroom.

Prosecution attacked Arbuckle's character by producing a witness claiming he had bribed him 3 years ago for the key to Rappe's dressing room. The story was shaky and the defence let it pass.

Prosecution called physical-training instructors who testified that Virginia Rappe was a healthy, athletic girl who'd never had a day's illness in her life. Defence countered with several witnesses who established she suffered from cystitis and was well known for tearing at her clothes in the manner described when having an attack.

At last Roscoe Arbuckle was called to the stand. He quietly told the events from his point of view. He'd gone to his room to change out of his pyjamas. When he tried to open the bathroom door he found Miss Rappe on the floor in front of the toilet. She'd been vomiting. He squeezed through the door and picked her up. He held her while she vomited again then sat her down, wiped her face, gave her water and helped her to the bed. He then went to get help from the other party-goers. When they returned, Miss Rappe was in a frenzy tearing at her clothes. The 'girls' then took care of her. He later returned to the room to find Mrs Delmont massaging Rappe with some ice. There was a piece of ice lying on her body. He picked it up and said, 'What's this doing here?' Mrs Delmont said, 'Leave it there, I know how to take care of Virginia'. He replaced it and tried to cover the girl with the bedspread. Mrs Delmont got angry and told him to get out of the room and leave her alone. 'I told Mrs Delmont to shut up or I'd throw her out the window, and I went out of the room'.

The jury was impressed by his simple, direct testimony and even more impressed when the prosecution cross examined him. They grilled him for 3 hours and his calm responses never faltered. They asked over thirty questions about the victrola; twenty-eight questions about how Delmont came to be there and more than 200 questions about the time on the hotel clock. At the end of the day, spectators in the courtroom stood and cheered him.

Arbuckle was that rarity, a truly jolly fat man. He had no meanness or malice or jealousy in him. Everything seemed to amuse and delight him. He was free with his advice and too free in spending and lending money. I could not have found a better-natured man to teach me the movie business, or a more knowledgeable one.

– Buster Keaton

The defence team felt confident when the jury returned. However, the jury was hopelessly deadlocked – ten to two said not guilty. The judge declared a mistrial.

The Second Trial

Most of the evidence in this trial was the same as in the first, but there were exceptions. Zey Prevon admitted that the district attorney had forced her to lie. The man who made the bribery accusations was found to be a bootlegger who'd been arrested for assaulting an 8-year-old girl, and was a fugitive from a chain gang. More witnesses stepped up to tell of Rappe's habit of ripping off her clothes. Genuine fingerprint experts testified that the prosecution evidence had been faked. McNab was so confident that he didn't call Arbuckle to testify – so confident, in fact, that he made no closing argument because 'the jury had all the facts'. The verdict: guilty, ten to two. The jury deadlocked. There would be another trial.

McNab underestimated the power of the publicity surrounding the case. The jury took his refusal to call Arbuckle or make a closing statement as an admission of guilt.

The Third Trial

The publicity circus had compromised Arbuckle's chances. For the past 7 months the papers had been full of shocking accounts of Hollywood debauchery. People were told that the rich and powerful men of Hollywood were working behind the scenes to pervert the course of justice. The court of public opinion had been fed a daily dose of histrionic lies. Arbuckle's films had been banned all over the United

States. Delmont was touring the country with a one-woman show. Billing herself as 'The woman who signed the murder charge against Arbuckle', she promised to 'rip wide the screen which hides Hollywood and the movie colony'. In this environment it would be impossible to find a jury that hadn't been prejudiced.

McNab had other problems: Zey Prevon had left the country and was hiding out in Cuba. The 'Taylor Scandal' broke (the unsolved murder of director William Desmond Taylor), producing a new wave of hysterical tales about Hollywood orgies, sexual perversity and murder.

The defence's strategy had been to be gentle on the character of Rappe and the show-girls to avoid alienating the jury, but now the gloves were off. McNab's cross-examination of Alice Blake was so vicious that she collapsed on the stand. He criticised the judge at every opportunity. He called abortionist Josephine Roth to testify that Rappe had been her patient five times: four for abortions, and one to give birth to a baby boy when she was 14 years old. He raised an incident where Mack Sennett had his studios fumigated because Virginia had introduced crab lice there. McNab couldn't know what the jury was thinking but he knew he was risking every-thing. He knew that attacking the dead girl was a huge risk and, if he was wrong, Arbuckle could spend 10 years in jail. The jury retired to consider the verdict.

Six minutes later they returned. The decision was unanimous. Five of the six minutes they had taken were used to compose a statement:

Acquittal is not enough for Roscoe Arbuckle. We feel that a great injustice has been done him. We feel also that it was our only plain duty to give him this exoneration. There was not the slightest proof adduced to connect him in any way with the commission of a crime.

He was manly throughout the case and told a straightforward story on the witness stand, which we all believed.

The happening at the hotel was an unfortunate affair for which Arbuckle, so the evidence shows, was in no way responsible.

We wish him success and hope that the American people will take the judgment of fourteen men and women who have sat listening for thirty-one days to the evidence that Roscoe Arbuckle is entirely innocent and free from all blame.

An Unhappy Ending

Six days after Arbuckle's acquittal, Will Hays of the censorship board banned him from working in movies. His days of stardom were over. He continued to work under an assumed name and died of a heart attack 12 years later. The morality clause now standard in film contracts is still known as the 'Arbuckle Clause'.

FALSE
PROPHETS

Fallen evangelist Jim Bakker being
escorted to the courthouse in Charlotte,
North Carolina, by federal marshals.

MOTIVATION

anger
charity
envy
faith
gluttony
greed
hope
lust
pride
sloth

THE PREACHER
AND THE PROSTITUTE:
JIMMY SWAGGART

MAIN CULPRIT:
Jimmy Swaggart (1935–), evangelist preacher

SCANDAL:
Busted for shenanigans with a prostitute

WHY:
'Demons' made him do it

If I do not return to the pulpit this weekend, millions of people will go to hell.
– Jimmy Swaggart

Evangelist Jimmy Swaggart speaking while holding the Bible. His hypocrisy seemed to know no bounds – as he was exposed in a sex scandal after having damned other Ministers of the Assembly of God for similar behaviour and expelled them from the church.

On Sunday, 21 February 1988, more than 8000 people crammed into the Family Worship Center in Baton Rouge, Louisiana, to hear a remarkable sermon. Jimmy Swaggart, the fiery televangelist and head of a huge worldwide religious empire, stood before his congregation, his voice shaking with emotion, and declared, 'I have sinned against you'.

Swaggart was known as the scourge of sinners, fornicators and pornographers. He had recently helped to bring down two fellow televangelists who had strayed from the path of righteousness. Now, as his wife and son looked on and television cameras recorded every agonising moment – it was his turn to repent.

The Televisual Preacher

Swaggart's training in evangelism began early. He was born on 15 March 1935 into a poor family in the small town of Ferriday, Louisiana. His cousin and best friend, future rock and roller Jerry Lee Lewis, was born in the same year. Both boys learned to play piano, and at night they would sneak into Haney's Big House, a now legendary black dance hall in Ferriday, where they were exposed to the infectious rhythms of blues and boogie woogie. Jimmy's parents, Willy and Minnie Bell Swaggart, embraced the Pentecostal church in 1943, and it wasn't long before 8-year-old Jimmy was 'speaking in tongues' – the ecstatic babbling, believed to be inspired by the Holy Ghost, which was one of the highlights of any Pentecostal meeting.

Jimmy began to preach on street corners, sometimes singing and accompanying himself on the accordion. In 1952 he married Frances Anderson and they had a son, Donnie. They spent 10 years living out of a car as they drove from one revival meeting to the next while Jimmy honed his preaching skills. He also recorded some gospel albums and they sold well. In 1967 Swaggart built a house in Baton Rouge that became the headquarters for his ministry. Two years later, he started a syndicated radio show and, in 1973, began to broadcast on television. With his passionate, theatrical preaching style and musical interludes, Swaggart was a natural for television.

Swaggart belonged to the Assemblies of God, a hugely successful Pentecostal sect founded in 1914. By the 1980s, he was its biggest star. His Baton Rouge complex housed the huge World Ministry Center, the 7500-seat Family Worship Center, the Jimmy Swaggart Bible College and a host of buildings devoted to the ministry's mail-order business and other ventures. Swaggart's television broadcasts were seen in 195 countries, and he was bringing in up to $150 million every year.

Such figures inevitably attracted media interest in the ministry and its finances and, in early 1983, a reporter named John Camp made a television documentary about the Assemblies of God. While researching Swaggart, he heard rumours that the evangelist had been seen with prostitutes. Camp's sources within the organisation dismissed them. With Swaggart, he was told, it just wasn't possible.

Meanwhile, there were rumours circulating about two other prominent Assemblies of God ministers, Marvin Gorman and Jim Bakker. Gorman was pastor of a thriving church in New Orleans, had a popular television program and was set for bigger things. Back in 1981, Swaggart had been told about a liaison between Gorman and a female member of his congregation. When confronted, Gorman admitted there had been a relationship involving kissing and petting, but said that they had never had sex. Swaggart believed him. Rumours of this and other affairs continued, however – some of them, it was said, spread by Swaggart, who saw in Gorman a potential rival.

In 1986, Swaggart learned that Gorman had been having a long-running affair with another minister's wife. A highly charged meeting took place in Swaggart's home at which Gorman admitted to the affair, but denied there had been any others. Swaggart called Gorman a liar and demanded he step down from his pastorship immediately – the Assemblies of God prescribed a 2-year period of penance and rehabilitation for adultery. Gorman begged for time – he was due to finalise a $16-million loan the following day to buy a new church and two radio stations – but Swaggart was inflexible. Gorman resigned and the following Sunday a statement was read to his former congregation accusing him of 'numerous adulterous and illicit affairs'. Gorman was expelled from the Assemblies of God and went bankrupt.

Jim Bakker was a far bigger fish than Gorman. With his wife, Tammy Faye, he ran the PTL Christian cable television network and Heritage USA, a religious theme park complete with a water slide and a fake volcano. The Bakkers were raking in about $100 million a year. Swaggart despised their gaudy style, conspicuous wealth and what he saw as an insufficiently stern attitude to sin.

Bakker was one of the few who defended Gorman after Swaggart brought him down. 'If he gets Gorman, he'll get me next', he was heard to say. He had reason to be worried. Rumours of Bakker's homosexual activities had been floating around for a while, and there was another story that PTL had paid a large sum to a church secretary so she wouldn't talk about her relationship with him. Swaggart kept the pressure on Bakker, and was finally instrumental in forcing him to step down from his executive positions at PTL – an act which led to his eventual imprisonment.

Jimmy Swaggart had made his position clear. 'You cannot cover sin', he said. 'It has to be exposed'.

Meetings in a Motel Room

'Pornography is as addictive as alcohol, drugs or gambling – and this is a proven fact! ... Addiction takes only a short time and then escalation sets in. 'Old' pornography is not as stimulating as "new" pornography. There's no thrill in going over what has been previously viewed. You need a steady diet of "bigger and better thrills".'

So said Jimmy Swaggart in the booklet *Pornography – America's Dark Stain*. He was speaking from experience.

One day in 1986, a 26-year-old prostitute named Debra Murphree was standing on a corner of Airline Highway in New Orleans. It was a strip of mainly run-down motels, some of them brothels. A tan Lincoln car pulled up. Inside it was a man wearing a sweatband, T-shirt and jogging pants slit at the front, with a handkerchief over the opening. She asked him if he wanted a date and he said, 'All I want to do is jack off awhile ... look at your tits'. He offered her $10. She was insulted and demanded $20.

Swaggart became a regular customer, meeting Murphree every 2 weeks or so. At first they drove around in his car while he asked her to undress. 'He'd always try to talk me into pulling my pants off and facing him sideways with my legs spread apart', she recalled. Once he asked her to strip naked and get out of the car in front of other people, but she refused, fearing he would drive off and leave her like that. Later, they met in the room she rented in the Travel Inn, which had a sign on the window reading, 'Positively no refunds after 15 minutes'. Across the road, a giant billboard proclaimed, 'Jesus said: "Unless a man is born again he cannot see the Kingdom of God." Your eternity is at stake.'

Early on, Murphree told him he looked just like Jimmy Swaggart. He said, 'A lot of people tell me that, but my name's Billy'.

Their meetings settled into a regular pattern. After dropping her at the motel, Swaggart would drive around for a while, making sure there were no police about. Having satisfied himself that there was no 'heat', he would go to Murphree's room and put $20 on the table inside the door. He never left a tip.

Swaggart liked Murphree to recreate poses he had seen in pornographic magazines, or get her to stand over him so he could look up her dress. They engaged in oral sex, during which he always wore a condom. On several occasions, he asked her to find another girl so he could watch the two of them together, but

THE PROSTITUTE

Debra Murphree was born in Patoka, Indiana, in 1961. The daughter of a railway worker, she was raised as a Methodist. In high school, however, she 'got a little wild', as she put it. She was married at 16, had a daughter and two sons over 5 years, then left her husband and started working for an escort service in Nashville. She fell in love with a cocaine dealer and the couple moved to New Orleans. By 1987 she was seeing up to ten clients a day. Shortly after gaining notoriety, as the girl in the motel room with Jimmy Swaggart, she was charged with soliciting (a charge unrelated to Swaggart), fined $500 and sentenced to 6 months in prison.

she said she didn't know anyone in the area well enough. Once, briefly and despite his later denials, they had sexual intercourse. His visits rarely lasted longer than 20 minutes.

One day, he noticed a photograph of Murphree's 9-year-old daughter in the room. He started asking questions about her, and wanted to know if Murphree would let her watch them having sex. She didn't like that kind of talk. 'You can do whatever turns you on', she told him, 'but don't mention my daughter again'.

Prostitute Debra Murphree, meets the press following the release of the July edition of *Penthouse*, which featured her story, complete with pictures.

Swaggart's visits to Airline Highway always took place in broad daylight. He had gained a lot of publicity over the Bakker case, and stated on several occasions that he himself had nothing to hide. He must have realised how much of a risk he was taking. He didn't know that a trap had already been set.

Marvin Gorman was suing Swaggart and his associates for $90 million, and had heard the rumours about the prostitute. His son Randy, who was both a minister and a reserve deputy sheriff, began to cruise Airline Highway, and met Murphree about the same time she started seeing Swaggart. He didn't tell her his name, and she knew him as 'the cop'.

Murphree had told a few of the other working girls that she was seeing Swaggart. None of them seemed intererested, but when she mentioned it to 'the cop', he was very interested. He started to ring her every day and gave her his beeper number so that she could contact him when Swaggart appeared. She threw it away. She didn't have anything against Swaggart. As she said later, 'He never tried to hurt me or got loud'.

Randy Gorman had booked a room in the motel next to the Travel Inn, directly across from Murphree's room. A stakeout man was installed there, along with a camera.

On 17 October 1987, at around 2 pm, Murphree was in her room when she saw Swaggart's car drive past. She went out and waved to him. He asked if there were was any 'heat' and she replied that it was safe. Swaggart parked the car and went to her room.

At that moment, Marvin Gorman received a phone call at the warehouse where he had set up a new church. The message was 'He's here. Hurry up.'

Swaggart put his $20 on the table. Murphree, hearing a car door slam, looked out of the window and saw 'the cop' running towards the motel next door. 'I don't like the look of this', she said. Swaggart stood up, grabbed his money and asked if Murphree would meet him later.

He then left, got into his car and started to back out, but realised he had a flat tyre – the stakeout man had seen to that. He changed it, but put the spare on the wrong way round. He was rectifying this when he heard a man call out, 'Jimmy!'.

Busted

Marvin Gorman walked over to him. Swaggart offered his hand but Gorman refused to shake. They got into the car. According to Gorman's account of their meeting, Swaggart kept asking him what he wanted, and offered to help him get his ministry back. Then Swaggart broke down and admitted that he had been seeing prostitutes for years. 'If those women go to hell', he said, 'I don't know what I'm going to do'. Gorman said he wasn't interested in condemnation, he just wanted Swaggart to confess to the church elders and get his own life back together. 'How could you be living this kind of life and attack me?', he asked. Swaggart apologised and said he would make things right.

The following day, Jimmy and Frances Swaggart met with Gorman and his attorney. Gorman laid down his demands. Swaggart would retract his allegations about Gorman having multiple affairs, confess his own sins and undergo counselling. Frances, a hard-as-nails businesswoman, who controlled much of Swaggart's empire, wanted to know if Gorman would drop his lawsuit if her husband did all this. Gorman said he wasn't discussing the lawsuit. The meeting ended with Swaggart agreeing to Gorman's terms.

Then Swaggart stalled. He and Frances must have wondered how many would believe a disgraced figure like Gorman, who also happened to be suing them. When they didn't hear any more from him, they assumed he had been bluffing. He hadn't told them he had photographs.

In February 1988, Gorman's patience ran out. He took his evidence to the Assemblies of God elders – 200 colour photographs of Swaggart and other men entering and leaving Debra Murphree's room. The following day, a Friday, Swaggart flew to the Assemblies of God headquarters in Springfield, Missouri. Elders arrived from all over the country for a meeting which lasted 10 hours. Rumours about Swaggart were flying around the Assemblies of God, and that evening there was a report on the ABC news.

'I Have Sinned'

On Sunday morning, Jimmy Swaggart, wearing a dark blue suit, stood in the Family Worship Centre and faced his people. 'I do not plan in any way to whitewash my sin', he told them. 'I do not call it a mistake, a mendacity; I call it sin … I have no-one but myself to blame. I do not lay the blame for the charge at anyone else's feet. For no-one is to blame but Jimmy Swaggart'. He apologised to his wife, his son and daughter-in-law, the Assemblies of God, his ministers, other evangelists, anyone who had ever watched him on television – oh, and Jesus Christ.

Swaggart said that his ministry would continue but he would be stepping down from the pulpit for an unspecified time. At no point did he indicate the exact nature of his sin. He ended by reciting Psalm 51. 'Wash me thoroughly from my iniquity', he wailed, 'and cleanse me from my sin'. As he finished he was mobbed by supporters. Others wept and hugged each other.

That night, millions saw Swaggart's contorted, tear-stained face on television. One of them was Debra Murphree, who was now living in Florida. 'He's talking about me', she realised. She quickly went out and found herself an agent.

The Louisiana district council of the Assemblies of God met to decide Swaggart's fate. Most of them were his friends, and they came up with a 2-year plan of rehabilitation, which would have seen him preaching again after 3 months. There were howls of outrage from church members about the leniency of this, and the Springfield elders asked them to reconsider. Swaggart's supporters noted that he had come clean about his sins, and some of them were saying his liaison with the prostitute had been a brief one. However, then Debra Murphree popped up in a television interview, giving all the sordid details of their year-long association – including Swaggart's interest in her young daughter.

The Springfield elders overruled the Louisiana council. Swaggart, they announced, must stop preaching for a year, and cease distribution of his tapes. Swaggart could not accept these terms. He resigned from the Assemblies of God.

Aftermath

Swaggart's followers had to choose between him and the Assemblies of God, and many left his ministry. Most of the students and faculty of the Jimmy Swaggart Bible College resigned. Swaggart's television show went from the number one religious program to number seven. He was forced to lay off staff, halt building projects and sell the corporate jet. Swaggart's travails also caused a significant downturn in Louisiana's economy that year.

The July 1989 issue of *Penthouse* featured a long interview with Debra Murphree and black-and-white photographs of her in Swaggart's favourite poses.

And yet, despite his public humiliation, Swaggart began to claw his way back. He kept on preaching, downplaying what he had done in New Orleans. 'There has never been anything in my life at any time that has been deviant or abberrant', he declared. Instead, he blamed demons for his lapses. He said that the evangelist Oral Roberts had cast out the demons over the phone, and he was now morally pure. The crowds were turning up to hear him again and his television ratings were on the rise.

Then, in October 1991, the demons were back. Swaggart, in the middle of a successful tour, drove into a carpark in Indio, California, and picked up a skinny, 31-year-old prostitute named Rosemary Garcia. As she got in, she saw several pornographic magazines on the passenger seat. Swaggart asked her if she knew a motel that showed pornographic films. Then he spotted a police car. He panicked and tried to stuff the magazines under his seat, causing the car to swerve. The cop pulled him over, looked at his licence and told Swaggart to get out of the car. The next thing he knew, several other police cars had arrived on the scene.

After this incident, most of the people who had continued to support Swaggart abandoned him.

Jimmy Swaggart is still preaching and making television programs. He occasionally hits the headlines, as he did in 2004 when he said that if he caught a homosexual making eyes at him, he would 'kill them and tell God he died'. (He later apologised for this and said he had been joking.) While he used to preach to many thousands, however, Swaggart's audiences now number in the hundreds. His Baton Rouge complex, or what remains of it, is a virtual ghost town.

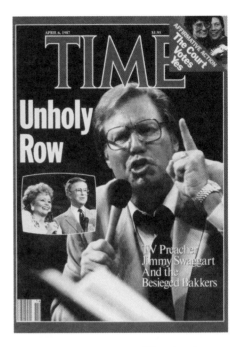

Swaggart made it onto the cover of *Time* when the row broke out between him and the Bakkers. The story of sex, fraud, theft and hypocrisy was irresistible to the press.

'MAN RAPED BY BANANA': THE REVEREND CANAAN BANANA

MAIN CULPRIT:
Canaan Sodindo Banana (1936–2003); President of Zimbabwe (1980–87) and Methodist minister

SCANDAL:
Drugged and raped one of his male aides

WHY:
Sexual deviant and closet homosexual in a country where homosexuality was punishable by 10 years' jail

… a mortuary of pathological lies and a malicious vendetta of vilification and character assassination.
— Canaan Banana

Zimbabwe's former president, Canaan Banana, 1986. A warrant for Banana's arrest was issued when he failed to appear in court after being found guilty on ten sex-crime charges.

In late 1983 Jefta Dube was a 21-year-old Zimbabwean policeman. He was fit, handsome and one of the stars of the police football team, the Black Mambas. They were playing against the State House Tornadoes, the team belonging to Zimbabwean President, the Reverend Canaan Banana, who was also widely known as Zimbabwe's number one football fan. Banana was impressed with Dube's grace and agility, his strength against his opponents and skill on the ball. Some days after, Banana summoned Dube to his presidential office and offered him a job as an aide-de-camp on his personal staff. He wanted Dube to join his football team and promised him promotion and the chance to travel abroad. For Dube, this was a great honour, and a chance to advance his career. Banana, after all, was Zimbabwe's first black president, having held the job since independence in 1980. He was also a revered revolutionary, poet, diplomat and man of the people. Dube accepted gladly. Things were looking up for him it seemed.

However, 12 years later Dube, having risen to the rank of police inspector, was arrested for shooting a colleague dead. When his case came to trial in 1997, he freely admitted the killing, but claimed diminished responsibility. He was sentenced to 10 years in prison. So what went wrong with Dube's life? The answer, he claimed, was Canaan Banana.

For the most part, life was relaxed working as a State House aide, especially if the reason for your appointment was to play soccer. The position of president was largely ceremonial, but Banana was a popular figure and a leading peacemaker in the battle between the Shona and Nbele – tribal factions in Zimabwean politics and society – that led to significant bloodshed. As such, there was no-one queueing up to kill him. It seemed Dube had landed a high-prestige, fairly low-stress job.

But there was more to the president's fond regard than Dube's soccer ability. In his trial, Dube claimed Banana raped and sodomised him, then forced him into a homosexual relationship which lasted for roughly 3 years. According to Dube, Banana's treatment turned him into an alcoholic and a depressive. It was also why he shot his colleague: he teased Dube incessantly by calling him 'Banana's wife'.

By the time Dube went to trial, Banana had been retired from the presidency for 10 years and was leading a comfortable life as professor of theology at the University of Zimbabwe, as well as dabbling in matters of national and African diplomacy. If the allegations were true, it would be a sad fate for a man who, by usual standards, had given much to his nation without asking for too much back.

Landing a Plum Job

Canaan Sodindo Banana was born in 1936 near Bulawayo in Zimbabwe. He received a mission-school education and was ordained as a Methodist minister in

1962. He became a proponent of liberation theology, a movement which used a socialist interpretation of Christ to promote the rights of the poor, particularly those in the developing world. Increasingly, he began to preach against the racist white regime of Ian Smith in Southern Rhodesia (the former name for Zimbabwe). He wrote an updated version of the Lord's Prayer that started 'Our father who art in the ghetto' and included lines such as 'Teach us to demand our share of the gold/Forgive us our docility/As we demand our share of justice'; this made him a national figure. In 1976, he defected from the moderate liberation leader Bishop Abel Muzorewa to the militant ZANU, led by Robert Mugabe. During the Rhodesian civil war he was detained and placed under house arrest on a number of occasions. When the nation of Zimbabwe was declared in 1980, Mugabe became prime minister and picked Banana as an ideal figurehead for the nation's first president. Banana's credentials were impeccable and, importantly, he was from the minority Ndebele tribe, while Mugabe was from the majority Shona.

Canaan Banana was not a regular name in Zimbabwe and ranks with the Philippine's Cardinal Sin as one of the most unfortunate names in late 20th-century history. In 1982, while he was president, Banana introduced laws making it a criminal offence to make jokes about his name. But when the Dube scandal broke the press had a field day with headlines such as 'Man Raped by Banana'.

Banana brought to the largely ceremonial position of president a moral energy and pastoral quality. He was an avuncular figure, who was also a theologian and poet. While he was known for his Mao suits, he also knew how to play the populist card in the largely rural nation by appearing in the newspapers and on television in overalls and gumboots while scattering feed in the chicken farm that he had established at State House. He played guitar and was Zimbabwe's number one football fan. He functioned as a peace-maker in a new nation with considerable internal tensions.

Although his role as president was largely ceremonial, Banana often used it to good effect. In 1987, his influence in getting Mugabe and his major rival, Joshua Nkomo, to negotiate after the massacre of 20,000 people in Matabeleland, saved thousands of lives. Mugabe decided to change the constitution soon after, by merging the roles of prime minister and president, a position he took for himself. Banana was generously retired at full salary for life and took up a position as professor of theology at the University of Zimbabwe. He also became a key emissary for the Organisation of African Unity – an important body in African trouble spots.

The Rape Allegations

When he heard of Jefta Dube's allegations in court, Banana responded that they were 'a mortuary of pathological lies and a malicious vendetta of vilification and character assassination'. Was there a chance that someone was fitting Banana up? The world of Zimbabwean politics had darkened since Banana's tenure and, with Robert Mugabe now in full control, people had been known to disappear.

Torture was on the unofficial menu and it was nothing for the government to destroy a possible adversary.

There had been whispers about Banana's sexual orientation in the past and the judge in Dube's murder trial was inclined to believe his story. He shortened his sentence on the grounds of diminished responsibility, saying Dube's sorry tale of the events leading up to the shooting carried a ring of truth.

Soon after, the police were called in to investigate the former president. In Africa, official justice can be an extremely capricious thing, and it wouldn't have been unusual for the case to disappear. Yet while Banana was a political ally of Mugabe, he was accused of something Mugabe hated; homosexuality. Mugabe was known for his denunciation of gay men, having famously claimed they were 'lower than pigs or dogs'. He once derided Tony Blair, whose government has been harsh on the poor record of Mugabe's failing quasi-dictatorship, as a 'gay gangster leading the gay government of the gay United gay Kingdom'. In 1995, the same year Dube shot his colleague, Mugabe told supporters at a rally, 'If you see anyone behaving like a homosexual, arrest them and take them to police'. In Zimbabwe, sodomy was a criminal offence punishable by up to 2 years in jail.

If he rescued his former ally from charges of sodomy, Mugabe would be risking his own credibility in an area where the population was in broad agreement with him. While not opposed to the idea in principle, in this case it would have been politically foolish for Mugabe to intervene in the 'natural course of justice'. On the other hand, allowing Banana to be mashed in court might at least give a veneer of impartiality to Mugabe's crony state. There was also the possibility it might even help Mugabe's popularity with the people. At the very least, it would create a diversion from the nation's worsening economic troubles.

With the judicial system allowed free rein to function, the police investigation into Dube's allegations was extremely thorough. In July 1997, Banana was charged on eleven counts: two of sodomy, three of attempted sodomy and six of indecent assault. And not just with Dube. Other victims included policemen and soldiers assigned to protect him, as well as his cook, a job seeker and a hitchhiker. He was released on bail pending his trial.

Banana's legal team tried valiantly to prevent the trial from taking place. They argued that the adverse publicity made it impossible for him to receive a fair trial. The Zimbawean supreme court didn't agree. The trial opened before Zimbabwean High Court Judge President Godfrey Chidyausiku and two assessors on 1 June 1998. Banana was supported by his wife, Janet, in court and pleaded not guilty.

Most of that day was given to the evidence of Dube. Soon after taking up his new post in 1983, Dube was surprised when Banana asked him to have dinner with his family. Dube obliged and ate with Banana, his wife and children. He remembered it as a silent dinner. Banana's lawyer would later argue that it was strange Dube remembered so little of the dinner. But it's easy to see that the young man, suddenly in the intimate space of Zimbabwe's first family, would feel out of place and petrified by the experience. The dinner was no doubt excruciating for Dube, but not as excruciating as what was yet to come.

After dinner Banana and Dube returned to the presidential office suite at State House. Despite being a Methodist cleric, Banana broke out the whisky and Dube settled down with his boss to play a few games of cards. Later in the evening, the talk turned to ballroom dancing, a favourite hobby of the president. When Dube confessed he didn't know how to ballroom dance, Banana offered to teach him. He put on some music and began to show Dube the basic steps. He grabbed Dube's waist, placed his hand on his shoulder and ordered him to obey his instructions.

As they practised, Banana held Dube tighter and tighter. Disturbingly, Dube could feel the president pressing his erect penis against him. The clinch tightened and Banana started to French kiss him. Dube managed to pull away and tell Banana that he wanted to go home. As he was leaving, Banana patted Dube on the buttocks and told him they would meet again. That night Dube went to his aunt's house and cried; his big opportunity all of a sudden had turned into a nightmare.

Canaan Banana and his wife, Janet, as they arrive at the courthouse in Harare, 1997. While Banana was in jail Janet left him and gained asylum in London.

It must have taken some strength of character that night for Dube to tell his president 'no'. The next time, however, he wasn't quite so lucky. Dube wasn't invited for dinner this time. They went straight to the presidential offices where Dube was given a soft drink. The drink was probably spiked because soon after Dube started feeling dizzy and the next thing he knew Banana was all over him, kissing him and removing his clothes. Dube blacked out. The next thing he knew it was dawn and he was lying naked under a duvet on the presidential carpet. There was semen on his buttocks and thighs. A semi-dressed Banana was standing over him smiling and said, 'While you were asleep, we helped ourselves'.

What followed was an enforced homosexual relationship which lasted for almost 3 years. In 1984, when Dube resisted the president, Banana had him detained for 3 days in a military prison. He also blackmailed Dube by making him sign confessions that he was guilty of derelicting his duty. If he didn't have sex with him, then Banana would make these public and Dube's career would be over.

At various times Dube approached his senior officers, including a deputy police commissioner and a senior assistant police commissioner, to help him get transferred from State House, but they claimed their hands were tied. It was only 3 years later, upon the direct intervention of Vice President Simon Muzenda, that Dube was transferred to another city. But by then he'd had sex with Banana more times than he could count, and his life was already in ruins. He was unable to deal with his ordeal psychologically and it had made him an object of mockery among some of his colleagues, the combination of which would lead to the shooting of 1995.

During Banana's trial it became clear that Dube was only one of many young men Banana had sexually terrorised. Evidence was given that he had sexually harassed his cook and a State House gardener. The then commander of the army, General Solomon Mujuru, gave evidence that he had withdrawn his troops from State House, where Banana was technically commander-in-chief, as he was sick of Banana interfering with them. An airforce officer gave evidence that he had been forced to push Banana into the State House swimming pool to repel his advances. Other evidence told how Banana had extorted sex from a job seeker in a city hotel over a 2-year period on the pretence he was helping to find the man a job. He had also sexually abused a young hitchhiker. In all cases Banana had abused the authority of his position to get sex from these men.

Banana wasn't charged with rape because Zimbabwean law doesn't distinguish between consensual and non-consensual sodomy as a crime.

On 22 June, Banana's legal team, somewhat bizarrely, made a motion for the case to be dismissed due to lack of evidence. Perhaps they were hoping that, by creating a legal window of opportunity, someone behind the scenes might step in and rescue him from what was looking increasingly like a guilty verdict.

On the Run

After a 17-day trial, the judges retired to consider their verdict. On 26 November Banana was found guilty of sodomy and the other charges. When the verdict was delivered, Banana was not in court. Facing a possible sentence of 22 years, Banana had donned a false beard and slipped across the border to Botswana the week before. The judge put out a warrant for his arrest while the government tried to arrange extradition from Botswana in time for the sentencing hearing on 10 December.

When the Botswanan police tried to track him down, they discovered Banana had slipped across their border to South Africa. Although South Africa had an extradition treaty with Zimbabwe, homosexuality in South Africa had recently been decriminalised and there were rumours Banana would try and claim sanctuary there as a gay refugee. Another theory put forward by Interpol was that Banana might try to seek refuge in Chile.

At this time, however, there were tensions between South Africa and Zimbabwe. Zimbabwe had sent troops to fight with the government in the chaos afflicting the Congo, while South Africa wanted to find a peaceful solution. Mugabe was also finding it difficult being usurped by Nelson Mandela as Southern Africa's greatest post-colonial leader. The relationship wasn't helped when it was revealed Mandela had been in direct contact with Banana and had met him on 2 December at the same time as South Africa's police were claiming ignorance of his whereabouts. Words were spoken between Mugabe and Mandela and Mandela then spoke to Banana. When, on 16 December, Banana turned up at the Zimbabwean border in a Mercedes and was picked up in a police-owned Mercedes which whisked him away to Harare, it was widely assumed a deal had been struck and that it was unlikely Banana would serve any jail time – and he may even receive a presidential pardon.

Banana told the court he had absconded because of politically connected threats to his safety and said that he had needed to 'share dangerous information with his real friends'. However, if an agreement had been made to spare Banana jail time,

someone had forgotten to tell the Zimbabwean High Court. When the court convened to sentence Banana on 18 January 1999, he was sentenced to 10 years' jail. However, 8 years of this was suspended and the remaining 2 years were to be served concurrently. Banana was also fined $500,000 Zimbabwean (around $10,000 or £3000), with half the sum to go to Dube and the other half to the family of the policeman Dube had killed.

Canaan Banana with Robert Mugabe, President of Zimbabwe and a well known homophobe.

When the court dismissed Banana's appeal in May, he was jailed. However, he was treated leniently. Banana was sheltered from the worst of Zimbabwe's notoriously rough jails and placed in the new Connemara open prison in central Zimbabwe, where he coached the young male inmates in football. He also had special permission to travel to Harare on shopping trips. After 8 months he was released for good behaviour.

The life Banana returned to was radically different to the one he enjoyed before the scandal broke. While in prison, his wife left him and went to live with their daughter in London. He was defrocked by the Methodist Church, sacked from the University of Zimbabwe and dropped from the Organisation of African Unity. When he went onto the field as president of the Zimbabwe Football Association to meet the national team after his release, he was loudly booed. He died of cancer a little more than a year after serving his sentence, a man whose not inconsiderable achievements were doomed to be overshadowed by his sexual predation and unfortunate name.

MOTIVATION
anger
charity
envy
faith
gluttony
greed
hope
lust
pride
sloth

PRAISE THE LORD AND PASS THE LOOT: JIM BAKKER'S FALL FROM GRACE

MAIN CULPRIT:
James Orson (Jim) Bakker (1939–), evangelist preacher

SCANDAL:
Ripped off hundreds of thousands of his followers and allegedly raped his church secretary

WHY:
He was from a poor background and wanted it all

I sorrowfully acknowledge that 7 years ago I was wickedly manipulated by treacherous former friends and colleagues who victimised me with the aid of a female confederate. They conspired to betray me into a sexual encounter at a time of great stress in my marital life ... I was set up as part of a scheme to co-opt me and obtain some advantage for themselves over me in connection with their hope for position in the ministry.

– Jim Bakker

Disgraced televangelist Jim Bakker addressing his supporters. Bakker fraudulently stole from his church followers, hiding away $158 million in forty-seven different bank accounts.

Live by the tube, die by the tube. Just as televangelism's first couple Jim and Tammy Faye Bakker rose from rags to riches on television, they were taken down on-screen by rival preachers in a bizarre barrage of prime-time investigative 'hit pieces' that uncovered all – the sex, fraud, theft of millions and the hypocrisy. It was the spring of 1987 and Jim Bakker, who built up the immense (and lucrative) PTL evangelical network, was forced to resign under pressure from Jerry Falwell, Jimmy Swaggart and other stars of the multi-million-dollar industry that had risen with the Bakkers's made-for-television ministry. Night after night they were taking a beating on the other church shows as well as on such mainstream news magazines as *Larry King Live* and *Nightline*. Bakker was accused of stealing immense sums from the collection plate, seducing his secretary, bringing prostitutes into the church and other, even wilder sexual shenanigans. Swaggart, whose downfall would occur a few years later due to similar peccadilloes, called Bakker 'a cancer on the body of Christ'. The preachers had to get rid of one of their own to save their own revenues.

After the first couple of exposés, and amid behind-the-scenes manoeuvring by concerned leaders in the movement, who were afraid their credibility and profits would be ruined, Bakker resigned on 19 March 1987. But the televised 'lynching' was only getting started. Falwell, who had been Bakker's first boss, was summoned to rescue the PTL and its highly lucrative Heritage USA theme park. Instead, he let it go down in flames. 'God sent me there to bring an abrupt end to the immorality and financial fraud of this 'religious soap opera' that had become an international embarrassment to the Christian gospel', he declared, washing his hands of the matter. When minor-league televangelist John Ankerberg went on the air to accuse Bakker of having homosexual lovers, suddenly the Bakker affair was kicked up a notch on the scandal monitor. In the fundamentalist community where the Bakkers had made their millions, homosexuality was way beyond the pale.

A partly resurrected Tammy Faye Messner speaks on Fox television in 2005, in a brief return to the media.

An Image Problem for Jim

Audiences had already been treated to jaw-dropping tales of prostitutes, wife-swapping among the PTL staff and embezzlement. Bakker tried rescuing his image by granting long interviews on *Nightline*. Just before he was finally defrocked by the Pentecostal Assemblies of God, he and Tammy Faye were on camera to quell the fears of their baffled audience. They tried one of the most effective tricks in their fund-raising repertoire, the old 'fountain of tears' number. Tammy Faye stood by her man: 'I've been married to this man for 26 years, and I can tell you one thing: he's not homosexual, nor is he bisexual. He's a wonderful, loving husband.'

On screen, at least until that fateful spring of 1987, the Bakkers had been the squeaky clean, sweetly wholesome couple whose evangelical Christian mission purported to help millions. By the time the federal prosecutors were done with Bakker, and Tammy Faye's divorce lawyers had picked him clean, the facts beggared belief. When Bakker was finally caught, he had amassed a personal fortune of $158 million that he stashed in forty-seven different bank accounts – and they were only the ones in his name.

Big Spenders from Humble Beginnings

Where did all that dough go? The details of the lavish lifestyles of Jim and Tammy Faye Bakker made spectacular tabloid copy. For instance, they enjoyed the smell of cinnamon buns, so they spent $100 a day on fresh buns, to fill their hotel suites with the aroma. Jim needed a facelift ($25,000), while Tammy Faye went on a $10,000 shopping spree one afternoon in Manhattan. Their private jet burned through several $100,000 cross-continental trips a year. They bought an air-conditioned dog house – but unfortunately it proved too noisy for their pooch to sleep in. The gold-plated fixtures in their mansion in Palm Springs, one of many, cost $60,000.

The beginning of their undoing was the fateful night of 6 December 1980, when Bakker took his 21-year-old church secretary, Jessica Hahn, to the Sheraton Sand Key hotel in Clearwater, Florida for what she said was her deflowering. The clincher in the seduction was a line that has gone down in the history of hypocrisy: 'When you help the shepherd, you're helping the sheep'. Over the next few months, Hahn received $265,000 in hush money, and waited 7 years to surface with her charges. When she came out swinging in a civil suit, shining an unwanted spotlight onto Bakker's life, it wasn't long before other victims came forward as well.

The Bakkers' ascension to celebrity and mega-million-dollar riches was an entrepreneurial as well as evangelical parable. They were the ultimate small-town hucksters who built a huge, ostentatious empire. Even though they played the hokey southern accents to brilliant effect before a nationwide audience that equates a drawl with sincerity, they were both lower-class midwesterners. Jim Bakker was born and raised in northern Michigan, while Tammy Faye was from a poor Minnesota family. The couple met as undergraduates at North Central Bible College in Minneapolis. Mr and Mrs Bakker dropped out of school and became itinerant Pentecostal evangelists. In 1965, they answered the call of television, signing on with Pat Robertson, then a Virginia-based local television celebrity for whom the Bakkers started the instantly lucrative 700 Club, a show that promised God-given wealth to those who sent in donations they often could not afford. Robertson's fame was still regional – eventually he would become the nation's best-known arch conservative, a presidential candidate in 1988 and a crucial supporter of the winning Republican tickets of Ronald Reagan as well as both George Bush I and II.

The Bakkers left Robertson's fold for a Los Angeles television church and then started their own flock in 1974 with The PTL Club (short for 'Praise the Lord' and 'People that Love' – later, comedians would call it 'Pass the Loot'). They launched the *PTL Club* television show in 1974, at a moment when the American viewing public was not nearly as cynical or wary as they are today – having been ripped off by Bakker and others since then. The cult-like mass appeal of television evangelists caused pledges to roll in from dupes across the country. Coat-tailing the national prominence of officially recognized figures such as Billy Graham, whose crusade had been going strong for more than a decade, the exploitative generation of evangelists-entrepreneurs was just composing their business plans, and the fiscal outlook was bright.

STRANGER THAN FICTION

It was a scandal worthy of the fictitious Elmer Gantry. The eponymous villain of Sinclair Lewis's cynical novel of 1927 went from being a shyster lawyer to using his pulpit-sharpened rhetorical skills as a preacher to seduce young girls and separate old ladies from their savings. As the Bakker debacle played out, it prompted a 'literature' of its own, including an acclaimed documentary film, *The Eyes of Tammy Faye*, and a song by country and western star Ray Stevens entitled *Would Jesus Wear a Rolex on His Television Show?*

The Bakkers' gaudy headquarters was in Charlotte, North Carolina, where they started Heritage USA, a fundamentalist theme park complete with rides and a water slide. The acerbic journalist P. J. O'Rourke wrote that it 'was like being in the First Church of Christ Hanging Out at the Mall'. But there was no joking about the Bakker juggernaut which, by the end of the 1970s, had grown to 600,000 active members pouring $129 million a year into the coffers and expanding the theme park and television facilities to gargantuan proportions. Many were 'lifetime partners' who committed $1000 a year to the capital campaign. In total, 114,000 people fell for this package, which got them a suite at the Heritage Grand Hotel 'for life' and perks at the park.

Rolling in cash, Bakker began surrounding himself with a wacky bunch of devoted lieutenants, who turned a blind eye to the way he used fake foreign-mission projects to raise more cash for swimming pools and luxuries at Heritage Park. Even before the Jessica Hahn revelations, there were rumours of wrongdoing. Federal agencies had started sniffing around the offices of PTL in the 1970s. The Internal Revenue Service (IRS) was tipped off that Bakker's compensation was out of hand. Eventually the 'Eternal' Revenue Service went after him for $9 million in excess compensation, and the PTL was stripped of the tax-free status that most religious organisations in the United States enjoy. The Federal Communications Commission started looking into the fund-raising games that PTL was playing as early as 1979, but didn't file charges in return for PTL selling off its television station in 1982. Bakker simply bought his air-time and business went on as usual, to the tune of

$10 million in new donations every month. Even though his salary was only $200,000, he awarded himself multi-million-dollar bonuses each year. Meanwhile, Heritage USA grew so fast it became a quasi-Disneyland, the third-largest theme park in the United States. The Bakkers' book royalties also mounted to $8 million.

The Crumbling of an Empire

In 1987 the edifice crumbled. All the investigations came together in a group of criminal and civil lawsuits that had Bakker in the dock for months. By December 1988 Bakker faced federal indictment on fraud and conspiracy charges. 'Discovery' in a court of law is the uncovering before trial of secrets. It would be hard to conjure a discovery more shocking and extreme than the Bakker criminal trials. The jury found Bakker guilty on all twenty-four counts of fraud, and he received a 45-year sentence along with a $500,000 fine – which was a mere slap on the wrist for someone who, according to the most conservative audits, had stolen at least $3.7 million.

The fraud cases hinged on the 'lifetime' that promised a free room at Heritage USA. The prosecutors showed that Bakker lied by understating the number of partnerships already bought. He over-booked the luxury accommodations and funnelled the revenues into his slush fund, which paid to hush up Hahn as well as for the luxurious tastes of his wife. The hotels he said were underway never even reached the shovel-in-the-ground stage. Bakker was found guilty and served time in jail from 1989 to 1993, when he was released on parole. But Bakker's legal woes were far from over. His furious former partners also sued him for fraud in 1990. The only case Bakker won was a separate civil trial for securities fraud.

In 1987 Jessica Hahn claimed she was raped by Bakker and a fellow evangelist when she was Bakker's church secretary. However, the Assemblies of God paid her $265,000 to keep quiet.

Bakker claimed that, from the beginning, his downfall had been orchestrated by enemies inside his ministry who used Hahn, like a latter-day Delilah, to trap him. He never changed his tune: during his trial, his first ploy was an attempt to elude conviction by claiming he was mentally unfit to take the stand (his lawyer had tried the same stunt with John Hinkley, who attempted to assassinate President Reagan). Then he fell back on the Judas defence: 'I sorrowfully acknowledge that 7 years ago I was wickedly manipulated by treacherous former friends and colleagues who victimised me with the aid of a female confederate. They conspired to betray me into a sexual encounter at a time of great stress in my marital life ... I was set up as part of a scheme to co-opt me and obtain some advantage for themselves over me in connection with their hope for position in the ministry.' Then the defence attorneys tried the *cosi fan tutte* ('everybody does it') approach. 'If a man raises over $150 million for a business that competed with Disney and the major networks and kept $3 million for himself, he may be guilty of mismanagement, naiveté, even stupidity, but is it a crime? Do you think Falwell lives in a 5-room house?', Bakker's lawyer asked. None of this had an effect on the jury, however, and Bakker lost all his appeals.

Where Are They Now?

After Jim's conviction, Tammy Faye made an abortive attempt to carry on the ministry, then went into brief seclusion. But she found her way back to television, albeit briefly, with a talk show on the conservative Fox network. Having dumped Bakker and grabbed what she could in the financial settlement, she married Roe Messner, who turned out to be from the Bakker mould – he had been the crooked principal contractor who built much of the gaudy Heritage USA theme park, and funnelled millions of dollars off for his own bank account. He was convicted of bankruptcy fraud in 1996. He and Tammy Faye are still paying the IRS back-taxes.

Jessica Hahn is alive and well and living in West Hollywood, the neighbourhood of choice for porn stars. In 1988, she cashed in on the publicity and posed nude for *Playboy* three times and was a *Penthouse* centrefold.

Amazingly, Jim Bakker is back. After getting out of jail on parole in 1993, this Lazarus of the televangelical movement lived in a halfway house run by the Salvation Army. Then he quietly returned to his old ways. He resurrected his television act with a cable show called *The Jim Bakker Show*. He built a studio production complex in Branson, Missouri, where he tapes a weekly show and hosts retreats and conferences. He wrote a series of *mea culpa* books, beginning with the bestseller *I Was Wrong*, published in 1996, followed in 2000 by *Prosperity and the Coming Apocalypse* and *The Refuge: The Joy of Christian Community in a Torn-Apart World*.

In 1998 Bakker married Lori Graham, a 35-year-old blonde and a clone of Tammy Faye – her theological musings are part of the new empire. They adopted a 'rainbow tribe' of children from underdeveloped nations, who smile on cue for the cameras and help to raise money for foreign missionary efforts. The theme of his rants these days is the evil of avarice. Under the headline 'Dangerous Guessing Games', Bakker wrote a website sermon, which appeared in February 2006, comparing the Whore of Babylon to the modern-day lust for wealth. It read in part: 'Simply stated: the harlot is not a particular church; it is the economic system of this world.'

ON THE LAM

Director Roman Polanski (centre, in double-breasted
suit) leaving the courthouse with his lawyer in Santa
Monica, 1977, where he was appearing on the charge of
statutory rape of a 13-year-old girl.

MOTIVATION

anger

charity

envy

faith

gluttony

greed

hope

lust

pride

sloth

THE FUGITIVE: CARAVAGGIO'S LIFE ON THE RUN

MAIN CULPRIT:
Michelangelo Merisi da Caravaggio ('Caravaggio')
(1573–1610), Italian Baroque artist

SCANDAL:
Murdered a rival in a sword fight after a quarrel

WHY:
Was short-tempered and violent and may have suffered from
a mental disorder

*He was of a fantastic humour, indeed bizarre ... [a] marvel of
art, [a] wonder of nature.*
– Giulio Cesare Gigli on Caravaggio

Portrait of the artist, c.1600. The fiery tempered
Caravaggio was said to have a furrowed brow, coarse
features and a 'shifty' look about him.

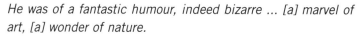

In 1606 the most acclaimed artist in Rome was Guido Reni. While most of his fellow artists lived in cramped rooms in seedy parts of town and scrambled for work, Reni dwelt in the palazzos of his patrons, surrounded by servants and celebrated by princes and cardinals and even the Pope himself. His work was popular as his style harked back to Raphael, the Renaissance's most beloved master of light, harmony and beauty. Consider Reni's painting of St Michael – although it depicts the archangel's triumph over Satan, Reni's Michael is a graceful, elegant figure, more like a dancer striking a pose than a heavenly warrior casting the devil into hell.

However, Reni's contemporary, the artist Michelangelo Merisi da Caravaggio (better known as 'Caravaggio'), believed that, by rights, Reni's wealth, fame and status should be his. He was the greater painter – his style, with its dramatic contrast of light and dark, broke new ground; the composition of his paintings was more dramatic, more intellectually, emotionally and even spiritually stimulating than Guido Reni's.

Shattering Conventions

In spite of Reni's popularity, there were some in Rome who agreed with Caravaggio that he was the best in town. His three paintings from the life of St Matthew had won him the attention he yearned for and everyone who saw his Entombment of Christ hailed it as a masterpiece. But Caravaggio's temperament compelled him to shatter conventions and even his greatest supporters found it hard to forgive him for his famous work Death of the Virgin.

The Carmelite friars who commissioned this painting in 1605 expected Caravaggio to paint it in the new historically accurate style – no choirs of angels and no golden light falling from heaven. Yet the painting Caravaggio delivered was much more true to life than the friars had bargained for. He depicted the Virgin Mary sprawled on a cot in a bare room, the pallour of death on her face, her body swollen from its final illness and her feet bare and unwashed. Worse, everyone recognised that the model for the Blessed Virgin was one of Rome's most notorious prostitutes. The Carmelites rejected the painting and Caravaggio's reputation suffered as a result.

Reputation, esteem and honour were everything to Caravaggio. He was from a small provincial town outside Milan and his father had been a stonemason. Caravaggio wanted to leave his humble origins behind and become a gentleman, but his rise up Renaissance Italy's social ladder progressed very slowly. Consequently he grew more short tempered and more sensitive to slights – real or imagined. Natural-born gentlemen who had estates and ancestral titles could afford to laugh off petty affronts, but Caravaggio felt he could not. At the slightest provocation he would reach for his sword. However, the greatest scandal in Caravaggio's life was yet to come.

Murder on the Tennis Court

It was a little before sunset on Sunday, 29 May 1606. While two acquaintances watched, Caravaggio and one of his closest friends, Onorio Longhi, were playing a game called *palla a corda*, a 16th-century forerunner of tennis, on a court near Campo Marzio, the Field of Mars in Rome. In the time of the Caesars this had been a parade ground for the Roman legions, but by Caravaggio's day it was reduced to just a small piazza in the most densely populated part of town.

As Caravaggio and Longhi played their game, Ranuccio Tomassoni walked past with his brother and his two brothers-in-law. The Tomassonis were a wealthy, politically well-connected family who virtually ruled the Campo Marzio neighbourhood. It was common knowledge that Caravaggio and Ranuccio didn't like each other, although no one could actually pinpoint the source of their animosity. Nonetheless, on that warm spring night Caravaggo and Ranuccio challenged each other to a game of *palla a corda*. To make it interesting they bet ten *scudi* (the modern equivalent of about £6 or $15).

Caravaggio's friends and Ranuccio's relatives stood on the sidelines watching the ball speed back and forth across the court, its dull thud against the racquets marking each volley and return. At the end of the match, both players claimed to have won and each demanded the ten scudi. Then, before the onlookers knew what had happened, Caravaggio and Ranuccio had drawn their swords. Unlike the gentlemanly art of fencing, there was no subtle thrust and parry to this fight. Both men were out for blood. Like madmen they chased each other around the piazza, hacking and slashing with their weapons. Ranuccio got in two nasty blows, slicing open Caravaggio's neck and nearly severing one of the artist's ears. As the blood soaked his shirt, Caravaggio lunged at Ranuccio, burying his blade in his enemy's gut. Ranuccio dropped to the ground while Caravaggio collapsed into the arms of his friends. Howling with rage and grief, Ranuccio's family bore him home where he survived just long enough to make his last confession to a priest. As for Caravaggio, his friends were afraid to take him to his house where he was sure to be arrested for murder. Instead they hid him at the home of an acquaintance named Andrea Rufetti, about 1½ kilometres from the site of the brawl.

Caravaggio's hiding place did not remain a secret for long. Within a few days the clerk of Rome's criminal court visited the bedridden painter to conduct a preliminary interview. Pointing to Caravaggio's bandaged neck and ear he asked what happened. 'I wounded myself with my sword in falling on the streets', Caravaggio replied, then added, 'I don't know where it happened, and no one was present'. The clerk was sceptical, which made the painter obstinate. Stating, 'I can say no more', Caravaggio ended the interview.

But it was not quite over. Invoking his authority as an official of the court, the clerk ordered Caravaggio to remain at Rufetti's house while preparations for his trial began. The painter gave his word that he would stay put, but the very next day he fled Rome, hiding in small towns in the Alban Hills, about 40 kilometres outside the city, until he could make his way to the villa of an old patron, Duke Marzio Colonna. The duke offered Caravaggio his protection and in return Caravaggio painted two pictures for his benefactor, *Mary Magdalene* and *Supper at Emmaus*. Meanwhile, a court in Rome tried Caravaggio *in absentia*, found him guilty of murder and promptly placed him under the most severe death sentence, *banda capitale*, which authorised anyone to kill the fugitive anywhere he was found.

The 'Black Hole' Personality

Caravaggio was not always a violent man. In fact, his police record did not begin until 1600, when he was 27 years old – well past the usual rambunctious, adolescent stage of being oversensitive and short tempered.

By 1600 he had built up an impressive body of work: *Boy with a Basket of Fruit*, *The Lute Player*, *Bacchus*, the almost-comical *Boy Bitten by a Lizard*, the serene *Penitent Magdalene* and the frightening *Medusa*. One of the most remarkable aspects of Caravaggio's early paintings is his genius for still lifes. He did not invent the genre – artists in the Netherlands, Spain and Italy had been experimenting with it for years – but Caravaggio's were so good that they set the standard for future artists. Furthermore, he had won the favour of Cardinal Francesco Maria Del Monte. Artists in the 16th and 17th centuries needed a powerful, well-connected patron who would keep them busy with a steady stream of commissions, while using their influence to advance the artist's career. Thanks to Cardinal Del Monte, Caravaggio was asked to paint three pictures from the life of St Matthew for the Contarelli Chapel in San Luigi dei Francesi, the church of the city's French diplomats and French visitors to Rome.

The St Matthew paintings mark the revelation of Caravaggio's distinctive style – the play of light and shadow, the dramatic poses and gestures of the figures in the paintings and the true-to-life depiction of violence. These paintings made Caravaggio the most talked-about artist in Rome, but they didn't make his fortune. He was still living in shabby rooms in a miserable part of town. To make matters worse, Guido Reni arrived in Rome at this time and soon art critics and patrons

WAS CARAVAGGIO GAY?

Among many art lovers Caravaggio's homosexuality is an accepted fact, the most common argument being the homo-eroticism found in so many of the master's paintings. Yet homo-eroticism, like beauty, is in the eye of the beholder.

Documents from Caravaggio's time refer to him as being frequently in the company of female prostitutes. Only one questionable document mentions homosexuality. This is a note by Richard Symonds, an English tourist, from 1650 – 40 years after Caravaggio's death. In this note Symonds says that the model for a painting of Cupid was the artist's 'owne boy or servant that laid with him'. Considering that it was 'common knowledge' in 17th-century England that all Italian men were pederasts, Symond's note perhaps tells us something about ethnic slurs 350 years ago but nothing concrete about Caravaggio's sexual preferences.

were contrasting Reni's graceful, light-filled, ethereal paintings of religious subjects with Caravaggio's dark, stark naturalism. Even the physical appearance of these two rivals were polar extremes. Caravaggio was pale, with dark, sunken eyes and a shock of unruly black hair. Reni was a blond, blue-eyed boy with a classic peaches-and-cream complexion. While Caravaggio was combative, Reni was an accomplished charmer. For all these reasons, and probably others, Caravaggio dismissed Reni as a hack. Once, in court, when a judge asked him why he couldn't get along with his fellow artists, Caravaggio answered that they were all *bagatelli* – meaning 'insignificant'.

The Entombment of Christ (or *Deposition from the Cross*), c.1602–04, is one of Caravaggio's masterpieces and demonstrates the dramatic poses and the theatrical contrast of light and dark, known as 'tenebrism'.

Professor S. Giora Shoham, a criminologist at Tel Aviv University, has suggested that the violent outbursts, which began in 1600, that marred Caravaggio's life, were the result of a 'black-hole personality'. This is where someone who feels their talent is not appreciated, or that they not receiving the attention they deserve, can retreat into paranoia and view themselves as a good person unjustly persecuted by wicked outside forces. A common reaction of a black-hole personality is to strike out at persecutors, even if the result is to pay serious consequences for such behaviour.

It's only a theory and it is difficult, if not impossible, to diagnose anyone 400 years after their death. Nonetheless, Professor Shoham's premise could explain the recurring violent encounters that marked the last years of Caravaggio's life.

Artichokes and Fried Balls

The first incident from the records of the Roman police in 1600 tells how Caravaggio, while out walking with some friends, encountered a rival artist named Federico Zuccaro with a group of his cronies. Caravaggio was already nursing a grudge against Zuccaro for standing in front of his St Matthew paintings at San Luigi and sneering, 'What is all the fuss about?'. As the two groups passed each other, Caravaggio overheard one of Zuccaro's friends say, 'Let us fry the balls of such scum as you'. Stopping in his tracks, Caravaggio began abusing Zuccaro and his entourage in the foulest language. Soon this war of words escalated to stone-throwing, then climaxed when Caravaggio and one of Zuccaro's friends, an ex-soldier from the Pope's own fortress, Castel Sant' Angelo, drew their swords. The two factions fell back screaming as passersby and nervous shopkeepers cleared the street as the two enraged antagonists threw themselves at one another. At first it appeared that the two duellists wouldn't stop until one lay dead on the pavement, but the fight broke up after Caravaggio sliced open his opponent's hand.

Two years pass before Caravaggio's name reappears in the police records. This time he was arrested for libel. A second-rate artist named Giovanni Baglione had been bad-mouthing Caravaggio and dismissing his work as derivative. Caravaggio responded by circulating scurrilous poems that called Baglione a 'prize prick' and encouraged him thus: 'Take your drawings and … wipe your bum with them'.

In another incident in 1604, Caravaggio was arrested for hurling a plate of artichokes in the face of a waiter. Standing before the magistrate the artist defended himself saying the waiter had treated him 'like a beggar'.

For the Love of Lena

On 29 July 1605, about an hour after dark, a young notary named Mariano da Pasqualone was strolling through the Piazza Navona, one of Rome's loveliest open spaces, when Caravaggio leapt out of the dark and attacked him from behind. Before the notary or his friend could react, Caravaggio struck Pasqualone on the head with his sword, leaving an ugly gaping wound, then fled. In the dark Pasqualone's friend could make out only two details: the attacker held either a sword or a large hunting knife and he was wearing a black cape over one shoulder. He didn't recognise the man, but Pasqualone said, 'It could not be anyone but Michelangelo da Caravaggio'.

The source of the quarrel was a young woman named Lena, a lovely, respectable girl from a poor family. Caravaggio was beginning a new painting, *The Madonna of Loreto* (also known as *The Madonna of the Pilgrims*), and he offered the beautiful Lena a generous fee if she would serve as the model for the Virgin Mary. Lena's mother gave her permission, so the young woman often came to Caravaggio's house to pose while he painted.

As it happened, Pasqualone had fallen in love with Lena and proposed marriage. Lena refused. Hurt and humiliated, he accused her of nursing an infatuation for Caravaggio, whom he denounced as 'a cursed man'. Lena must have repeated Pasqualone's insult because once again Caravaggio's uncontrollable temper flared. He hunted Pasqualone through the streets of Rome and, when he found him in the Piazza Navona, he put aside all pretensions of being a gentleman, struck down his enemy from the rear, then ran away.

Even Caravaggio realised that with this vicious attack on Pasqualone he had pushed his luck. Rather than wait for the police to take him to jail, he ran from Rome and kept running until he reached Genoa. Meanwhile, Caravaggio's friends in Rome tried to keep him out of prison. Cardinal Del Monte did some lobbying on behalf of his favourite artist, although even he conceded that Caravaggio 'is a very odd person'. Finally, Pasqualone agreed to drop all charges against him in return for complete admission of guilt and an abject apology – in writing.

Caravaggio complied. 'I am very sorry for what I did', he wrote. 'I beg [Signore Pasqualone] for his forgiveness and peace.'

While Caravaggio was humbling himself before Pasqualone, new troubles were waiting for him back at his house. His landlady, Prudenzia Bruna, fed up with a tenant who was 4 months behind in his rent, confiscated all of Caravaggio's possessions and locked him out of the house. In a vengeful fury, Caravaggio pelted Bruna's windows with rocks.

Six days later Prudenzia Bruna came to court demanding that Caravaggio pay his back rent and compensate her for damaging her venetian blinds. In a comical moment she produced as evidence her ruined blinds and the rocks that had broken them.

The Escape

For a man as highly strung as Caravaggio, life in Italy after his conviction must have been unbearable. Anyone, friend or stranger, who struck him down would win the thanks of the Roman court. And so, in 1607, he sailed from Italy to the island fortress of Malta.

The Knights of St John (popularly known as the Knights of Malta) ruled the island from their magnificent capital, Valletta, a city built of golden stone on a rocky peninsula that soared above the sea. Almost immediately after his arrival on the island Caravaggio was introduced to the Knights' Grand Master, Alof de Wignacourt. Caravaggio ingratiated himself with his host in the one way that was certain to please – with pictures. He painted two handsome portraits of Wignacourt and a dramatic painting of the beheading of St John the Baptist, the Knights' patron saint. The painting still hangs in the Knights' church in Valletta.

Wignacourt was so pleased with Caravaggio's work that he made him a Knight of St John. The Knights were such an exclusive military order that the grandest noblemen in Europe competed to join. Yet Caravaggio, a stonemason's son, had jumped to the head of the line – thanks to his talent rather than his pedigree.

THE KNIGHTS OF MALTA

In about 1120 a crusader knight opened a hospital for pilgrims visiting the Holy Land. The nurses were monks – as well as formidable fighters sworn to defend the Holy Land – who formed the Knights of the Hospital of St John of Jerusalem.

In 1291 the Saracens drove all crusaders out of the Holy Land and the Knights settled on the island of Rhodes where they defended Christian Europe against Muslim pirates. They still ran a hospital and kept their monastic vows.

In 1522 the Turks attacked Rhodes and the Knights fought heroically for 6 months, only surrendering when their supplies ran out. They were allowed to leave Rhodes unharmed but homeless, until, in 1530, the king of Spain gave them the island of Malta. In 1565 the Turks attacked and the siege was marked by incredible brutality. After 4 months the Turks retreated, inspiring hundreds of young noblemen to want to become Knights. But they were very selective, making Caravaggio's swift admission into their order even more remarkable.

However, that was in July. By October, Caravaggio was a prisoner in the Knights' dungeon. (Even though the Knights were monks, there was nothing 'soft' about them; in one battle with the Turks, the Turks bound the headless corpses of captured Knights to wooden crosses, then floated them into the harbour – the Knights responded by using the heads of fallen Turks as cannonballs.)

Carravagio's crime against the Knights was the usual one – drawing his sword in anger. But this time he had confronted a superior and, in the strict hierarchy of the Knights of St John, such an affront was unforgivable. Caravaggio was imprisoned in a cell that was a 3-metre deep pit, carved out of solid rock. No prisoner had ever escaped this cell, yet somehow Caravaggio scrambled out, used a rope to rappel down the fortress walls, then made his way to the harbour where he found a ship to carry him to Sicily.

The frustrated Knights went forward with Caravaggio's trial anyway. They stripped him of his knighthood, deprived him of his privileges and in their own words, 'expelled and thrust [him] forth like a rotten and fetid limb from our Order and Community'.

Caravaggio's fellow artists and art collectors were especially welcoming to him in Sicily – and soon the commissions were flowing in. But he was still a hunted man. Friends in Sicily noticed that he was extremely nervous, and he went to bed fully dressed and armed with a dagger. So it seemed very odd to the artist's Sicilian supporters when, in summer 1609, he announced he was making a trip to Naples. Caravaggio's friends in Rome had been petitioning the Pope to pardon him so he could return home. The rumour of such a pardon might have drawn Caravaggio to Naples – from there it was only a short sea voyage up the coast to Rome's port, Civitavecchia.

The Death of the Virgin (detail). Carmelite friars commissioned this painting in 1605, but rejected it because it was too true to life – and the model for the Blessed Virgin was a notorious prostitute.

As he waited in Naples for the papal pardon, he went often to the Osteria del Cerriglio, a beautiful, fashionable tavern that was a favourite with artists and poets. It was here that four assassins ambushed Caravaggio, stabbing him about the face and neck. The wounds were so serious that word spread that the artist was dead. He survived, but he was left permanently disfigured.

In summer 1610, the long-awaited pardon finally arrived. Caravaggio was on his way home when he fell ill in Port'Ercole, an insignificant town on the edge of a mosquito-infested marsh. Records from the period describe his illness as 'a fever', which suggests that he had contracted malaria. He lingered for a few days, then died on 18 July 1610.

A few years after Caravaggio's death one of his friends, Giulio Cesare Gigli, tried to sum up the man. In terms of personality Gigli said, 'He was of a fantastic humour, indeed bizarre'. But Caravaggio was a 'marvel of art, [a] wonder of nature'.

MOTIVATION

anger
charity
envy
faith
gluttony
greed
hope
lust
pride
sloth

'HE WOULDN'T TAKE NO FOR AN ANSWER': ROMAN POLANSKI

MAIN CULPRIT:
Roman Polanski (1933–), international film director

SCANDAL:
Convicted of raping a 13-year-old girl then fled the United States to escape prison

WHY:
A tragic and difficult life may have led to sexual deviation

It was not consensual sex by any means. I said no repeatedly but he wouldn't take no for an answer. I was alone and I didn't know what to do. It was very scary and, looking back, very creepy.
– Samantha Geimer

Holocaust survivor, Oscar-winning movie director, convicted rapist and fugitive from justice, Roman Polanski, pictured with a friend, 1976.

Jack Nicholson's home stood in a quite enclave of three houses, all owned by Marlon Brando, on the heights of Mulholland Drive, one of the most exclusive addresses in Los Angeles. In 1977 Nicholson, the star of *Chinatown* and *One Flew Over the Cuckoo's Nest*, rented one of the Brando houses. A second house in the enclave was home of character actress Helena Kallianiotes, who had appeared with Nicholson in *Five Easy Pieces*, and who served as gatekeeper and caretaker to the three houses. The third house was unoccupied. An electric gate at the entrance to the little cul de sac kept out the curious, the star-struck and the tabloid journalists, ensuring the privacy of Brando's tenants and their guests.

One of Nicholson's close friends was film director Roman Polanski, a Polish émigré who had come to Hollywood to make his fortune. In 1968 Polanski broke free from the mould of being a director of foreign art films (such as *Knife in the Water*) by directing the box office hit *Rosemary's Baby*. Starring the waif-like Mia Farrow as the 'unholy mother' chosen to bear the child of Satan, the movie was a sophisticated yet frightening horror film, loved by both critics and audiences. Polanski followed up this success 6 years later with *Chinatown*, a film noir masterpiece that made Polanski one of the hottest properties in Hollywood and elevated Jack Nicholson to superstar status.

On 10 March 1977, Polanski pulled up to the gate of the Brando compound. Kallianiotes recognised him and buzzed him in. As she followed the director's car up to Nicholson's house, Kallianiotes happened to notice a young girl in the front seat beside the 44-year-old Polanski.

Nicholson wasn't home. He was on a skiing vacation in Aspen, Colorado. His girlfriend, actress Anjelica Huston (daughter of the film director and actor John Huston), was staying at the house, but she wasn't home either. Nonetheless, Kallianiotes opened the front door and let Polanski and the girl in. The teenage girl's name was Samanatha.

Laying the Groundwork

Polanski represented their visit as part of a photography shoot. He was working for *Vogue Homme*, a French men's magazine famous (or notorious, depending upon one's point of view) for its erotic photographs of young women. The editors had hired Polanski to photograph beautiful young girls from around the world. One of Polanski's friends, Henri Sera, was dating Samantha's older sister. It was on Sera's recommendation that Polanski had visited Samantha's mother at her family home in the San Fernando Valley.

For the meeting, Polanski had brought along a copy of the French edition of *Vogue*, the highly regarded fashion magazine for women. He never mentioned that he was in fact working for the much racier *Vogue Homme*. Polanski's deception worked: the mother was dazzled by the idea of her daughter appearing in *Vogue*. Convinced that Polanski's assignment was legitimate, the woman brought out her daughter and introduced Samantha to the director. In terms of physical maturity, Samantha was precocious. In every other way, however, she was a little girl; shy and uncertain of herself around strangers. Polanski was smitten. He assured the mother that Samantha was exactly what he was looking for.

Polanski took the first set of pictures in the family's backyard. At the end of the session he made an appointment with the mother for another round of photos with the girl – this time he would pick up Samantha and take her to Jack Nicholson's house. To reassure the mother, he promised that he would not be alone with her daughter, and that Anjelica Huston would be there.

Champagne with a Quaalude Chaser

Inside Nicholson's house, Polanski produced a bottle of champagne from the refrigerator. Samantha was reluctant to drink. She said alcohol made her feel funny. But Polanski encouraged her to have some and every time she took a sip he refilled her glass. By this time Kallianiotes had gone back to her own house.

Alone at last with Samantha, Polanski produced a Quaalude tablet, a sedative, which he cut into three pieces. He cajoled her until she swallowed one of the pieces. The combination of the champagne and the Quaalude disorientated the girl and, while she was in this confused state, Polanski led her outside to the jacuzzi where he persuaded her to pose topless, and then completely nude. After taking a few photos, Polanski stripped off all his clothes and climbed into the hot tub with her.

Now Samantha panicked. She insisted on calling her mother, but the champagne-and-Quaalude cocktail made it difficult for her to think straight as she spoke:

'Are you all right?', the mother asked.

'Uh huh', Samantha answered.

'Do you want me to come pick you up?'

'No', Samantha said.

But once she had hung up, Samanatha had second thoughts. She told Polanski she felt sick and wanted to go home. Instead, he pointed her towards a bedroom and suggested she lie down for a while. She had been lying on the bed for only a short time when Polanski, still naked, entered the room, climbed on the bed and began kissing her. Samantha kept saying, 'No! No!' but, groggy with the alcohol and drugs, she had no strength to fight back. While 13-year-old Samantha was in this helpless state, Polanski raped and sodomised her.

Suddenly someone knocked on the bedroom door. Leaping up, Polanski opened the door a crack. It was Anjelica Huston. Although the door was only slightly ajar Huston could see the rumpled bed and someone beneath the sheets. It made her feel angry that Polanski had used Nicholson's house for an afternoon assignation while she was a guest there.

Promising, 'We'll be out in a few minutes' Polanski convinced Huston to leave them alone. Once the door was closed, he returned to the bed where he again tried to rape the girl. Failing, he quickly dressed and went out to speak with Huston.

About 20 minutes later Samanatha emerged from the bedroom, dishevelled and obviously unwell. Huston kept asking her, 'Are you OK?'. The girl replied that she was, but also insisted, 'I want to go right home'. Polanski, however, seemed in no hurry to leave. He kept trying to make conversation with Huston. Finally, raising her voice, the actress said, 'Roman, are you going to take her home?'.

Scrabbling now, Polanski collected his camera equipment and escorted the girl out to his car and drove her home.

What Samantha's Sister Heard

Home at last, Samantha rushed straight to her bedroom, where she called her boyfriend and told him everything that had happened. Out in the bedroom hallway, Samantha's older sister overheard the entire conversation. She was horrified.

Meanwhile, Polanski was in the living room showing Samantha's mother the pictures he had taken. The woman had expected high-quality fashion photos. Instead, she flipped through a pile of amateurish snapshots. The poor quality was disappointing, but what really upset her were the pictures of her daughter topless. The mother demanded that he give her the photos. Polanski refused and, after the argument escalated, Polanski grabbed all the pictures and bolted.

A moment later the older sister came into the living room where she repeated to her mother everything she had just heard Samantha tell her boyfriend. The mother then called the police to report that her daughter had been raped.

The next night, two police officers and two deputy district attorneys confronted Polanski in the lobby of the Beverly Wilshire Hotel. They had a warrant to search his hotel room. As they walked towards the bank of elevators, Polanski reached into his pocket then raised his hand to his mouth. He was about to pop something in when

EARLY CAREER HIGHLIGHTS

Rosemary's Baby (1968). Mia Farrow, John Cassavetes and Ruth Gordon. An Oscar for Best Supporting Actress (Ruth Gordon); Italy's David di Donatello Award for Best Foreign Actress (Mia Farrow); and the French Syndicate of Cinema Critics Award for Best Foreign Film.

Macbeth (1971). Jon Finch and Francesca Annis. The British Academy of Film and Television Arts Award (BAFTA) for Best Costume Design.

Chinatown (1974). Jack Nicholson, Faye Dunaway and John Huston. An Oscar for Best Original Screenplay; BAFTA Award for Best Screenplay, Best Direction (Roman Polanski) and Best Actor (Jack Nicholson).

Tess (1979). Nastassja Kinski and Peter Firth. Oscars for Best Cinematography, Best Art Direction/Set Decoration and Best Costume Design; France's Cesar Award for Best Director, Best Film and Best Cinematography.

one of the policemen spotted what he was doing and quickly grabbed his wrist. Opening Polanski's fist he found a Quaalude tablet – the drug that Samantha had said Polanski had given her at Jack Nicholson's house.

Up in his hotel room Polanski appeared cool and unconcerned. He made himself comfortable in a large chair and invited his visitors to take a seat. Looking around the room, one of the deputy district attorneys discovered a collection of slides of young girls, so Polanski fetched a slide viewer so his guest could see the pictures more clearly. When the officers said that he was being charged with raping a minor, Polanski smiled and replied that the girl's entire story was a lie. The champagne, the Quaaludes, the sex – none of it had happened.

Back to Jack Nicholson's House

From the hotel the police and the deputy district attorneys took Polanski to the police station where he was booked. Then they all drove to Jack Nicholson's house. Kallianiotes was nowhere to be found and it took persistent banging on Nicholson's front door before Anjelica Huston opened up. She had been packing to leave and, from her facial expression and tone of voice, she made it clear that she didn't appreciate the interruption, even from the police. It was even more obvious to the lawmen that she was not happy to see Roman Polanski again.

While the police searched the house, one officer went off to the kitchen with Huston where they could talk privately. Huston shattered Polanski's story, saying she had found him in a bedroom by the pool area, that he came to the door naked and that, when Samantha emerged from the room about 20 minutes later, her clothes were rumpled and the girl appeared dizzy. In terms of his sexual tastes Polanski, Huston told the cop, was a 'freak'.

The mother's complaint, the photos of young girls found in Polanski's room and the statements made by Anjelica Huston were enough. The police charged Polanski with suspicion of 'unlawful sexual intercourse' with a 13-year-old girl. He was released on $2500 bail.

As the preparations for the trial began, Polanski hired Doug Dalton, a Hollywood lawyer with movie-star good looks. The prosecutor assigned to the case was an incorruptible young Mormon called Roger Gunson. After hearing the evidence, a grand jury indicted Polanski on six felonies, including rape by use of drugs, perversion and sodomy. If Polanski was found guilty on all six counts he could

THE PIANIST

Starring Adrien Brody, *The Pianist* (2002) won forty-four awards from film critics around the globe, including: Oscars for Best Actor (Adrien Brody), Best Director (Roman Polanski) and Best Screenplay Based on Material Previously Produced or Published; BAFTA Awards for Best Film and the David Lean Award for Direction; Cesar Awards for Best Actor (Brody), Best Director, Best Film, Best Cinematography, Best Music Written for a Film, Best Sound and Best Production Design; The David di Donatello Award for Best Foreign Film. Polanski was also presented with a Golden Palm at the Cannes Film Festival for this film.

spend up to 50 years in prison. The judge set the trial date for 9 August 1977. By a cruel twist of fate, this was the eighth anniversary of the gruesome murder of Polanski's wife, Sharon Tate, and their unborn son in 1969.

Living on Boiled Flowers

If anyone deserves to be a sympathetic character, it is Roman Polanski. He was born in Paris in 1933 where his Polish-born father, Ryszard, and Russian-born mother, Bula, had settled. The Polanskis were Jewish. As Roman was growing up, Adolf Hitler was formulating his plan to dominate Europe and exterminate all of Europe's Jews.

Had the Polanskis remained in Paris they might have been able to emigrate to South America or to the United States. But instead they moved back to Ryszard's home-town, Cracow, which placed the family directly in the path of the Nazi invasion.

The details of what the Polanskis suffered during the Nazi occupation of Poland are hard to pin down. However, this much is certain; with their fellow Jews the Polanskis were confined inside the Cracow ghetto where Nazi guards were free to shoot and kill any Jew for any reason. When he was 6 or 7 years old, young Roman witnessed one such execution. A group of elderly Jews was being herded down the street for transportation to a death camp. One old woman who could barely walk taxed the patience of the Nazis by staggering behind, so one of the officers drew his pistol and shot her in the head.

In 1941, Bula Polanski was seized in a round-up. One version of the story says that 8-year-old Roman was with her at the time; he survived because his desperate mother threw him off the truck that was heading for Auschwitz.

Roman and his father lived in a one-room hut in a dark interior courtyard of the ghetto. Out of compassion they had taken in a boy of about Roman's age named Stephen, whose parents had been abucted by the Nazis. But they were not together long.

In the liquidation of the ghetto, Roman's father was sent to the Mauthausen concentration camp. Little Stephen, like hundreds of other small children in the ghetto, was shot in the schoolyard. However, Roman escaped, slipping through a hole in the barbed-wire fence.

Roman's father had managed to get some money to acquaintances, a family of Catholic Poles who promised to shelter his boy. It was a tremendous risk as the Nazis killed Christians who were caught sheltering Jews. Now 8-year-old Roman hurried to their house. For a time he lived with this family; then he was sent to live in the countryside with a family of peasants.

Roman was much safer in the country than he had been in the city but the challenge now was finding enough to eat. The family's plot was small – not enough to feed them all. In a 1971 interview with talk-show host Dick Cavett, Polanski recalled scavenging in the woods for berries and mushrooms and living on boiled flowers, sometimes supplemented with a little milk or sugar. A photo from 1946 reveals the effect the war had on Roman Polanski. Although he was 13 years old at the time, he appears no bigger than a 6-year-old child. Today Polanski stands 1.65 metres tall.

A Stranger at the Door

In March 1969, a short, slender young man with long hair and crazed eyes knocked on the door of the Polanskis' home on Cielo Drive in Benedict Canyon. Sharon Tate, Polanski's wife, asked the stranger what he wanted. He replied that he was looking for a man named Terry Melcher. One of Sharon's friends came to the door and told the visitor that Melcher was the previous tenant, and that he didn't live there any more. At that, the stranger walked away.

A 1969 police mug shot of Charles Manson, the mad-eyed leader of the cult known as the 'Family'.

That brief encounter at her front door was the only time Sharon Tate ever met her murderer, Charles Manson.

Tall and curvaceous with long, honey-blonde hair and enormous brown eyes, in 1969 Tate was still building her acting career. She had appeared in fifteen episodes of the 1960s sit-com The Beverly Hillbillies and had had bit parts in The Americanization of Emily and The Sandpiper. What she hoped would be her big break came in 1967 when she was cast as one of the three female leads in Valley of the Dolls.

Terry Melcher, the man Manson wanted to see, was one of the biggest music producers in the United States. He had worked with some of the top bands of the 1960s, including the Beach Boys, the Byrds and the Mamas and the Papas. As a favour for a friend, Melcher had let Manson audition for him, but declined to offer him a recording contract. It is possible that Melcher, the man who rejected Charles Manson, may have been the killers' original target.

Helter Skelter

Around 11 pm on 8 August, Charles Manson waved goodbye as members of his 'Family', Charles 'Tex' Watson (aged 23), Susan Atkins (aged 21), Patricia Krenwinkel (aged 21) and Linda Kasabian (aged 20), drove off in a battered Ford to kill some 'rich pigs' at 10050 Cielo Drive, LA.

Polanski was not home that night. He was in London working on The Day of the Dolphin. Sharon, whose baby was due in about 2 weeks, was at home with three close friends. With her that night was Abigail Folger, the heiress of the Folger coffee fortune, and her chronically unemployed lover Wojtek Frykowski, one of Polanski's old friends from Poland. Also in the house was Sharon's ex-fiancé Jay Sebring, a handsome Hollywood hair stylist. A little after midnight, Frykowski was passed out on the couch in the living room, Folger was reading in her bedroom and Sharon and Sebring were sitting together on Sharon's bed talking. That is how the killers found their victims as they entered the house.

Sometime between 12.30 and 1 am, just as she was going to bed, one of the Polanskis' neighbours heard three or four sounds that she thought could have been gunshots. Since she heard nothing else, she turned out the lights and went to sleep.

About the same time, 1 kilometre downhill from the Polanskis' house, a counsellor at a camping ground heard a man screaming, 'Oh, God! No! Please don't!'. Then the screaming stopped. Unnerved by what he had heard the counsellor climbed into his car and drove up to the hilltop neighbourhoods, but he saw nothing unusual.

At 8 am the next morning, Polanski's housekeeper let herself in by the kitchen door. As she walked into the living room she froze. The furniture, the carpet and the walls were splashed with blood. The front door was open and through it she could see pools of blood on the flagstone path. And out on the lawn lay a body, soaked in blood.

Screaming and completely terrified, the woman ran from the house. As she hurried down the driveway she passed a parked car; something was sprawled on the front seat. She slowed just enough to peer inside: it was another corpse. Hysterical now, she ran to a neighbour's house pounding on the door as she shrieked, 'Murder! Bodies! Blood!'.

The first police officers to arrive at the crime scene were nauseated by what they found. The body in the car was Steven Parent, an 18-year-old acquaintance of the Polanskis' groundskeeper. He was just leaving when he had encountered the four killers from Manson's Family. Parent had been the first to die; he was shot three times in the chest and once in the face.

On the front lawn the police found two more bodies. Abigail Folger had been cut down as she tried to flee and stabbed so many times that her white, ankle-length nightgown was dyed red with her own blood.

CHARLES MANSON'S 'FAMILY'

Charles Manson lived in the hills above Los Angeles at the Spahn Movie Ranch, a ramshackle site that had once been a location for Hollywood westerns. Living with Manson were his 'Family', about thirty-six young men and women who ranged in ages from early teens to late twenties. Fuelled by sex, drugs and Manson's own lame attempts at rock music, Manson revealed to his followers his apocalyptic vision of racial and class warfare that would cleanse American society. Manson believed that the senseless slaughter of a group of rich white people would so terrify white society that it would come to the conclusion that the killings must be the work of black criminals and rise up to kill every black man, woman and child. From Los Angeles the war between white and black, rich and poor, would fan out until the United States was drowning in blood. Manson and his Family called this blood-letting 'Helter Skelter'.

Nearby was the body of Wojtek Frykowski. He had fought his attackers, and his resistance appeared to have driven them mad. He had been shot twice, stabbed fifty-one times and his skull was bashed in.

Inside the house, concealed behind a large sofa in front of the fireplace, lay the bodies of Jay Sebring and Sharon Tate. Sebring had been shot once and stabbed seven times. Sharon had been stabbed sixteen times, in the back and in the chest. Later one of the killers testified that, in her final moments, Tate had pleaded for her life and the life of her baby, but the killer replied, 'Look bitch, I have no mercy for you'.

On their way out of the Polanski house, one of the killers ran back inside, dipped a towel in Sharon Tate's blood, and printed the word 'PIG' on the front door.

Hearing of the massacre, Polanski was both devastated and frightened. When he returned to Los Angles he went into hiding – the killers had not yet been found and the police and Polanski feared he also might be a target.

The Deal

Eight years after Polanski lost his wife, he was facing trial for the rape of a 13-year-old girl. However, considering the seriousness of the charges against him, Polanski was treated leniently by the court. He was not a US citizen but a citizen of France, yet the court never confiscated his passport. He was permitted to go about his business, including travelling overseas to scout locations.

The prosecutor, Polanski's attorney and the judge in the case had even arrived at an informal agreement regarding sentencing – 90 days in jail in return for Polanski pleading guilty to unlawful sexual intercourse. Even after Polanski began to appear around Los Angeles and Beverly Hills in the company of 15-year-old Nastassja Kinski – a relationship which Polanski insisted was entirely innocent, but which the judge interpreted as a sign of the director's utter contempt for the court – the judge still agreed to abide by the deal he had hammered out with the attorneys.

It could be argued that the prosecutor let Polanski off the hook. Since the night he was arrested, Polanski had changed his story dramatically several times. Originally he denied that he had had sex with Samantha. Then he said that he had not planned to have sex with the girl, that their going to bed together had been spontaneous. Later he modified his story again, saying she was a willing sexual partner. It was also said that, in his more candid moments, Polanski complained to friends that in sexually sophisticated Europe no one would think twice about a 44-year-old man coupling with a 13-year-old girl.

Finally, the judge ordered Polanski to the California state prison in Chino for a psychiatric evaluation. It was understood among all parties that the time Polanski spent in Chino would count towards his ultimate 90-day sentence. The evaluation took 42 days, at the end of which Polanski emerged furious, fairly boiling over with resentment for having been locked up with what he described as 'the scum of society'. But he believed that at least his ordeal was now over.

He was mistaken. He still owed the state of California 48 additional days behind bars. Once his attorney made this clear to him, Polanski drove straight to the Los Angeles airport and bought the last first-class seat on a flight to London.

In London, a lawyer advised Polanski to travel to France immediately. England had an extradition treaty with the United States, while France did not. Polanski left at once for Paris. Meanwhile, back in Los Angeles, the judge issued a bench warrant for Polanski's arrest. It was an empty gesture. Polanski was beyond the reach of US justice and he has kept his distance from the United States ever since.

As for Polanski's career after he went on the lam, it has been decidedly chequered. *Tess*, released in 1979 and dedicated to Sharon Tate (her last gift to Polanski was a copy of the Thomas Hardy novel), is still acclaimed both for Nastassja Kinski's luminous performance and for Geoffrey Unsworth's superb cinematography. Given the magnificence of the film, Hollywood felt obliged to nominate Polanski for an Oscar as Best Director, but members of the Academy of Motion Pictures played it safe by giving the award to Robert Redford for *Ordinary People*.

The films that followed – *Pirates*, *Frantic*, *Bitter Moon*, *Death and the Maiden*, *The Ninth Gate* – generally met with a rocky reception from critics and audiences. But all changed with *The Pianist* in 2002.

The 46-year-old Polanski, with 20-year-old girlfriend Nastassja Kinski, at a press conference, 1979.

Reviewers and movie-goers were ecstatic about the film. It won forty-four film awards around the globe. But as the media hailed Polanski's accomplishment, they also brought up the story of the rape, his flight from justice and his lack of remorse over what he had done. Members of the film industry and the public debated whether such a man deserved awards and prizes. In the midst of the debate, an unexpected ally rallied to Polanski's side.

Young Samantha, now Samantha Geimer, a 38-year-old wife and mother of three living in Hawaii, wrote a guest column, which was published in *The Los Angles Times*. 'I believe that Mr Polanski and his film should be honoured according to the quality of the work', Geimer wrote. 'What he does for a living and how good he is at it have nothing to do with me or what he did to me. I don't think it would be fair to take past events into consideration. I think that the Academy members should vote for the movies they feel deserve it. Not for people they feel are popular.'

And so, with Samantha's blessing, Hollywood awarded Polanski an Oscar for Best Director for *The Pianist*. Since Polanski was (and is) a fugitive, he did not re-enter the United States to attend the award ceremony. On Oscar night, actor Harrison Ford, the star of *Frantic*, accepted the award on behalf of Roman Polanski.

THE CASE OF THE VANISHING ARISTOCRAT: LORD LUCAN

MAIN CULPRIT:

Richard John Bingham (Lord Lucan) (1934–unknown)

SCANDAL:

Accused of murdering his children's nanny and beating his wife before vanishing from existence

WHY:

Gambling problems caused a separation from his wife and he wanted custody of his children

Help me! Help me! I've just escaped from being murdered! My children, my children! He's in the house! He's murdered my nanny!
– Lady Veronica Lucan

Johh Richard Bingham, Earl of Lucan, and Lady Veronica Lucan after their marriage, 28 November 1963.

On the evening of Thursday, 7 November 1974, a dazed and injured woman staggered into a pub in the upper-class London suburb of Belgravia, shouting 'Help me! Help me! I've just escaped from being murdered! My children, my children! He's in the house! He's murdered my nanny!'. The woman was Lady Veronica Lucan, and she had clearly been savagely beaten around the head. This incident marked the beginning of one of the most extraordinary tales of scandal in high places, and one of the world's most enduring mysteries – the fate of Lady Lucan's presumed attacker, her husband, Lord Lucan.

Richard John Bingham, known as John, was born on 18 December 1934 into a family of some notoriety. His great-great-grandfather, the 3rd Earl of Lucan, was the general who gave the order for the ill-fated Charge of the Light Brigade. John's father, the 6th Earl, was an ardent socialist and Labour government minister, but John was a throwback to the old school, a dyed-in-the-wool aristocrat who looked down on the 'lower' classes and expected the highest quality of life for a minimum of effort.

John was educated at Eton where he was to discover the great passion of his life – gambling. He spent 2 years in the army, then began a career as a merchant banker. In 1963 he married a former model, Veronica Duncan, whose sister had married his close friend Bill Shand Kydd. In early 1964 John's father died and he became the 7th Earl, while Veronica became the Countess of Lucan. Later that year their first daughter, Frances, was born. It was also around this time that John won £26,000 (around $64,000) playing cards in just two nights. He decided to give up merchant banking and become a professional gambler. His friends nicknamed him 'Lucky'.

Lucan spent most of his nights at the Clermont, an exclusive casino in Berkeley Square, London, owned by John Aspinall. He would gamble until dawn, go home for a few hours' sleep, then be back at the club for lunch. Lady Lucan usually insisted on accompanying him. Inevitably, the routine began to take a toll on their marriage. The situation deteriorated when Lady Lucan suffered from post-natal depression after the birth of their son, George. Lucan initially appeared sympathetic, but after a while he started telling his friends that his wife had 'gone mad'. He wanted to book her into a psychiatric hospital, but she refused to go.

Lucan had inherited a fortune of £250,000 from his family, but his relentless gambling had eaten it away, and any luck he once had at the gaming tables seemed long gone. Money became an issue and Lady Lucan was particularly concerned about his refusal to put aside funds for the children's education. She continued to suffer from depression after the birth of their second daughter, Camilla, in 1970.

In 1974, the couple separated. Lucan moved out of their house at 46 Lower Belgrave Street and into a basement flat in nearby Elizabeth Street. He told his friends that Lady Lucan was not well enough to look after the children, and obtained temporary custody of them. A bitter battle in the High Court followed. Lady Lucan admitted that she had a problem with depression, but maintained that it was not nearly as serious as her husband thought. Lucan taped their telephone calls in an attempt to gain evidence against her. It was all to no avail. In June, his wife was awarded custody of the children. Lucan was devastated.

Regaining custody became an even greater obsession for him than gambling. He hired detectives to watch Lady Lucan, and made further tape recordings during his access visits to the children.

Meanwhile, Lucan's finances were approaching collapse. He had heavy expenses, overdrafts at four banks, and the custody battle had cost him £40,000 (about $98,000). He began to sell off the family silver.

Lucan spent the first weekend of November with his children. A few weeks before this, Lady Lucan had engaged a new nanny, 29-year-old Sandra Rivett. The children told Lucan that Sandra's night off was Thursday, when she went out with her boyfriend.

The Body in the Basement

It was on the following Thursday evening at around 9.45 pm that Lady Veronica Lucan made her dramatic entrance into the Plumber's Arms pub screaming for help.

Two policemen arrived at the Lucans' house 15 minutes later and forced open the front door. They walked along the elegant hallway and came to the entrance to the stairs which led to the basement. There were bloodstains in the stairwell and, using a torch (the light above the stairs wasn't working), they saw a large pool of blood with a man's footprints in it on the basement floor. They made a quick search of the rest of the house. In one bedroom they found a bloodstained towel lying on the bed. On the

Lady Veronica Lucan, pictured about a week after the murder of her nanny and the mysterious disappearance of her husband, Lord Lucan.

floor above they found the Lucan children. The two youngest were asleep. The eldest, Frances, aged 10, was awake and asked, 'Where's Mummy and Sandra?'.

The police then made a more thorough search of the basement, which contained the kitchen and breakfast room. The walls were splashed with blood, as were some broken cups and saucers lying at the foot of the stairs. A metre or so away there was a large canvas US mailbag from which blood was seeping. Inside was the body of Sandra Rivett. She had been bludgeoned around the head. A bent and bloodstained length of lead pipe wrapped in surgical plaster was also found.

The light bulb had been removed from the fitting above the stairs – this was the only light that could be switched on from the floor above, and it sat on a chair.

In hospital, Lady Lucan gave a statement to the police in which she named her husband as the attacker. She has never wavered from this.

According to Lady Lucan's account, Sandra had gone downstairs to make a cup of tea at about 8.55 pm. The two younger children had already been put to bed, and Frances was in her room watching television. When the nanny had not returned after 20 minutes, Lady Lucan went to look for her. She saw that the basement was in darkness and called out Sandra's name. A man emerged from the cloakroom and attacked her, hitting her with a heavy object. She screamed, and when he told her to be quiet, she recognised her husband's voice. Lucan tried to push his gloved fingers down her throat but she managed to grab hold of his testicles and the attack ceased.

They both collapsed onto the stairs. Lady Lucan asked him where the nanny was and he admitted that he had killed her. 'I think we'd better go upstairs and have a chat', he said.

They went upstairs, running into Frances, who was told to go to bed, which she did. In their bedroom, Lady Lucan lay down while Lucan paced around, trying to decide what to do. There was an awkward silence which Lady Lucan later described as having the mildly absurd air of aristocratic standoffishness. Lucan went into the bathroom to get a cloth to wipe her face. When he had the tap running, she took the opportunity to escape from the house and run the 30 metres to the Plumber's Arms.

Lucan Flees

Around 10 pm, Madeleine Florman, a friend of Lucan's who lived nearby, was woken by frantic ringing on her door. She thought it was local youths just mucking around and ignored it. However, 20 minutes later she received a phone call from an agitated man she recognised as Lucan, but he soon hung up. Police later found bloodstains on her doorstep.

A few minutes after the call to Florman, Lucan rang his mother and told her that there had been a 'terrible catastrophe' at the house. He had been passing by when he noticed a fight going on inside. Veronica was injured and there was a lot of blood. 'Oh, God, Mother', he added, 'there was something terrible in the basement. I couldn't bring myself to look'. He asked her to fetch the children, and then hung up.

Lucan then drove 68 kilometres to the home of his friends Ian and Susan Maxwell-Scott, who lived in Sussex. He was driving a blue Ford Corsair that had been lent to him by a gambling buddy Michael Stoop (his own car, a Mercedes, was having

THE MURDERED NANNY

Sandra Rivett was a vivacious redhead who was popular with the Lucan children and their mother. Rivett had separated from her husband and had a son who was being looked after by her parents, Albert and Eunice Hensby, who lived in a caravan park in Hampshire. Her boyfriend was a 27-year-old Australian pub manager named John Hankins. He had asked her to return to Sydney with him but she had not yet given him an answer at the time of her murder. At the inquest into her death, her parents complained that she seemed to have been forgotten amid all the infighting in the Lucan family over Lord Lucan's guilt or innocence.

engine problems). Arriving at the Maxwell-Scotts' he found that Ian was in London, but Susan let him in and poured him a whisky. Lucan was in a terrible state, she later said, wearing flannel trousers with a damp patch on them that looked as if a stain had been wiped off. He told her he had been through an experience 'so incredible that I don't think you or anyone else could possibly believe it', and gave an expanded version of the story he had told his mother. Having seen the fight he had let himself into the house and gone down to the basement, where he slipped on a pool of blood. The attacker had fled. Lady Lucan had cried out that the man had killed Sandra, and accused Lucan of hiring him to kill her.

Lucan asked if he could use the phone to ring his mother. The conversation was brief. She told him the children were now safe at her flat, and asked him if he wanted to speak to the policeman who was with her. He said he would ring the police in the morning.

Lucan then tried to ring his friend Bill Shand Kydd, but was unable to reach him. He sat down and wrote two letters to him, which he gave to Susan to post. She asked him if he wanted to stay the night, but he said he had to 'get back and straighten things out'. He drove off at 1.15 am.

There has been no verified sighting of Lord Lucan since then.

On the following Monday, the Ford Corsair was found in the port town of Newhaven, south of London. There were bloodstains in the front of the car and, in the boot, a length of pipe wrapped in surgical plaster that matched the one found in Lower Belgrave Street.

SIGHTINGS

Lord Lucan has been sighted on just about every continent. In 1974, police in Melbourne, Australia, arrested an Englishman they thought was Lucan after he made some suspicious financial transactions. He turned out to be the errant British MP and failed businessman John Stonehouse, who had faked his own death.

In 1975, Lucan was reported to be a frequent guest at a hotel in Cherbourg, France. He has been seen sobbing in a gym in British Columbia and working in Queensland, Australia. Lord Lucan has turned up in Sicily, Ireland, South Africa and the Netherlands.

Taking Sides

It soon became clear that Lord Lucan, peer of the realm, was not being treated like a normal murder suspect. Although Lady Lucan had told police within hours of being attacked that he was responsible, it was not until the following Tuesday – 4 days later – that the police issued a warrant for his arrest. The media displayed a similar deference. While the story was all over the front pages, the initial focus was on Lucan's mysterious disappearance. That he might have been the killer was not actually mentioned.

Lucan's blood relatives and friends immediately closed ranks, united in the belief that he was innocent. They were considerably quicker off the mark than the police. The day after the murder, John Aspinall organised a lunch where Lucan's friends discussed how they could help the missing earl – when he reappeared. Later, the police would accuse the 'Clermont set', as they were dubbed by the media, of doing everything they could to obstruct the investigation. Meanwhile, Susan Maxwell-Scott had not thought it necessary to report to the police the incident of Lucan's late-night visit. They only learned of it when they traced her through the postmarks on the letters he had written to Shand Kydd from her house.

The main reason all his supporters believed Lucan was innocent was a simple one – he just didn't seem capable of such a violent attack.

The division between the pro- and anti-Lucan sides was evident at the inquest into Sandra Rivett's death. Lady Lucan sat alone, completely ignored by Lucan's mother and his other supporters.

DEAD LUCKY

In 2003 a book called *Dead Lucky* appeared, co-authored by a former Scotland Yard detective, Duncan McLoughlin. It claimed that Lucan had been living in Goa, India, under the name Barry Halpin, and had died there in 1996. A photo of a long-haired and bearded man, bearing a passing resemblance to Lucan, was reproduced around the world. As soon as the book was published, friends of Halpin came forward. They recalled a somewhat eccentric schoolteacher who worked in Britain and Australia before dropping out and ending up in Goa. He played the guitar and the tin whistle. He sounds like an interesting fellow, but unfortunately he wasn't Lord Lucan.

Bill Shand Kydd read the two letters out. In the first, Lucan repeated his story of interrupting a fight in the house, and said his wife would blame him. 'V. [Veronica] has demonstrated her hatred of me in the past and would do anything to see me accused. For George & Frances to go through life knowing their father had stood in the dock for attempted murder would be too much. When they are old enough to understand, explain to them the dream of paranoia, and look after them.' The second letter dealt with an upcoming auction of some of the family silver – in it Lucan asked that the proceeds from the auction be used to clear his overdrafts.

There was also a third letter, which fellow gambler Michael Stoop received on the Monday after the killing. In this, Lucan talked about 'a traumatic night of unbelievable coincidence', and wrote that all he cared about was that the children be protected.

The QC acting for Lucan's mother did his best to talk up Lady Lucan's alleged hatred of her husband. But the inescapable fact was that all the forensic evidence supported her account. The blood found in the basement had been mainly Group B (Sandra Rivett's group), while that on the staircase was mainly Group A (Lady Lucan's). Both types were found on the lead pipe. There was no evidence whatsoever of another attacker.

The jury took just half an hour to reach their verdict – the cause of Sandra Rivett's death was 'murder, by Lord Lucan'.

A 'Night of Unbelievable Coincidence'

The police version of events was that Lucan had acted alone. He had intended to kill his wife and, in the dark, had mistaken Sandra Rivett for Veronica Lucan (they were the same height and of a similar build). This is certainly the most commonly held view of the case, but there have been other theories.

Some have chosen to believe Lord Lucan's account – that he interrupted an attack by someone else. As he was the only person with any motive to kill Lady Lucan, and no-one has given a reason for Sandra Rivett being a target, it has been suggested that the attacker was a burglar. While a burglar could have killed the nanny (and even had a sack to put her in) there would have been no reason for him to wait 20 minutes or so and then attack Lady Lucan. The biggest obstacle to this theory, though, is the matching length of lead pipe found in Lucan's car boot.

In his book, *Trail of Havoc*, Patrick Marnham argued that Lucan hired a hitman to do the job. He noted that the Lucans' daughter Frances, when giving her account of the night, put the time of events 20 minutes earlier than in her mother's version. (Frances used the beginning and ending of certain television programs as a reference point.) If Frances's timetable is accurate, Lucan, who was seen at the Clermont earlier that evening, would not have had time to get to the house and murder the nanny. As a professional hitman is unlikely to have chosen a lead pipe for a weapon, Marnham suggested that the man Lucan hired had been unable to carry out the murder and, at the last moment, sent a drunken replacement who bungled it. However, there is no real evidence for this theory.

Police use an auto-giro in their attempts to search for the missing Lord Lucan, England, 1975.

If Lucan did act alone, there remains a mystery almost as baffling as his disappearance. How could he have believed that the crime would achieve its aim – the return of his children? Even if everything had gone to plan and he had succeeded in killing his wife, bludgeoning her to death would have inevitably left a lot of blood and other physical evidence at the scene. He would then have had to dispose of the body, presumably transporting it in the boot of his car, which again would have left bloodstains. He could have tried to dispose of the car as well, but how would he have explained its disappearance? It looks like this was one gamble 'Lucky' Lucan could never have won.

Dead or Alive?

Most of Lucan's friends believe he took his own life just hours after the murder. 'Lucan killed himself out of shame for having botched it', said John Aspinall. 'He reckoned that if he wasn't around any more, there would always be a question mark over his guilt, which would be good for his children.'

Lady Lucan believed he got on a ferry at Newhaven and jumped overboard. Others have claimed that Lucan bought a speedboat before the murder (he had been a keen speedboat racer in earlier years). 'He tied a stone around his body and scuttled the powerboat he kept at Newhaven and down he went', said Aspinall. The journalist Charles Benson, who went to Eton with Lucan, had another theory. 'He had almost certainly found the means of disposing of the body. He had probably found a desolate spot, a pothole in deep undergrowth. So he shot himself in the very place he had earmarked for Veronica's body.'

Others continue to believe that Lucan is alive. A lifelong gambler, they reason, would surely have taken the risk of escaping, and Lucan had many rich friends who could have helped him do this.

It's an odd thing to say, but when you're being attacked by someone you love, it seems to hurt less.

– Lady Veronica Lucan

In 2004, on the 30th anniversary of the murder, Scotland Yard announced that they were relaunching their investigation into the case. They had prepared a computer-generated image of how Lucan would now look, and would also be applying DNA techniques.

In the same year, Lucan's son George appeared in a television documentary, saying he believed his father was innocent. The killer, he said, was a burglar Lucan had hired to rob their home as part of an elaborate insurance fraud.

In 2002 Lady Lucan gave a rare interview. Still living in Belgravia, now estranged from all three of her children, she vividly recalled the night of the murder. 'John hit Sandra so hard that the pipe bent', she said, 'and this actually saved my life, because when he attacked me, he couldn't land it with the same force. It was wrapping around my head rather than bashing through it.' She said that she had long ago forgiven her husband. Noticing an oil portrait of Lucan on the wall, the interviewer asked why she kept it there. 'Well, it's only a piece of decoration, isn't it? And it's honestly quite a good likeness. If I threw it out, I would only have to find something else to replace it. What would be the point of that?'

DOUBLE LIVES

British Labour politician John Stonehouse, who faked
his own death and went on the run, pictured returning
to London to face the music, 1975.

MOTIVATION

anger
charity
envy
faith
gluttony
greed
hope
lust
pride
sloth

THE SCAM ARTISTE EXTRAORDINAIRE: THERESE HUMBERT

MAIN CULPRIT:
Thérèse Humbert (1856–1918), French fraudster

SCANDAL:
Perpetrated huge scams on the strength of a bogus inheritance for more than 20 years

WHY:
Need for survival plus an overactive imagination

The greatest swindle of the century.
– French lawyer, after successfully convicting the Humberts

Thérèse Humbert c.1903. Also known as 'La Grande Thérèse', she lived in a world of illusion and fantasy and managed to convince many influential people that she was an heiress. She and her family perpetrated such large-scale fraud that, when it was discovered, it rocked the very fabric of the French economy.

A crowd had gathered around the fashionable Humbert mansion on the Avenue de la Grande Armée in Paris, 9 May 1902. They had come to witness the court-ordered opening of the famous strongbox, the contents of which Thérèse Humbert had used as collateral to borrow a staggering amount of money over a period of 20 years. The anticipation was immense. The box had long been thought to contain papers pointing to wealth of over one hundred million francs. Everything the Humberts owned had been secured by the contents of this box – their Paris mansion, numerous country estates and a merchant bank. With none of the Humberts available to be present at the event, and no key able to be found, it was left to locksmiths wielding hammers to break the box open. When they did, the news spread like wildfire that all that was inside was an Italian coin, an old newspaper and a trouser button. One of the greatest scandals of the century was revealed for all to see.

At the height of her fame, Thérèse Humbert, the daughter-in-law of former French justice minister, Gustav Humbert (also her half-uncle), lavishly entertained the cream of Parisian society in her mansion situated on one of Paris's most expensive streets. Yet the edifice of her social triumph had been built on a lifetime of lying and the day the strongbox was opened it all came crashing down around her, landing her in jail. The shockwaves of her downfall rippled through French society causing resignations, massive embarrassment, financial ruin and even suicide among the powerful and innocent alike. In some ways, La Grande Thérèse, as she was known, was the precursor to today's internet scams, yet she was so much more elaborate, artistic even. While reprehensible in terms of its impact upon its many unsuspecting victims, the performance of La Grande Thérèse, and her ability to sustain it for so many years, was the work of a top-flight illusionist, whose imagination's sustained capacity to defy reality, indeed bend reality to meet her desires, was phenomenal.

Birth of a Scammer

The story begins with the young Thérèse Daurignac, a girl of unspectacular parentage with an overactive imagination and a talent for enchantment to make people believe her unlikely tales. She was born in the town of Aussone near Toulouse in the south of France. Both Thérèse's parents were illegitimate. Her facility for fantasy was inherited from her father, Guillaume, a foundling supported by the local priest, and who became an eccentric and visionary. Guillaume's romantic dream-world, in which he was the descendant of an illustrious castle-dwelling family, was the foundation for his daughter's world-beating lies. Thérèse combined this fantasy world with the business acumen that came from her mother, Rosa – one of the many illegitimate children fathered by a financially wily, yet parsimonious, bachelor farmer. It was Rosa who, for most of Thérèse's childhood, kept the family afloat by running a successful boutique selling lingerie to the wives of the wealthy burghers of rapidly industrialising Toulouse. Her much older husband dabbled in the esoteric arts of bone-setting, fortune-telling and faith healing.

The initial phases of Thérèse's childhood were relatively prosperous. Her family was earning a good living, they had a small farm, she had brothers and sisters and friends – but the wheels fell off after the death of her mother. Had it been her father who had died, it's unlikely she would have had to hone her capacity for fiction to the extent she did. But her remaining parent, already an old man, retreated further into his fantasy world of necromantic projects and Thérèse, only 14 years old, became the effective head of the family.

The Beginnings of the Scam

Thérèse had always told stories to entertain her friends. They loved her concoctions because, in an age without television, movies or radio, she was able to make life seem more glamorous than it actually was. For instance, she came up with the idea that her friends pool all their jewellery so they would each seem like they owned a lot more than they did.

Yet when her mother died, it fell to Thérèse to beg and borrow in order to keep her father and five younger siblings clothed and fed. It wasn't long, however, before Thérèse, who was a great lover of finery, realised the same charm she used to cajole eggs from farmers could equally be applied to the dressmakers and hairdressers of Toulouse. While not beautiful, men in particular were enamoured of her earthy Toulousian French that was spoken with a beguiling lisp. The shopkeepers gave her credit partly because their enjoyment of her talk was stronger than their desire to be paid.

Thérèse began to secure her borrowings with the claim that she was the heiress to the Château Marcotte – an estate on the border of France and Spain that she would lay claim to for the rest of her 'career'. The source of the provenance was usually attributed to a kindly spinster aunt but, at this stage, Thérèse was prone to imaginative riffing and the details of the story varied from one telling to the next.

While the Château Marcotte story served her well, the patience of Toulouse's shopkeepers wasn't endless. When she was 17, and the shopkeepers were already becoming suspicious, Thérèse made the extra claim that she was betrothed to the son of a Bordeaux shipping magnate – in a loveless match that was being forced upon her to honour an agreement between their two fathers. On this basis, she managed to scam a bridal trousseau. However, it wasn't long before her creditors woke up to her latest stunt and collectively sent Thérèse and her family bankrupt. The family was split up and the farmhouse sold. Now in disgrace, Thérèse and her father moved to Toulouse to look for work.

A Fortunate Hitch

In Toulouse, one of Thérèse's mother's half-sisters, Marie Emily Thénier, had done particularly well for herself. While working as a maid, she had cleaned the rooms of a law-student lodger called Gustav Humbert. He took a shine to her and they were eventually married. While Thérèse's family were on the skids, their relatives the Humberts were headed towards the top echelons of French society. Gustav had

become a professor of law at Toulouse University, then a socialist politician. His pioneering work on the French Third Republic had made him a hero of the progressive left, who bestowed on him the honour of life senator in 1875. Gustav and Marie had two children. Their son Frédéric, who studied law, was intelligent but lacked the gumption of his father. In 1878, Thérèse married Frédéric Humbert in a double wedding – the other couple were her younger brother, Emile, and Frédéric's younger sister. The Daurignacs and the Humberts were thus inextricably entwined.

A French cartoon, c.1903, titled 'The Humbert Affair', depicting Thérèse Humbert reaping the fruits of borrowings made on the imaginary inheritance of the non-existent Crawford. When the scam was made public, many victims were too embarrassed to come forward.

The wedding was the most spectacular that the village of Beauzelle, just outside Toulouse, had ever seen. Thérèse's wedding costume alone cost more than 5000 francs – about the same price as renting a flash Parisian apartment for a year. The shopkeepers of Toulouse must have been impressed by the social standing of her bridegroom and once again were gulled into providing her credit on the basis of her inheritance story.

The fact that she got away with it, taught Thérèse a useful lesson: one of the strange paradoxes of the confidence trickster's art is that the more outrageous the demand you make, the more likely people are to accede to it. The wedding, whose costs were traditionally the responsibility of the bride's family, was never paid for. Before long, the shopkeepers of Toulouse were shaking their heads at how they had let themselves fall under her spell yet again.

A Family Affair?

If it's easy to envisage how an array of farmers and provincial shopkeepers would have fallen under Thérèse's spell, it's more difficult to see why Gustave Humbert, a future minister of justice with an impeccable reputation, would have permitted his children to marry such relatives of dubious ethics and origins. Especially since, unlike many, he must have been aware of Thérèse's true ancestry. The locals were puzzled and gossip abounded. In retrospect, the most likely answer lies in Therese's imaginary Château de Marcotte. While Gustave Humbert had risen spectacularly through society, he lacked money. The idea of a daughter-in-law with an inheritance was therefore tempting. Thérèse had the attributes of being intelligent, charming and ambitious. Moreover, Gustave may have preferred Thérèse, rather than hitching his family to the propertied classes who, in many cases, were the natural enemies of the Third Republic. Whether at first Gustave was enchanted by Thérèse and actually believed her story, or whether he saw the potential to leverage her imagination, is difficult to know. Perhaps he even saw her utilisation of fake inheritances as a brilliant form of class warfare. It's improbable that someone clever enough to be a celebrated lawyer, top-class university professor and eventual French minister of justice should be so naive to have kept believing in his half-niece and daughter-in-law's schemes.

Not long after the marriage, Gustave used his social authority to arrange a mortgage of the Château de Marcotte for more than 700,000 francs. Gustave was appointed minister of justice in 1882, the highest legal office in the land. That same year, he was the intermediary in the mortgage of Thérèse's second property, an equally imaginary plantation of cork oaks in Portugal, which had apparently been left to her by a man her mother had nursed back to health when he had a heart attack outside her shop. A doctor from the southwest of France advanced the sum of 60,000 francs to the newly appointed justice minister against his daughter-in-law's inheritance of the estate. From this point on, there's little doubt that the Humberts, both father and son, were complicit in Thérèse's scams. Although a hero of the Third Republic, Gustave compromised his integrity in exchange for money. His involvement in Thérèse's schemes, as a conduit to important people and a form of moral security, made it possible to expand the operation to a Parisian and national scale. Without Gustave's support it's difficult to believe that Thérèse's outrageous caper would have gone as far as it did.

Solid Air

Having finalised the script of the inheritance, the Humberts began to use the money they borrowed to acquire actual real estate, which they also proceeded to mortgage. In a short period of time they went from owning castles in the air and renting a dingy apartment in Paris to being significant landholders. Their first purchase, a house in a fashionable part of Paris was followed by a chateau in the Fountainebleau forest, 15 kilometres from Paris, complete with its own private lake. On a family trip to Narbonne in the south of France the following year, the Humberts returned, having paid the astronomical sum of 2 million francs for the family seat of Comte de Toulouse-Lautrec (whose son Henri was the famous French painter). The purchase was purely for display, as none of the Humbert family would ever live there. But how could the Humberts' capacity to repay be doubted when they were known to own such an esteemed chunk of France?

Thérèse now had the political connections and 'assets' to launch herself into the upper reaches of French society. Sophisticated Parisians were as besotted with the husky-voiced provincial ingenue as the Toulousian shopkeepers had been and, importantly, equally prepared to advance her credit. The Humberts bought a newspaper, L'*Avenir de Seine et Marne*, which their loyal friend Armand Parayre ran as a radical muckraker. It supported the progressive cause of Gustave and campaigned successfully to get Frédéric elected as a Republican deputy to the French parliament. At the same time, Thérèse expanded the family's property portfolio with the addition of two more country estates and, the *pièce de résistance*, a city mansion more than four stories high in the ultra-fashionable Avenue de la Grande Armée – one of the majestic Baron Hausmann-built streets running from the Arc de Triomphe.

France was in the grip of industrialisation. Massive fortunes were being made and consumed. It was an era of extravagance and upheaval which came to be known as the *Belle Epoque* ('beautiful era'). Thérèse had landed in a slice of history perfectly suited to her peculiar skills where the flow of cash, love of risk and luxury, general optimism and the new elite – which had emerged from the Third Republic – all created an environment conducive to the kind of scam she was involved in. Before long, Thérèse had become one of the most esteemed hostesses in the nation, with presidents, ministers and plutocratic financiers all paying court to her in her opulent Paris home. As her figure thickened with age, her expenditure on dresses rose astronomically, while her signature fashion items were her extravagant hats piled high with jewels, bird feathers and fruit – they captured perfectly both the excess of the age and the fanciful character of one of its chief exploiters.

As the money continued to circulate feverishly through the family's hands, they did what any sensibly greedy family in a similar situation would do – they started their own bank. The Rent Viagère, which launched in 1893, drew in many more, often smaller investors, and was backed by little more than a fancy prospectus with unauthorised pictures of the President of South Africa (a country renowned for its diamonds, a subject dear to Thérèse's heart) and the Pope. It was a runaway success – perhaps, if given a few more decades, it may well have turned the family into genuinely successful bankers.

LIVING THE HIGH LIFE

In the front section of the Humbert house Thérèse was at the pinnacle of her social splendour, entertaining guests such as Sarah Bernhardt and Emile Zola, while the president of France, Felix Fauré, was a regular at the Humbert table. Her supporters were the elite of the French Republic and included the police chief and the chief justice of the appeal court, as well as the upper echelons of French freemasonry. Thérèse had reached a position where she was seemingly untouchable.

As her social standing took off and her Paris residence became one of the capital's most exclusive salons, the exotic story of Thérèse's strongbox became famous throughout all of France. In a cynical age such as our own, it's difficult to imagine how people would keep lending money on the unknown contents of a never-opened strongbox, but once one person of reputation had done so, others tended to follow, especially since Thérèse was also known for offering some of the highest interest rates in town.

Crawfraud

Having succeeded twice in mortgaging non-existent properties, Thérèse's imagination began to explore the full potential of the practice. Her subsequent wealth and social status were derived from her ability to get people to lend her lots of money using these imagined estates as security.

The safe which Thérèse Humbert claimed contained a fortune in trust for her, when, in fact, it held an old coin, a newspaper and a trouser button.

In the early stages, her beneficiary and the story behind it tended to change according to her whims. Over time, the heart attack victim nursed by her mother became a fellow resident of her lodging house in Toulouse, who Thérèse had nursed, and who had died, but not before writing her into his will.

Eventually a master version of the story emerged. In this story, Thérèse was on a train in 1879 when she heard groaning from the neighbouring compartment. She went to investigate and found a man having a heart attack. She saved his life by putting her smelling salts under his nose. Robert Henry Crawford turned out to be an American millionaire. He sent her a letter 2 years later saying that he had written her into his estate, which was worth the astronomical sum of 100 million francs.

However, it's not as simple as Crawford keeling over and Thérèse getting the cash. While she needed a dead man, the pay-off needed to be postponed. At this point the legal expertise of her husband and father-in-law became invaluable. They concocted a further fiction that Crawford had left her a strongbox with bearer bonds worth 100 million francs. In the strongbox was also Crawford's final will naming Thérèse as sole beneficiary. However, there was also a competing will leaving the fortune to Crawford's two sons and Thérèse's younger sister, Marie. A third document apparently recorded an agreement in which the Crawford sons granted Thérèse guardianship of the fortune while the dispute was being resolved, while a crucial fourth document was an offer by the Crawford brothers to waive their claim on the 100 million if Therese paid them 6 million francs and allowed one of them to marry the younger sister also named in the second will. It was this story that enabled Thérèse to borrow large amounts of money at high interest, based on the argument that if she could put together the 6 million to pay off the Crawford brothers, then the rest of the 100 million would be hers.

In 1885, when she had leveraged well over 6 million, Thérèse sued the Crawfords in the civil tribunal of the Seine, for violating the agreement that was the fourth tenet of the contents of the strongbox, claiming that when she had offered the 6 million francs, the Crawfords had welshed on the deal. She won the case, but was able to perpetuate the scam when the Crawfords — who it must be remembered didn't exist — appealed, and the matter conveniently remained in a state of legal suspension for years, as it climbed its way slowly from court to court. Thérèse was therefore able to continue borrowing money on the basis of her 100 million-franc inheritance.

The Dark Side of the Scam

Thérèse's scam was a family affair and only those related by blood were aware that the foundation of the family's new wealth was pure illusion. How they managed to pull it off for so long seems almost a miracle, and was only possible because of the charismatic hold that Thérèse had over the rest of her family.

The Humbert–Daurignacs occupied various roles that were neccesary to give the scam legs. Gustave was the *éminence grise* who gave the family an aura of respectability, while Thérèse was the creative genius and figure of wonder who had French society dancing to her tune. Her husband, Frédéric, was the details man, honing the scams, keeping the ship running as tightly as possible given the necessary extravagances — and his wife's tendency to incautiously improvise upon the inheritance story, something which would trigger their eventual undoing.

When you are making a fortune by ripping people off, there are bound to be dissatisfied customers. For the most part, Thérèse was able to charm or trick them but, when that failed, there was Thérèse's brother, Romain, who operated the blackmail, extortion and physical violence side of the family business. It was he, for instance, who deflected a revolver pointed by the wife of a ruined newspaper owner at Thérèse. (The woman was arrested by Humbert-friendly police and locked up in a mental asylum.) Romain occupied concealed apartments accessed through a hidden door behind the stairway in the mansion on L'Avenue de la Grande Armée. His apartments, which included a couple of cells, had a tradesmen's entrance from another street which was where lawyers and tradesmen came to complain about being scammed and from where the threats were dispensed. Whereas Thérèse's imagination was aimed towards high society, Romain was enamoured of the law. When Gustave Humbert died in 1894, the scam lost a moderate presence and both Thérèse and her brother became more sociopathic in the achievement of their goals.

Thérèse began to keep a suicide register which began with the collapse of the Girard Bank, one of the Humberts' major creditors, in 1895. When the desperate president, Paul Girard, visited Thérèse seeking repayment and she refused, he shot at her but missed, then went home and killed himself. The Humberts then attempted to bribe the bank's receiver, Monsieur Duret, over dinner, but it ended up with Romain beating him up. Duret lodged a lawsuit in which the Humberts were represented by the leader of the French bar, Maitre du Buit. The case was settled in 1896 for 2 million francs, but not before the Humbert affair was described in court by Duret's lawyer 'as the greatest swindle of the century'. Yet the insult was largely perceived as political, an attempt by the conservative right to get at some of the progressive Third Republic's favourite citizens.

With such a large payment to make and quickly, the Humberts were forced to forage far and wide for loans. The wheels were starting to fall off. As they became more desperate to raise money, the rates they were forced to pay got higher. Yet, amazingly, it would be another 6 years before their paper empire would come crumbling down around them. One of the next businessmen to take on the Humberts, didn't even get a chance to kill himself. In 1899, Paul Schotman of the Lille distillery firm, Schotman et fils, was found dead on a train, after refusing to lend the Humberts an extra 7 million francs, on top of the 2 million he had already advanced. On hearing the news, the murdered man's brother and cousin rapidly paid up. Romain was strongly suspected of having commissioned the hit, but the Humberts' high-ranking contacts in the police department ensured he wasn't officially connected to the crime.

PLAYING AT LIFE

Despite the fact they didn't exist, over the years, there were numerous sightings of the Crawford brothers. They turned up sometimes to brief lawyers, or were reported in the news as having papers served on them by a bailiff.

A further delay to settlement was Thérèse's younger sister Marie's refusal to marry an American, which was also part of the fourth condition of the plot.

At an exclusive dinner party held by Thérèse, Robert Crawford Jr tried to put a magnificent jewel-encrusted engagement ring on Marie's finger, but she determinedly brushed him aside. The Crawfords, who spoke French with American accents were played by Thérèse's brothers, Romain and Emile Daurignac, acting to a tight script – an extension of the make believe and dress-up games their big sister had made them play as children.

The Truth Catches Up

It was a poor piece of improvisation by Thérèse, however, which set off the chain of events that would lead to her downfall. In 1901, Thérèse met a simple request from a court judge for the Crawfords' American address, by replying '1302 Broadway, Manhattan' off the top of her head. When the court checked out the address, the response from America was that Crawfords had never lived there. As a consequence, the judge ordered the opening of the strongbox at the petition of one of the Humbert's many creditors.

Once that order had been given, there was no way out. Two days before the opening, the Humberts slipped out of Paris, leaving their loyal offsiders and friends, the Parayres to carry the can. Once the fraud was revealed, the shockwaves reverberated through French society. The Humbert's lawyer resigned as head of the bar, as did several other prominent people close to the Humberts. The Rente Viagère was declared bankrupt and thousands of people lost their life savings, while the scandal sheets were full of lists of important people who had lost large sums in the scam, including the Empress Eugènie, many from the top of France's financial world, jewellers and other luxury merchants, as well as the president's son.

Six months later, the Humberts still hadn't been found. When the conservative right claimed on 6 December 1902 in parliament that the investigation had been muzzled by the Humbert's progressive Republican friends – which it had – there was a riot that led to the suspension, then abandonment, of the session.

Two weeks later, however, with her old friends in the police probably finding it politically impossible not to arrest them, the Humberts were found hiding in Madrid and were brought back to Paris to face trial. It was one of the most anticipated trials in France and dominated the daily news. Creditor after creditor took the witness stand. Thérèse Humbert was in debt for much more than 100 million francs. Yet the establishment, eager to avoid further embarrassment as well as the revelation of some of its own less-than-sanitary financial dealings, made a deal behind the scenes. The sentences were rather light: 5 years for Thérèse and Frédéric, 3 for Romain and 2 for Emile. In return the Humbert–Daurignacs were to remain silent. They fulfilled their part of the bargain and, once their sentences had been served, none of them was ever heard of again.

MOTIVATION

anger

charity

envy

faith

gluttony

greed

hope

lust

pride

sloth

PORTRAIT OF A SHADOW: THE SECRETS OF ANTHONY BLUNT

MAIN CULPRIT:
Anthony Blunt (1907–83); Surveyor of the Queen's Pictures

SCANDAL:
Was exposed as an MI5 double agent and Russian spy

WHY:
An anti-fascist and subversive by nature

Sir Anthony Blunt, British art historian and Surveyor of the Queen's Pictures was exposed as a former Soviet spy and became known as 'the spy with no shame'.

Last Thursday, in response to a priority written question from the hon. Member for Hartlepool (Mr. Leadbitter), I thought it right to confirm that Professor Blunt had indeed been a Soviet agent and to give the House the salient facts. Today we have an opportunity to debate the whole matter.
– British Prime Minister Margaret Thatcher

Even though it was the comfortably familiar ritual of tea as usual with the queen mother that afternoon of 25 May 1951, Sir Anthony Blunt had more on his mind than making palace chitchat with his royal second cousin, and deciding where to hang a recently cleaned old master painting. At that very moment, Guy Burgess and Donald Maclean, his close associates in the now-notorious Cambridge spy ring, were each packing a single suitcase of their most treasured possessions. They were secretly getting ready to defect to Russia, just in the nick of time, before they were exposed. Elsewhere in London, Kim Philby, another member of the ring, considered the fallout from the impending news. Blunt knew he would be next.

Having committed treason in wartime, they all faced dire criminal charges. But it was Blunt, the 'fourth man', who was the most prominent of them all and would cause the biggest stir. He was the leading light of the British art world, a constant presence at court, a familiar face in the corridors of power and on television – not only as an expert on paintings and drawings but as a 'public intellectual' with close ties to the royal family. The defections of Burgess and Maclean put him in a particularly precarious position, with perhaps as much to lose as he had risked during his covert career as a double agent inside MI5 during World War II, siphoning sensitive military intelligence to his Russian handlers.

After two decades of rapidly eroding secrecy, during which Burgess's drunken indiscretions in London's gay underground had threatened all their lives with exposure, Blunt knew that the disappearance of the first two traitors would leave a trail that would eventually lead to Philby, the next of their crew to be outed. Then the lens would be turned on him – the long-rumoured shadow figure in the most notorious espionage drama of all, a story worthy of John le Carré.

But one would never have guessed at this underlying nerve-wracking complexity from the unperturbed demeanour of Blunt, whose teacup silently returned after each sip to its saucer where it reposed without a tremor all afternoon. It was the quintessential Blunt performance. He would return as usual to his spartan flat on the top floor of the elegant Courtauld Institute – home to many of the most gorgeous Impressionist paintings in Europe and his academic fiefdom for three decades. His boyfriend would have dinner and a decent gin and tonic waiting. Of all Blunt's secrets, his homosexuality was probably the least secure. The knowing royals turned a blind eye, as did his (mainly gay) colleagues in the art world and, more surprisingly, fellow soldiers who were aware of his soap opera-style love life during the war.

The news broke on June 7 1951. As headlines around the world announced the hunt was on for 'the missing diplomats' Burgess and Maclean, the mounting heat brought out the natural sphinx in Blunt. He professed complete surprise at their disappearance.

Even at the height of his career as a public servant, Blunt was an enigma to his closest friends (including members of the royal family). Distinguished, devoted, diligent and dull, he scarcely seemed the James Bond type. But every stage in his life led him deeper into deception as the stakes grew perilously higher, both in terms of the official secrets he stole, and the escalating values of the art he controlled. His double lives were almost kaleidoscopic in their variety. He hid his homosexuality behind a suave and icy demeanour that frequently attracted the aggressive desire and unrequited love of a number of aristocratic women. He ascended to a high-level position in the War Office, beginning in 1939, that gave

Guy Burgess, a diplomat recruited by the Russians as an agent, along with Blunt, Philby and Maclean.

him access to thousands of sensitive documents that he passed to his Soviet handlers. As the Surveyor of the Queen's Pictures, he was a close adviser to the sovereign and the most powerful figure in the British art world. He was a courtier in the upper echelons of power, both political and cultural, who used his privileged access to repeatedly betray authority – a habit he picked up early in life.

From his school days onwards, the habit of deception had been a necessity to Blunt when it came to his sex life. Until 1967, sodomy was a federal offence, punishable by prison, and close friends of Blunt with a preference for young boys (including Guy Burgess) had barely survived career-threatening brushes with the law, not to mention blackmail. It was due to careless behaviour, as much as the diligence of government investigators, that drove Burgess into exile.

The Fourth Man Unmasked

Blunt's secret survived the onslaught of press and official calls for inquiries that followed the sensational flight of Burgess and Maclean. It even held tight when, 12 years later in 1963, Kim Philby was unmasked when he too fled to Moscow. The moment of truth, when it all came crashing down for Sir Anthony Blunt, can be pinpointed with complete exactitude.

It was the afternoon of Thursday 15 November, 1979. The Surveyor of the Queen's Pictures, and about-to-be-exposed Russian agent, was cowering in a friend's house in Hammersmith, having been tipped by the cabinet secretary that, during question session in the House of Commons, Prime Minister Thatcher was to reveal the hidden identity of the 'fourth man' in the Cambridge spy puzzle. Standing before her fellow Conservatives and to the delight of the Labour party members across the aisle, Thatcher read a prepared statement that confirmed the published rumours that had shocked the nation just hours before: Sir Anthony Blunt, the most prominent and powerful figure in the English art world, had confessed to passing top-level secrets from British Intelligence to the Russians during World War II. By the end of the day, Buckingham Palace had issued a terse announcement of its own that Blunt had been stripped of his knighthood. It was said the Queen, to whom Blunt (a blood relative) had been a close adviser for nearly four decades, never spoke his name again. The Queen Mother, more forgiving, told friends that she felt it was a shame but she still admired him.

Inside the corridors of power across the world, the response was uniform disbelief. The most hotly pursued secret agent in history had been standing before them front and centre on the public stage in the spotlight of the media all along. The press had a field day. It became open season on Blunt's homosexual affairs, shady dealings in the high-stakes art field and the lurid details of his friendships with those known traitors, his Cambridge pals: Kim Philby, Guy Burgess and Donald Maclean. Blunt was the only one who had not fled the country. It turned out that he had made a deal with the Tory government back in 1964 that gave him immunity from prosecution, in return for information he volunteered in a debriefing with MI5 about the Cambridge spy ring.

Blunt's carefully guarded private life fell apart. His boyfriend, John Gaskin, who had been in hiding with him all through the ordeal, attempted suicide by jumping from the balcony of their top-floor apartment at the Courtauld Institute. Blunt's academic and honorary titles were summarily withdrawn, and his lawyer was powerless to defend him against the attacks as the scandal grew to extremes. He died just 4 years later, wasted away by the stress and drinking.

A Life of Deception

From his childhood to the unforgettable instant of his unmasking in 1979, Blunt had practised the ironic contrast between appearance and reality. He was the son of a Bournemouth clergyman and an aristocratic Scot (his mother's family line included the Earl of Strathmore – the father of the future queen mother, Blunt's most staunch royal supporter). Blunt was a brilliant student at Marlborough, one of England's top boarding schools. He immediately became the centre of a close circle of rebellious aesthetes who called themselves the Anonymous Society. The lifelong habit of forming clandestine groups began during his schooldays, spent in the company of simpatico members of exclusive cliques and secret societies, some of them faintly notorious. While most middle-class parents dispatched their boys to Marlborough to mingle with the scions of the rich and titled, the artsy set eschewed the socially advantageous sports like rugby and cricket to outdo one another in extravagant passions for art (as well as for pretty younger boys). They took their love of beauty to rebellious extremes. In a telling anticipation of the secret lives to come, the name the tiny circle of aesthetes gave themselves – their Anonymous Society – distinguished itself for its antagonism towards the establishment and the propriety of the other boys.

Blunt's love of art was a self-taught passion that began while still at Marlborough. He would go to London and linger at Zwemmer's, an art-book shop in Charing Cross Road that had opened in 1921 and which had books with colour plates as well as prints that Blunt could borrow and take back to school. At the age of 16 he published his first essay, which argued that the more 'indecent' the art, the better. Not surprisingly, Oscar Wilde was his patron saint.

The Anonymous Society was the first of several secret clubs for Blunt. At Cambridge he was one of the Apostles, and was quickly tapped to be one of the bright young things of Bloomsbury, which, in the late 1920s, represented the avant-garde elite. Like his earlier exclusive coteries, Blunt's Bloomsbury set was infamous. It recruited many Cambridge intellectual stars often while they were still undergraduates. A veritable cult, it had its high priests in the writers Lytton Strachey and Virginia Woolf, the economist John Maynard Keynes, as well as Blunt's hero, Roger Fry – whose avant-garde taste in art was part of the dangerous allure. Blunt became Fry's protégé. They called themselves 'a conspiracy of the self-elected, answerable only to each other'. There was a strong gay undercurrent to the high-minded gatherings. Defiance of the establishment came naturally to Blunt, whether he was subverting the authority of the school, the morality of the age or the status quo in art.

Perfectly Placed

The making of a spy blends talents with a touch of ideology. An outstanding undergraduate career in mathematics and art history at Cambridge led Blunt to a coveted fellowship at Trinity College. He was inducted into the Soviet cause by a committed communist professor of economics named Maurice Dobb, one of many leading Cambridge intellectuals whose anti-fascist passion in the 1930s made them the perfect quarry for the Soviet spymasters.

The first of the Cambridge golden boys to be recruited was Kim Philby who, by 1933, was a confirmed communist. Philby did not actually travel in the same fast set as the more socially adept Maclean, Burgess and Blunt, but was considered a catch because his father, St John, was well connected to the Saudi royal family (and the NKVD – the predecessor to the KGB – mistakenly assumed he was also British military intelligence). Another element in the equation was sex. Philby's reluctant final conversion to communism came when he was caught in a 'honeytrap' in Vienna, the target of a beautiful woman working for the Russians. If the new recruits were gay, as they knew Blunt and Burgess were, it was all the more convenient because it set them up for blackmail. Blunt was not the most politically rabid of the crew. He was one of many left-leaning British intellectuals who went to Spain in 1935 in an ill-fated attempt to check fascism – costing the lives of many of the best and the brightest.

Maclean, Burgess and Blunt's handler was Alexander Orlov, an NKVD agent who arrived in London in 1934. The Soviets knew that the young, wealthy and socially competent set which Blunt emblematised would have the best prospects of penetrating the upper reaches of Whitehall and the War Office.

Blunt's career as a spy began slowly enough – his handlers essentially left him alone for the first year until after he was (amazingly) made a part of MI5's highly sensitive but gentlemanly B division, thanks to his gift for languages. His sexual orientation was not as easy to hide as he thought (behind his back his colleagues knew all about it) and, for that reason, he was not as trusted as his spymaster hoped. But he was good at signing up new talent. Blunt deftly recruited his Cambridge cohorts, the charming and flamboyant Guy Burgess and Donald Duart Maclean.

THE POWER OF ART

Blunt had such influence in the London art world that all he to do was stroll into a gallery or auction house and glance at a picture – soon the rumours of his interest would push the value of the work up.

The clever Blunt soared to the upper ranks of trusted strategists during the war. Stationed at first in France, he was brought back to London when Germany invaded. His assignment was the surveillance of neutral missions in London. He attended meetings of the Joint Intelligence Committee, and had complete access to the work of the Secret Intelligence Service, as well as all of MI5's documents, including the Bletchley Park codebreakers' reports. Many of these sensitive papers, including the 'Ultra' material from the code breakers, were passed on to his Soviet handlers.

Even during the war Blunt was conducting art historical research and writing books. After the armistice, his reward for serving his country well was the plum job of Surveyor of the Queen's Pictures, which put him in charge of the largest private collection in the world and brought him into daily contact with the royal family, which treated him as a confidante. When Blunt was exposed, his constant proximity to the queen was one of the most shocking aspects of his betrayal.

The Spy with No Shame

The art world is a circle – you are either in or you're out. As Surveyor of the Queen's Pictures and director of the Courtauld Institute, Blunt was at its very centre. When a figure like Blunt ascends to the Olympian heights that he attained, especially through association with the House of Windsor, then he is in a position to dictate the fates of others – artists, curators, dealers, collectors, critics, museum directors and publishers. He sets the canon, and his opinions move the prices.

In Blunt's time, as market values for paintings began to soar, there were scores of lawsuits contesting attributions. Blunt wielded his formidable power in ways that at first seemed relatively innocuous. Few cared for the French artist Poussin, so nobody really bothered if Blunt deemed one of his drawings to be genuine. As the stakes rose, however, the temptation to run the risk of discovery by his peers made it all the more sweet to manipulate the market. Unlike some of the art world's most notorious players of this game – Bernard Berenson and Lord Duveen being the champions – Blunt was not in it entirely for the money. But when he did

Anthony Blunt at a press conference, 20 November 1979, following revelations that he was the fourth man in the British Philby, Burgess and Maclean spy ring of the 1950s.

authorise fakes or re-attribute paintings and drawings, it enabled friends to make a killing in the market.

The most egregious of his ruses was pulled off in the 1960s when he authenticated a Castiglione and a Pontormo that had actually been painted by the gifted forger Eric Hebborn, one of Blunt's closest and most dangerous friends in the gay circle of London art experts. Some biographers have even suggested that Blunt went along with the scam as a way to thumb his nose at the British art establishment, rather than for the money.

Both in espionage and in art, the secret to Blunt's success in deception was that in person he was polished and diffident – the ideal canvas on which strangers could paint their own portrait of the connoisseur, courtier or the traitor.

He became known as 'the spy with no shame'. But even the unmasking of Anthony Blunt does not mark the final resolution of his story. The most spectacular of Blunt's many deceptions is the most elusive and baffling: his self-deception. How could a mind of this analytic power and ironic bent miss the deep-seated contradiction between his role as a traitor and his belief that he was serving his country? Many of Blunt's biographers, even the most critical among them, defend his treason by pointing out that Blunt may actually have believed he was countering the forces of fascism, thereby benefiting Britain, by helping the Russians. He was not alone in his belief that communism could improve Europe. Many of the most brilliant minds at Oxford and Cambridge had taken a similar turn to the left in the 1930s. The relative pittance Blunt received from the KGB for his services (bonuses of a hundred pounds on a few occasions, one larger payment for a particularly juicy batch of information) could scarcely be the entire basis of his motivation. What is even more likely is a deeper psychological attraction to danger and to subversion. His illicit love life was mischievously flaunted at inappropriate times as boyfriends came and went from his apartment at the Courtauld. His career is filled with stories of his love for the underdog. The Russians were in need of information that Blunt could steal and pass to Moscow. His habits in the art world were similar. Although he was constantly in the limelight when at the peak of his power as celebrity curator, Blunt was irresistibly attracted to the shadowy figures in the wings. His choice of the artist he would champion in his earliest scholarship was an underdog. The neo-classical, 18th-century French painter Nicholas Poussin had been unfashionable so long that it took a determined effort on Blunt's part to restore him to the canon of European masters. Could it be that in the end the reason for Blunt's addiction to deception was simple bloody-mindedness, the urge to wreck all authority from within?

MOTIVATION

anger

charity

envy

faith

gluttony

greed

hope

lust

pride

sloth

GOOD VERSUS EVIL: THE PETROV AFFAIR

MAIN CULPRITS:
Vladimir Mikhaylovich Petrov (1907–91) and his wife, Evdokia Petrova (1915–2002), Russian diplomats and spies

SCANDAL:
Defected to Australia at the height of the Cold War, sparking a political incident that changed the face of Australian politics

WHY:
The death of Stalin made the Petrovs' future back in Russia uncertain and unsafe

No friends, no future, I wish I was dead. No-one could dream of our misery.
– Vladimir Petrov

Vladimir Petrov applied for political asylum in Australia in 1954, on the grounds that he could provide information on a Soviet spy ring operating out of the Russian embassy in Australia.

Evdokia Petrova wasn't afraid; she was terrified. As she sat by her desk at the Russian embassy in Canberra, Australia's capital, she smoked one cigarette after another. It was the middle of April, 1954, and she had not heard from her husband, Vladimir, in over 10 days. He had simply disappeared. Of course she knew he was a spy, as she was herself, but his latest mission was hardly dangerous. He had just gone to Sydney on a routine operation and had not been heard from since.

No-one at the embassy appeared to have the slightest sympathy or empathy for her predicament; in fact quite the contrary. She had been placed under virtual 'house arrest' since 6 April, and requested to remain within the embassy confines. To make matters worse, she was denied access to newspapers, magazines or the radio. Why, after all her years of dedication to the Soviet regime, was she being treated this way? Of what were they keeping her ignorant? Evdokia was being frozen out. She had seen this happen to others back in Russia, but she never thought it could happen to her. Her blood ran cold.

She began to hear whisperings from her embassy colleagues that her husband had been taken prisoner by the Australian Security Intelligence Organisation (ASIO), and some even said that, on the balance of probabilities, he was already dead. If these awful rumours were true, what would become of her?

Back in Russia, political changes were taking place. With Stalin dead, and without the protection from his supporters that they once enjoyed, Evdokia and Vladimir Petrov were being criticised and rebuffed. According to their superiors in Moscow, the Petrovs were not carrying out their espionage functions with sufficient diligence and vigour. Evdokia began to wonder whether her husband may have defected. Although he seemed to enjoy the Australian lifestyle, he had never mentioned defection to her. She assured herself that he wouldn't be so selfish as to endanger her family back home by embarking on such a rash course. Would he? Her mind began to disintegrate and depression took hold. What also frightened her were the crowds that had begun milling outside the embassy. As she looked out of her window on the second floor, she could see buses, full of tourists, stopping outside the front gate to have a good look. Were they looking at her? She must be paranoid; it was just the pressure getting to her.

However, the arrival at the embassy of two armed and burly members of the Soviet State police only added to her confusion and terror. Known as Karpinsky and Zharkov, they arrived on 16 April 1954, and informed Mrs Petrov that their job was to 'escort' her back to the Soviet Union. No reasons were given.

On 19 April Evdokia, flanked by the two men, arrived at Mascot airport in Sydney. Unbeknownst to her, the Australian prime minister, Robert Menzies, had publicly announced Vladimir Petrov's defection, and the media, along with over 1000 members of the public – mostly Eastern European immigrants – were waiting to catch a glimpse of his wife.

What the crowd witnessed that day was a drugged and crying Mrs Petrova being dragged across the tarmac to a waiting aeroplane. The mob surged towards her and people were heard to scream, 'Don't go back – if you do you will be killed!'. Another yelled, 'Don't let her go, she doesn't want to go'. The crowd encircled Evdokia in an attempt at rescue and jostled with the aides. In that moment, as the flashbulbs exploded, Australia had its very own spy case with an unlikely, but very photogenic, heroine. Evdokia was about to become a freedom fighter, a Cold War symbol of good, against the evil of Soviet tyranny. The Petrovs had unknowingly carved their place in Australian Cold War history.

However, the question on everybody's lips was whether the Australian government and, in particular, the prime minister would intervene and save Evdokia from certain punishment and possibly death on her return to Moscow. Even spies were worthy of rescue. Politically, the Petrovs could be of great use to the Australian prime minister.

The Cold War in Australia

The Petrovs had arrived in Australia in February 1951, ostensibly to provide consular support at the Russian embassy. Australia was entering a period of conservatism that was cloaked by the Cold War. It was only 5 years since Churchill had made his famous statement that 'an iron curtain' had 'descended across Europe'. The 'iron curtain' he was referring to was of course communism, and it was the opinion of most Western leaders that the Bolshevik idea should have been 'strangled at birth'. Australia, due to the economic destruction of Britain during World War II, had begun to see its future within the American orbit. Even Prime Minister Robert Menzies swallowed his 'Britishry' and adapted Australia's foreign policy accordingly.

As a couple, the Petrovs were an unlikely match. Apart from being of humble, lower middle class origins, they were complete opposites. Vladimir was moonfaced, overweight and drab. He wore the same bland, grey gabardine overcoat with matching suit and hat, day in, day out. He drank massive amounts of brandy and his slide into alcoholism was showing on his features. He chainsmoked, his hair was wet with perspiration and his hands shook. His hearing was poor and, in his stilted Russian accent, he could hardly hold a conversation in English without regularly asking for things to be repeated or explained. Evdokia,

MAYHEM AT MASCOT

At Mascot, in a handwritten statement, Evdokia Petrova wrote: 'I was upset and had been crying a lot for some days – I was not well. Immediately, I left the car with the men, the crowd started to shout to me – 'Don't go back'. Some of the crowd caught hold of me by my belt – I was very frightened of the crowd ... the crowd were pushing – I lost one of my shoes – my handbag was broken – two buttons were torn from my suit'.

on the other hand, was like a breath of fresh air. She was trim, beautifully groomed and manicured and spoke English fluently. Known to enjoy 'shopping' above all other pastimes, she was fashionable and accessorised her wardrobe with style and panache. From all accounts, the Petrovs' relationship was rocky and in many respects was a marriage in name only. In addition to having to cope with his heavy drinking and womanising, Evdokia found her husband secretive and unresponsive, selfish and egotistical. The lack of closeness between them was exemplified when, in early 1954, Evdokia had no idea that her husband was contemplating defection.

The Spy Who Came in from the Cold

In April 1951, Vladimir Petrov was promoted to Third Secretary at the Russian embassy in Canberra. This middle-ranking diplomatic position provided him with the cover he needed to go to Sydney and Melbourne to carry out surveillance and espionage. His formal duties included deciphering intelligence from Moscow, establishing a local network of spies, organising the surveillance of Soviet immigrants and infiltrating Russian émigré and refugee groups. Despite considerable effort, he made little progress in his spycraft. His only real success lay in re-activating the former Russian agent Andre Fridenbergs in Sydney – code-named Sigma, Fridenbergs provided information on the Latvian government that was occupied by Soviet forces. Evdokia's job function at the embassy was primarily administrative in nature. However, sometimes her espionage function involved ciphering and assistance in the field.

Vladimir, already suffering from an identity crisis brought about by his feelings of dissatisfaction with communism, preferred the sleazy side of Sydney and Melbourne nightlife, and was known to enjoy the company of prostitutes. He also liked to spend time at the Russian social club in Sydney, where he met Michael Bialoguski, a talented Sydney doctor and musician. Petrov's defection is essentially attributable to his friendship with Bialoguski. At the time of their meeting, Petrov had no idea that Bialoguski was a part-time spy for ASIO. Bialoguski cleverly targeted Petrov as a potential defector. He invoked and played upon Petrov's insecure personality. Bialoguski convinced Petrov that he would be arrested upon his return to Russia for being a 'Beria' sympathiser – Beria, one of Stalin's closest advisers, had been executed after Stalin's death. Petrov was still under the impression, though, that Bialoguski did not know he was a spy.

The two new friends wined and dined and spoke about the future. In essence, Bialoguski made Petrov feel important. He made him believe that he was destined for greater things. By February 1954, Petrov had confessed to Bialoguski that he was a clandestine Soviet spy and was disillusioned with the communist way of life. As he put it: 'I no longer believe in communism since I have seen the Australian way of living'.

Bialoguski, sensing a great opportunity, advised the deputy director of ASIO, Ron Richards, that Petrov was ripe for the picking and could be persuaded, with the right inducement, to defect. Richards offered Petrov £5000 to defect, on the condition that Petrov provide documentary evidence of espionage in Australia. In particular, ASIO wanted information on Soviet infiltration of the Department of External Affairs. Richards, while winning Petrov's trust, told him: 'We must trust each other on this. I mean, you do believe me when I say we will look after you'. Petrov, anxious to stamp his mark on history, agreed to provide Bialoguski with the requisite documents. In true spy fashion, the two met clandestinely at a number of bizarre locations in Canberra including the railway bridge near Queenbeyan, J. B. Young's shop and the Kingston hotel, which was opposite the Russian embassy. Petrov felt important. Despite the danger, he loved the surge of adrenalin as he waited to pass on the secret documents.

In ASIO, the coded terminology for defectors was 'cabin candidate' – Vladimir Petrov became known as 'Cabin Candidate 12'.

Meanwhile, however, Evdokia had absolutely no idea of her husband's actions. Indeed, it appears that he wanted to defect without her. Perhaps he wanted to start a new life without the 'baggage' that Evdokia represented?

On 2 April 1954, Vladimir Petrov arrived at an ASIO safehouse in Sydney. There he met Ron Richards and the head of ASIO, Brigadier Charles Spry. As Petrov consumed his brandy, the two linchpins of ASIO read the secret documents that he had collected over the last few months. That night they labelled the documents A–J. The documents provided the names of communists working within the Department of Foreign Affairs and the Australian Labor Party and would become important political weapons. Their significance would reverberate around the corridors of power for the next decade and would help bring about the self-immolation of the Australian Labor Party. Petrov provided the necessary explanations upon request. That night he signed a document requesting political asylum. His request read: 'I, the undersigned, wish of my own free will to seek political asylum in Australia'.

Evdokia the Freedom Fighter

On 13 April, Prime Minister Menzies announced to the press the defection of Vladimir Petrov. Sensing a great political opportunity, he announced before the House of Representatives a Royal Commission on Espionage in Australia. He predicted a major scandal; one which he could use to his own advantage. It would be seen that certain foreign embassies were being used to spy against Australia's interests. The fact that communists were later discovered to have infiltrated the Department of Foreign Affairs and the opposing Labor Party was an added bonus.

Menzies out-manoeuvred the Labor opposition leader, Herbert Evatt, by telling him that nothing important would be discussed at the last parliamentary sitting before the May election. He caught Evatt completely unawares, knowing that several members of Evatt's party had been fingered by Petrov and labelled as spies.

Exactly a week later, Menzies was rather taken aback when informed of the debacle at Mascot airport. A photograph, showing a frazzled Evdokia being dragged, with one shoe missing, by sinister Soviet cadres to an awaiting plane was being telegraphed across the world. Her facial expression showed abject terror. It would become one of the most famous photographs of the 1950s and became etched in the Australian national consciousness. The telex machine in Menzies's office ran hot. One message said: 'Freedom and humanity demand the grounding of the Petrov plane for complete investigation'; another was: 'Deeply shocked. Witness Mascot. Seeming cooperation (between) police and government airline with Soviet State police kidnapping Mrs Petrov. Still time for you to issue orders which would clear democratic name of Australia'.

Fearing accusations of allowing Evdokia to go to her probable death, Menzies instructed Brigadier Spry to approach her when her plane landed in Darwin on its way to Russia. Spry was instructed to do everything in his power to convince Mrs Petrova to defect with her husband. Politically, Menzies could not be seen to be inactive, and it was crucial that he took the initiative, as a general election was only weeks away.

On Evdokia's plane, even the flight staff became involved. They were encouraged by ASIO to try to convince Evdokia to stay. One air hostess, in particular, struck up a bond with Evdokia. She even gave her a pair of black suede sandals to replace the shoe she had lost on the tarmac.

A shoeless Evdokia Petrova, flanked by two Russian guards, is roughly escorted to a waiting aeroplane at Mascot airport, Sydney, 1954. This photograph would become an iconic anti-communist image of the 1950s.

Evdokia, trying to numb her misery with beer and cigarettes, confided in her new friend. Crying, she told her that, 'I think my husband is dead'. She was then told of her husband's defection. Her sense of terror and hopelessness turned into anger. Why had he not told her of his plans and how could he have put her through such unnecessary agony? Still believing that she was doomed to return to Russia, Evdokia told the stewardess that 'no one can help me, these men have guns'. Evdokia was told not to worry. The stewardess alerted the captain, who in turn alerted Darwin police. Upon their arrival in Darwin, the police violently disarmed Karpinsky and Zharkov, and Evdokia, to her relief, was separated from her captors. After speaking to her husband, via a specially arranged telephone call, Evdokia decided to defect. It was not an easy decision.

What now became known as the 'Petrov Affair' placed Australia squarely on the map of international affairs. The Petrovs' decision to defect occurred at the height of the Cold War. Evdokia became the perfect visual metaphor for the triumph of Western democracy against Soviet totalitarianism. By the following day, newsreels in cinemas were showing the Mascot imbroglio. Newspapers and magazines captured the mood. The headline of the *Daily Mirror* stated 'She Stays'. The *Melbourne Argus* named her 'Evdokia: Woman of the year'. She was given the flattering name of the 'Blonde Petrova'. Later, in 1956, she wrote: 'I found myself publicised like a film star ... I was like some strange creature never seen before ... a spy-film heroine'.

With an apprehensive expression, Vladamir Petrov arrives at the High Court in Melbourne, 1954, to resume his evidence in the Royal Commission on Espionage.

After she arrived in Darwin, the press stopped representing Evdokia in a helpless or tragic light. She was now depicted as a woman transformed by freedom. Touched by the 'Australian way', she was irrevocably changed. It was the beginning of an image in which she was portrayed not as a captive but a fashion icon, a lady celebrated for her taste and discretion. A typical photograph, taken a few weeks later, depicted Evdokia on the veranda of Government House. As the *Canberra Times* reported on 26 April 1954, 'She appeared to be enjoying a cup of tea and had changed from the costume which she had worn on the plane into a floral summer frock'.

After being granted political asylum, the Petrovs were provided with the aliases of Mr and Mrs Sven Allyson. They bought a home in Bentleigh in Melbourne, Victoria, and lived under a 'D notice', which was an agreement between the government and media to protect their privacy and identity. However, they continued to give assistance to ASIO and were responsible for naming approximately 500 Soviet agents. Only a handful of these resided in Australia. The government of the Soviet Union, furious with Australia's 'interference' withdrew all consular staff from the Russian embassy and sacked the Australian consular staff from Moscow.

The Political Consequences

The general election held on 29 May returned the Menzies Liberal government to power by a narrow margin. The full impact of the Petrov Affair had not yet filtered through to the political arena. The Royal Commission on Espionage, however, would provide Menzies with the necessary ammunition to virtually obliterate the political fortunes of the Labor Party. He would not have been so successful if the leader of the Labor Party opposition, Dr Herbert Evatt, hadn't acted so erratically. The purpose of the Royal Commission was to investigate the allegations of espionage made by the Petrovs and also to identify 'a nest of traitors'. The thread behind the questioning was that all identified communists were potential foreign agents. What riled Evatt the most was the allegation that members of his staff were involved in espionage. Even his press secretary, Fergan O'Sullivan, was named in the Petrov documents. Ultimately, no evidence of wrongdoing was attributable to O'Sullivan but his career was nevertheless ruined. However, instead of supporting O'Sullivan, Evatt dismissed him. The names of communists or communist party sympathisers were printed in the daily newspapers. Those named suffered the consequences: they lost their jobs, their children were bullied at schools and most were victimised in one form or another.

Evatt reviled the Royal Commission for its 'McCarthyist' leanings. He also alleged that many of Petrov's documents were forgeries and falsifications. According to most accounts, Evatt began acting irrationally. On 7 September, after a series of outbursts against the commissioner and witnesses, he was barred from participating in the proceedings. The commissioner declared: 'It has become apparent that you cannot disassociate your function as an advocate from your personal and political interest'. Thereafter, Evatt transferred his attack to the House of Representatives. He became obsessed with proving that a vast right-wing conspiracy existed. This conspiracy supposedly involved Menzies, ASIO, the Petrovs and the catholic right-wing element of the Labor Party. The right-wing faction of the Labor Party bitterly disagreed with Evatt's conspiracy theory. Labor caucus meetings became famous for their wild accusations and actual fist fights. So divided was the Labor Party, that the catholic right-wing split and a new party, the Democratic Labor Party (DLP) was formed. The Labor Party would stay out of office for the next 17 years until the election of Gough Whitlam in 1972.

Identity Crisis

Although the Petrovs were vindicated by the Royal Commission, their domestic situation was far from ideal. From all accounts they suffered terribly. When the Petrovs were finally united in Sydney in late April 1954, they had a furious row. Evdokia accused her husband of unmitigated stupidity. What, she asked, would happen to her mother and sister now?

Their first abode was at Palm Beach in Sydney. Neighbours of the Petrovs reported hearing Evdokia crying at night for months on end. Petrov wrote: 'No-one could dream of our misery'. Evdokia was even more eloquent: 'It was painful, painful.

MOONING AT RED SQUARE

At the Australian embassy in Moscow, an interesting discussion was taking place between two Australian diplomats following the Petrov defection. Dick Woolcott informed his friend Bill Morrison: 'One of us will be out of here in a fortnight. The Russians will reciprocate. They always do'. Morrrison disagreed and countered, 'If we're expelled I'll drop my daks [trousers] in Red Square'. Within 48 hours both men were expelled by the Soviet government. Morrison, true to his word, honoured his pledge. On the way to the airport, Morrison asked the cab driver to stop at Red Square. He got out of the cab, dropped his trousers and 'mooned' the Kremlin before dozens of startled Russians. Woolcott was laughing so hard that tears streamed down his face. Morrison jumped back in the cab and ordered the driver to make haste.

Because still somewhere, somewhere inside of me or in my husband always some kind of feeling that you left your country and you feel that you are just a defector'. With their £5000 'reward' they eventually settled in Bentleigh. Initially, they lived in fear of assassination. Vladimir rarely left the house except occasionally to go fishing or hunting. Evdokia fared somewhat better and eventually rebounded. Her sister Tamara migrated to Australia in 1965 and they developed a close bond. And Evdokia continued to indulge her favourite pastime of shopping. Still, there was something terribly sad about their existence. To avoid a potential media circus, Evdokia was unable to attend her husband's funeral when he died in 1985. Evdokia outlived her husband by more than 17 years.

MOTIVATION

anger

charity

envy

faith

gluttony

greed

hope

lust

pride

sloth

THE PSEUDOCIDAL POLITICIAN: JOHN STONEHOUSE

MAIN CULPRIT:

John Stonehouse (1925–88); British cabinet minister

SCANDAL:

After cooking the books of his personal companies, he fled the country, faked his own death and lived under various assumed names

WHY:

Money troubles from shady financial deals

How is it that the merest hint of scandal, based on the flimsiest of evidence and propagated by obviously maladjusted or twisted men can erase a lifetime of constructive endeavour motivated by the highest ideals
– John Stonehouse

John Stonehouse leaving Horseferry Road magistrates court, London, 5 November 1975. The British Labour MP faked his own death and was charged with fraud, conspiracy and forgery.

Many people commit suicide after being caught out in a scandal, but few have the imagination to fake it. In 1974, John Stonehouse, a tall, handsome, charming and narcissistic British Labour politician, did just this.

Stonehouse, whose career peaked as a British minister in the Harold Wilson Government of the 1960s, was born in Southampton, England, the youngest of four children. His parents embodied the ideals of the Labour movement. His father, William, was a former post-office engineer who became a trade union official, while his mother, Rosina, once a kitchen maid, conquered the English class system to become Mayor of Southampton in 1959.

Pictured with his wife, Barbara, John Stonehouse arrives at the House of Commons to take up his seat after winning the 1957 Wednesbury by-election.

His parents' lives exposed Stonehouse to politics from an early age. Otherwise, his childhood seemed fairly normal. At 18, he joined the airforce and trained in the United States to become a World War II pilot. When the war ended he entered university and graduated with a degree in economics from the London School of Economics, by which time he was married. In 1952, he left with his wife, Barbara, and their young family for Uganda, where he worked to introduce co-operative societies to the Africans. While on a trip to Rhodesia he was deported, and he was also later arrested in South Africa for arguing the cause of black Africans – which earned him a reputation as a bright young iconoclast of the left.

In 1957, several years after returning from Africa, Stonehouse was elected Member of Parliament for Wednesbury, a coal-mining town near Birmingham, England. Since it was common for British parliamentarians to have jobs outside of parliament, Stonehouse worked for the London Co-op. With more than a million members it was the biggest retail co-op in the world. Yet the bureaucracy and committee-style democracy of the Co-op frustrated him sorely – an early sign of his impatience with rules, regulations and social restrictions.

Labour Days

Stonehouse was a rising star of the British Labour Party. It was even tipped that he might go all the way and one day become its leader. When Harold Wilson became prime minister in 1964, Stonehouse was appointed a junior minister. He began as Parliamentary Undersecretary for Aviation, then became Undersecretary of State for the Colonies (1966–67), where he presided over the decolonisation of territories such as Botswana, Lesotho and the Seychelles. He was particularly proud of his work in Mauritius where, according to his somewhat immodest memoir, *Death of an Idealist* (1975), he 'snatched a complex agreement from the jaws of threatened chaos'. He returned to Aviation in 1967, this time as minister and was instrumental in getting the Anglo–French agreement for the production of the Concorde aircraft into place.

Stonehouse lobbied strongly on behalf of British manufacturers. But hanging out with business tycoons, Middle Eastern potentates and arms dealers may well have whetted his appetite for fast bucks and financial chicanery. While in the position of Minister of State for Technology (1967–68), he was made Privy Councillor, ostensibly as a reward for selling aeroplanes to Arabs. It was the pinnacle of his career.

Harold Wilson neither liked nor trusted Stonehouse. It was rumoured that Wilson gave him the job of Postmaster General (1968) in the hope that he'd make a mess of it and could be fired. While Stonehouse was a minister, he never made it into the cabinet – another indication of Wilson's belief that he flew too close to the wind. When Wilson lost the 1970 election, a disillusioned Stonehouse wasn't even part of the shadow ministry. It's been speculated that Wilson lost his trust in Stonehouse when a Czech defector named him as a spy – yet Wilson later said, 'I never thought he was a spy, but I always thought he was a crook'.

With a difference of opinion between Stonehouse and his party on his abilities, he was left on the backbench with time on his hands. He turned one hand to business, starting a number of companies. Then, when the Pakistani army mounted a genocidal campaign in East Pakistan (Bangladesh), slaughtering up to a million people, Stonehouse became one of Britain's most prominent advocates of the Bangladeshi cause while the likes of Kissinger and the United States backed the Pakistanis for geopolitical reasons. Stonehouse helped to create the first Bangladeshi postage stamps, and became a dual UK–Bangladeshi citizen when independence was achieved after the Indian army defeated the Pakistanis. At some point he also started sleeping with his secretary, the divorcee Sheila Buckley, who was almost 20 years younger than him. It was a combination of these three interests that led to his life-changing decision.

The Beginning of the End

It's difficult to know exactly when Stonehouse's money troubles began. But, by the time he was hit with the heat of a Scotland Yard investigation sparked by a *Sunday Times* article concerning his involvement in the establishment of a Bangladeshi bank, his financial affairs were a shambles. With his persuasive charm and ability to paint a picture with words, Stonehouse made a great salesman, but the flipside of this was the creative licence he took with reality. Whether his problems increased as a consequence of his ego trying to cover up his incompetence, or because he'd had his fingers in the till from the very beginning is difficult to know. Either way, he ended up breaking the law. Like many before him, Stonehouse dressed up his poor financial situation by continually shuffling money between his twenty companies in order to give the illusion of financial health. As the scrutiny from official investigations grew, it became clear, his stellar connections notwithstanding, that he wouldn't be getting away with it for much longer. Unless ...

First Attempt to Fake Death

Stonehouse bought a life insurance policy worth £185,000, presumably for his family's benefit. For his own benefit, he had already siphoned off a large sum of his company's money. On 4 November 1974, he made a frank speech in the House of Commons that dumped on some of his Labour colleagues. According to his memoir, it was several days later when he flew to Miami, with no less than two false passports, ready to 'kill' John Stonehouse and migrate to Australia as Joseph Arthur Markham – the name on one of the passports.

On arrival in Miami he checked through US immigration as Stonehouse, then again as Markham. He rented two hotel rooms, one under the name Stonehouse and one under the name Markham. Leaving all his Stonehouse things in the Fontainebleau Hotel, he gave his key to the hotel porter, undressed on the hotel veranda, then went for a long swim. When the beach was deserted, he returned to shore, picked up the Markham gear he'd stashed in the Eden Roc Hotel, and flew to Houston under the name George Lewis, having created the illusion that John Stonehouse had drowned.

From Houston he flew to Mexico City where he missed the connecting flight to Sydney. Instead, he flew to Los Angeles, where he booked into the Marriott Airport Hotel, which he described as a 'plastic place for plastic people'. It was a mistake. He'd stayed there several weeks before and it evoked memories of his life as John Stonehouse, mover and shaker, a paragon of plasticity. He started to get cold feet about leaving his old life behind. As part of his cover, he had organised a meeting with Harry Wetzel, the president of the aerospace company Garrett Corporation. He kept the appointment and, by the end of this meeting, in an office where there was a copy of a book of Escher prints his daughter had distributed in Britain, he decided not to go through with faking his death. He rang his wife to say he was coming home late, then raced back to Miami to pick up his luggage and passport. Although the pile of clothes was gone, no-one at the Fontainebleau Hotel had noticed Stonehouse was missing.

JUGGLING PERSONAS

Although I did not fully realise it at the time, I was operating on three levels. One the imaged man: cool, calm and apparently in command of all his senses carrying on the life normally expected of him. Two, the original man, who carried all the heavy layers of the imaged man as a burden and despised this role, suffering deep torment as the desperation of his position became more evident. Three, the Phoenix man: a make-believe person who was uncluttered with problems and tensions, and through natural relaxation, gave comfort to the other two. The first two men had to die for the strain of living for them was too great. I wanted them to die. I wanted to die. There was no other way.
– John Stonehouse,
Death of an Idealist (1975)

Second Attempt

According to his memoir, the next morning when Stonehouse woke, he was horrified by his lack of resolve. It was definitely a struggle, but this time he was determined to break free. He put his Markham things back in the Eden Roc hotel and repeated the same process all over again. This time, he caught a plane to Chicago with the intention of flying to San Francisco and from there to a new life in Australia. Yet after a flight full of mental trauma – including yelling 'Why do you do this to me!?' at the mirror in the aeroplane bathroom – he decided to turn around in San Francisco, fly back to Miami, and retrieve his Stonehouse identity. In Miami no-one had noticed he was missing once again. Stonehouse flew back to London, where he voted in parliament on issues he didn't believe in and played chess in between. He also went for a twenty-sixth anniversary dinner with his wife at their favourite Italian restaurant. In his memoir he claimed: 'I felt as close to her as I always had – very close'. However, he said nothing to her about his predicament.

Third Time Lucky

If Stonehouse's memoir is to be believed, he returned to Miami soon after, on a business trip, with the intention of remaining John Stonehouse and exorcising his previous two 'pseudocide' attempts. Yet when his business dealings didn't come off as planned, he fell into a depression that led to him once again leaving his clothes in a pile at the Fontainebleau Hotel and going for a long swim in the hope of giving the impression that Stonehouse had drowned. He left Miami and flew to San Francisco, where he stayed in the best room at the Fairmont Hotel for a single room price – a good omen perhaps for someone who was risking a good deal of social status by abandoning his identity.

Sheila Buckley became Stonehouse's mistress during his heydays in British politics. Almost 20 years his junior, she stuck by him through the whole ordeal of the trial, and they eventually married in 1978, shortly after his release from jail.

From San Francisco he flew to Honolulu where he hung out at Waikiki Beach for 5 days before flying to Australia and registering on arrival in Melbourne as Joe Markham. Success. He opened a bank account in Markham's name at the Bank of New South Wales and started to build his Australian life.

Almost inevitably, Stonehouse was to bring himself undone with his own cleverness. He had had the forethought to realise that Joe Markham might be connected to John Stonehouse – since the two had been at the same place at the same time in Miami – so it seemed he planned to make him vanish too and become Clive Mildoon; the name on his other false passport. This, together with the fact that he would have had to have got hold of his two false passports in England (the names of which were taken from deceased men in his former constituency), shows the premeditation of the events.

His scheme would have succeeded if it hadn't been for the smallest piece of bad luck. When he opened a new bank account in Mildoon's name at the Bank of New Zealand, he didn't know that a clerk from the previous bank was by coincidence in the bank at the same time. He noticed Stonehouse using different names to open the accounts and reported this to the police. The police, who had recently let the Great Train Robber, Ronnie Biggs, through their grasp, initially thought Stonehouse might be Lord Lucan, the British noble who had disappeared after allegedly murdering his children's nanny.

In order to confirm his second change of identity, Stonehouse had to leave Australia again. Under the name of Markham, he flew to Copenhagen via Singapore, Bangkok and Tashkent. In Copenhagen he read the British newspapers. This time his disappearance had not only been noticed (Stonehouse had told his mistress to raise the alarm), it had caused a sensation. Instead of the dignity afforded to the tragic death of a public figure, the papers were full of tales of his dubious character and questionable activities. Stonehouse was appalled by this treatment of his former self in the press. His memoir says: 'How is it that the merest hint of scandal, based on the flimsiest of evidence and propagated by obviously maladjusted or twisted men can erase a lifetime of constructive endeavour motivated by the highest ideals. Some British newspapers were full of smears and innuendo and unsubstantiated allegations. And each report cut deep into the psyche of Joe Markham, sitting lonely, isolated and without friends in a busy Copenhagen, preparing for Christmas.' However, Stonehouse wasn't alone. Although it's not mentioned in the memoir, Sheila Buckley was waiting for him in Copenhagen. Such omissions put the veracity of Stonehouse's account into doubt. At the end of their intimate rendezvous, Buckley asked Stonehouse to take her with him back to Australia, but he told her to be patient. He returned to Australia on Aeroflot via Moscow, New Delhi and Singapore. This time, he checked into Australia under the name Clive Mildoon.

> Markham and Mildoon, the names on Stonehouse's false passports, were identities that he had pilfered from the husbands of widows in his former British constituency.

Australian Life

In Melbourne, Stonehouse rented an executive apartment and began to build a new life for himself. He joined the Victorian Jazz Club and enjoyed going to their parties. He also joined a chess club. Still, he never quite freed his new self from his prior self. When he saw his picture in the Australian papers alongside the accusation that he was a Czech spy, he was at first horrified, but he was later relieved when Wilson cleared him of the allegation in the House of Commons.

There wouldn't be much time left for Clive Mildoon, however. Unknown to Stonehouse, plain-clothes police had moved into his apartment complex and were following his every move. On Christmas Eve 1974, while he was taking a 'walking tour of St Kilda', the red light district of Melbourne, the police pulled him over. They took him to the cells where they told him they knew he was John Stonehouse and the game was up. The brief life of his alter ego was over.

Loopholes and Home Truths

As a British politician, Stonehouse enjoyed a form of diplomatic immunity and, because he hadn't actually committed a crime in Australia, the Australian authorities, against British wishes, initially allowed him to stay. His wife, overjoyed that her husband was still alive, flew out laden with Christmas presents for him. She still didn't know about Buckley. However, the press did. The police had been checking the phone calls Buckley made in the hotel she'd been staying at and matched them to Stonehouse's Melbourne number. After 26 years of marriage, Mrs Stonehouse learned of her husband's infidelity from journalists.

A PLEA FOR PROTECTION

While the deportation battle continued between British and Australian authorities, Stonehouse wrote to a number of countries asking for residency including Sweden, Botswana, Mauritius, Kenya and Zambia. All refused him.

Despite the presence of Barbara Stonehouse, Sheila Buckley also raced to Australia to be with her lover. This fraught triangle moved up the eastern seaboard trying to stay one step ahead of the British media hordes until a furious argument on a Queensland beach saw Barbara Stonehouse return to London to start divorce proceedings, while Buckley stayed on with her man.

After 6 months and a massive worldwide fraud investigation, Stonehouse and Buckley were deported to the United Kingdom in June 1975. Stonehouse arrived home, still an MP, and was granted bail awaiting trial. Despite his disgrace, the thick-skinned Stonehouse took Buckley to tea in the House of Commons tea room. When he went to the Labour Party Blackpool Conference, he was booed and delegates shouted, 'Go back to Australia, scab!'. He responded by becoming a member of the English National Party.

After 68 days of hearings, at that time the longest fraud trial in UK legal history, John Stonehouse was found guilty on eighteen charges of theft, fraud, and deception on 6 August 1976 and sentenced to 7 years in jail. When Sheila Buckley received a 2-year sentence for her part in the affair, her mother cried out from the public gallery, 'Is it a crime to love a man?'. The court suspended Buckley's 2-year sentence, accepting that she'd fallen under the spell of Stonehouse's charisma, but they argued that she was aware of, and a participant in, his frauds. Following his conviction, Stonehouse resigned from the House of Commons on 27 August 1976, more than 18 months after he was first arrested.

Jail and Beyond

Stonehouse served only 3 years of his sentence and had open heart surgery while still in prison. When he was released in 1978, Sheila Buckley was waiting for him. Within a few weeks they were married and they eventually had a son.

John Stonehouse spent the remainder of his life with Sheila. He turned his hand to writing novels – an apt career change for someone with his imagination – until he died of a heart attack on live television in 1988. Given the fantastic adventures of his life, his literary career was solid rather than spectacular.

To the end of his life he blamed everyone and everything but himself for a catalogue of crime and deception that destroyed his political career.

– Stonehouse's Obituary

John Stonehouse was a man of great ambition and imagination who failed to live up to his promise, then failed to deal with this fact. His scandal and downfall is the story of an astronomical and charismatic ego that was allowed to get out of control.

PRIVATE
PERVERSIONS

Howard Hughes testifying at a
hearing before the Senate War
Investigation Committee, 1947.

PLEASURE THROUGH PAIN: THE MARQUIS DE SADE

MAIN CULPRIT:
Donatien Alphonse François de Sade, The Marquis de Sade (1740–1814)

SCANDAL:
Multiple rape, torture and bestiality, resulting in imprisonment and finally a mental asylum

WHY:
He was sexually abused as a child and was forced to witness orgies, but he was also spoilt and encouraged to feel that he had a God-given right to do as he pleased

There is no more lively sensation than that of pain; its impressions are certain and dependable, they never deceive as may those of the pleasure women perpetually feign and almost never experience.

– Marquis de Sade

A 19th-century engraving of Donatien Alphonse François de Sade, the Marquis de Sade, in prison. All together, de Sade would spend 27 years of his life incarcerated.

On a glorious spring day in April 1768 the weather belied the mood of Donatien Alphonse François de Sade. He was nervous. Exactly a week had passed since his sexual escapade with Rose Keller. Everyone seemed to know about the disastrous nocturnal affair and there were rumblings of a major public scandal. De Sade had already spent time imprisoned in the dungeon of Vincennes, and it was an experience he did not want to repeat. Unfortunately this new scandal was potentially even more damaging. On the grapevine, he had heard that police inspector Marais, the man responsible for his previous arrest, was on his case. Worse still, his mother-in-law, Mme de Montrevil, was petitioning the king to issue a *lettre de cachet* for de Sade's swift return to prison. Apparently, it was also she who had put Marais on his trail. De Sade's wife, Pelagie, had always been supportive, so why should his mother-in-law be so riled? As de Sade reflected on his experience with Rose Keller, he couldn't understand what all the fuss was about.

At the beginning of April 1768 de Sade had hired a cottage in Acrueil on the outskirts of Paris where he could freely indulge in sexual pleasure and experimentation. He regularly brought prostitutes and actresses to the cottage and gratified himself with abandon. On 3 April he met Rose Keller, an unemployed cook who had recently been widowed. There was something about her that atrracted him – possibly her innocence. De Sade took Keller to the cottage explaining that she would be paid for performing menial domestic tasks. However, immediately upon their arrival, de Sade ordered Keller to strip. When she refused, he ripped off her clothing and tied her naked to a bed. She pleaded for mercy, but unfortunately for Keller that just excited him all the more. To de Sade, sexual arousal was intimately linked to pain – in fact, pleasure and pain were indistinguishable sensations to him. Using a cat-o-nine tails, de Sade whipped Keller's buttocks until they bled. He then made incisions into her skin with a knife and proceeded to pour hot wax into the open wounds. The more she screamed, the more he enjoyed himself.

A GOD-GIVEN RIGHT

As a man of nobility, distantly related to the Bourbon family, de Sade believed that it was his God-given right to participate in any manner of sexual indulgence he chose. As he once wrote: 'I wanted to live in accordance with the promptings which came from my true self. Why was that so difficult?'

De Sade wanted all the privileges of nobility, but without any of the responsibilities. On another occasion, while reflecting on the notion of wickedness, he wrote: 'If you enjoy wickedness, it shows that Nature intended you to be wicked and it would be wicked not to be'.

Later, when de Sade had left the room, Keller took the opportunity to make her escape. Using bed linen to make a rope she climbed out of the window. Shortly after, local villagers found her roaming about nearby, bleeding and incoherent. After attending to her wounds, they took her to the local police station, heard her story, and formal charges were laid against de Sade.

Pondering the events of that night, de Sade felt that his only error had been to allow Keller to escape before he could pay her off for services rendered. He should have been more astute and never have left her alone. He believed it was his right to use her as he wished. But he felt he should have been more prudent and kept a closer eye on the intransigent 'common girl'.

By 10 April de Sade had offered Keller a very large settlement to keep her quiet. However, the rumours of the event, now having gained a life of their own, were growing in intensity and embellishment. Therefore de Sade decided to flee and lay low for a few months until his indiscretions were forgotten and he could return to Paris or to his Castle in Compte. At all costs he must avoid police inspector Marais. However, unknown to de Sade, Marais was at that very moment closing in on him and de Sade was arrested on 14 April and imprisoned for more than 6 months.

Formative Years

Donatien de Sade was born on 2 June 1740. His upbringing was peculiar to say the least. His mother had little time for her precocious son and did not believe in demonstrating love or affection. Almost immediately after birth, Donatien was sent to a nearby convent to be cared for. His father, the ambassador to the court of Elector of Bavaria, was also cold and embittered. Accused of financial mismanagement during his ambassadorship, he was never able to rise above his station as a member of the lower nobility. He was also a practising bisexual and he indulged his passions freely and often in front of his son. Although de Sade loved and respected his father, his devotion was not reciprocated and this affected him deeply.

PHILOSOPHY OF LIFE

During de Sade's early adulthood his philosophy could be summarised as: 'All human felicity lies in man's imagination, and that he cannot think to attain it unless he heeds all his caprices. The most fortunate of persons is he who has the most means to satisfy his vagaries.'

At the age of 5, Donatien was sent to live with his grandmother and five aunts where he was mollycoddled and his precocity encouraged. He would later comment, 'The flattery I received made me haughty, despotic and choleric'. Although four of his aunts were nuns, that didn't seem to prevent them from regularly participating in orgies. Sodomy, despite being illegal in France, was practised by many French aristocrats at that time, and Donatien's family was no exception.

Donatien was then sent to live with his uncle, the Abbé de Sade. Although a member of the clergy, the Abbé kept a mistress and owned a brothel. He was also bisexual, considered sex an important recreational pursuit and often attended orgies involving priests, nuns and prostitutes that were held within the walls of convents and abbeys. As a child, Donatien learned to despise the hypocrisy of church morality. He would later write that 'religions are the cradles of despotism'.

At the age of 10, he was uprooted again and sent to a renowned Jesuit School – the College Luis-le-Grand. There, strict religious education was fused with corporal punishment. Floggings took place on a weekly basis for all forms of misdemeanour. Donatien found that he enjoyed these floggings intensely and, unlike his peers, actually began to look forward to them. It is during this phase of his life that de Sade first came to associate pain with pleasure and also around this time he began to experiment with sodomy.

At the age of 15, he was transferred to an elite military academy and was soon admitted to the king's light cavalry. With the commencement of the Seven Years' War in 1757, de Sade was quickly promoted. By 1757 he was commissioned as a 'standard bearer' in the Carabiers. At the age of 18, stationed in Germany, he was involved in heavy fighting and distinguished himself. Again he was promoted, this time to Captain.

By all accounts, de Sade had grown into a dashing, handsome and charismatic leader, although somewhat foppish in appearance. His primary failing was his inability to accept criticism and his reluctance to learn from his errors. He was extraordinarily headstrong. His personality was arrogant, loud and uncompromising. He devoted himself to the pursuit of pleasure in all its forms, largely through spontaneous trysts with various actresses and prostitutes.

The Origins of Sadomasochism

After the Seven Year's War, de Sade resigned from the military. As a 'free spirit', he had found it difficult to accept the orders of his superiors. He returned to Paris and spent most of his time pursuing famous actresses and sexually experimenting with prostitutes. In April 1763 he became besotted with Mme Laure de Lauris from a noble Provençal family, and attempted to court her. When she eventually declined his invitations, he became enraged and, in a vindictive attempt to embarrass her, publicly accused her of giving him gonorrhoea. De Sade's father, who was becoming increasingly concerned by his son's lack of stability and frightening mood swings, swiftly organised a marriage between his son and Mme Renée-Pelagie de Montreuil. Although socially inferior, Pelagie's family was exceedingly wealthy. Despite meeting her only 2 days prior to the wedding, de Sade unenthusiastically acquiesced, simply to appease his father. They were married on 17 May 1763.

For many years Pelagie loved and supported her husband in every conceivable way, even procuring adolescent girls and boys for his sexual amusement. However, de Sade considered his wife plain, pasty and sexually unappealing. Philosophically, he was also opposed to the institution of matrimony. A few years into the marriage he wrote, 'The horror of wedlock, the most appalling, the most loathsome of all the bonds humankind has devised for its own discomfort and degradation'. His father, however, caring little for his son, was pleased with the marriage. He wrote: 'As far as I'm concerned, the best thing about the marriage is that I'll be rid of that boy, who has not one good quality and all bad ones.'

Within a few months of their union, de Sade convinced his wife to join him in organising Parisian garden parties. These 'parties' became celebrations of all manner of sexual deviation, especially group sex and sodomy. De Sade enjoyed shocking his playmates by combining sex with social taboos, especially blasphemy. Although not particularly fond of sexual deviation, Pelagie assisted, as she would do anything to ensure her husband's happiness. Unfortunately for her, by October 1763, de Sade became involved in his first major scandal.

The Testard Affair

Mme Jean Testard was an attractive prostitute. De Sade procured her favours for a specified fee and took her to a rented apartment. When Testard informed de Sade that she was Catholic, he lost all semblance of control. He assaulted her with a barrage of blasphemy and performed sexual acts on himself with a holy chalice and crucifix. When she complained of his sacrilegious behaviour, de Sade screamed 'if thou art God, avenge thyself!'. De Sade forced Testard to whip him with a cat-o-nine-tails and then he inserted holy wafers into her genitals. Brandishing a sword, he forced Testard to disavow God and repeat his blasphemous words. Frightened and repulsed, she managed to escape and the following morning reported him to the police. Ten days later, inspector Marais arrested de Sade and incarcerated him in the dungeon of Vincennes. Appalled by de Sade's behaviour, Marais warned all the brothel keepers in the town not to let their girls out alone with the monster. From this point onwards, Marais kept a vigilant eye on de Sade, and he would arrest and imprison de Sade on many occasions in the future.

A GODLESS ANARCHIST

With regard to God, de Sade maintained that, *'there is no God. Nature is sufficient unto herself; in no wise hath she need of an author'*. With regard to the law, he wrote: *'Are not laws dangerous which inhibit the passions? Compare the centuries of anarchy with those of the strongest legalism in any country you like and you will see that it is only when the laws are silent that the greatest actions appear.'*

Following the death of his father in January 1767, and with no-one to curb his excesses, de Sade became increasingly outrageous. He renovated his castle 'La Coste' and devoted a room to sexual literature and toys. He and his adoring wife also staged many 'special bacchanalian parties'.

Life after Rose Keller

After being released from prison following his assault on Rose Keller, de Sade's behaviour worsened still. His experimentation with sex became even more obscene. The threat of imprisonment had no effect on his spiralling descent into depravity and moral turpitude. He even used vomit and excrement during sex to shock his cohorts.

The year 1772 was a bad one for de Sade. In July, he organised a disastrous gathering. He gave his guests a variety of 'Spanish fly' (a type of aphrodisiac) but some of the guests became violently ill and required medical treatment. One of them, Marguerite Coste, went to the police and complained of being poisoned, raped and sodomised. De Sade, getting wind of an imminent arrest, went on the run again, This time he was to be sentenced to death for sodomy. He fled to Sardinia with Latour, his valet and homosexual partner. He also persuaded Pelagie's youngest sister, Anne-Prospere – with whom he had been having an affair – to join him.

More than 6 months passed before he was recaptured in Sardinia – de Sade's mother-in-law being behind his arrest. He was sent to the prison in Miolans. He convinced his captors that he was a model prisoner so they dropped their guard and, on 30 April 1773, he managed to escape. Arrogantly, he left a letter thanking the warden for his warm hospitality.

Once again on the lam, through his powers of persuasion he convinced his wife Pelagie to take him back. Within a few months, however, de Sade was back to his old tricks. This time he became obsessed with perverting the innocence of children. In his book *The Philosophy of the Bedroom*, he wrote, 'How delicious to corrupt, to stifle all semblances of virtue and religion in those young hearts'. Between June and August 1774, he used his wife to procure six teenage girls for his sexual amusement. Despite being wanted by the police, he audaciously imprisoned the girls in his castle at La Coste, treating them as his private harem. However, the father of one of the girls visited de Sade and attempted to shoot him. Lucky for de Sade, the gun misfired. Pelagie relocated all the girls to nearby convents. De Sade, however, was forced to flee, and he returned to Italy to spend the next 2 years in hiding.

Engraving of an orgy, as published in de Sade's novel *Juliette*. Sodomy, despite being illegal, was practised by many French aristocrats during the 18th century.

On 13 February 1777 inspector Marais finally caught up with de Sade. He was found guilty of multiple rape, torture and bestiality. This time he remained incarcerated for 13 years, most of which he spent at Vincennes, although he was ultimately transferred to the Bastille in 1784. Eventually, Pelagie, tired of her husband's antics filed for divorce.

During the term of this final incarceration, de Sade devoted himself to writing. Unable to carry out his debauched fantasies, he decided to encapsulate them in writing. By the time he was released in 1790, he was a bloated, dishevelled parody of his dapper years.

Literary Opus

The central unifying theme of de Sade's literary works is that eroticism is the mainspring of human behaviour. He argues that 'lust is to the other passions what the nervous fluid is to life; it supports them all, lends strength to them all … ambition, cruelty, avarice, revenge, are all founded on lust'. His writings, although abundant, are repetitive and often highly disturbing. Nearly all his works revolve around the subjects of rape, paedophilia, necrophilia, oral sex, sodomy, incest, bestiality, torture, group sex and the use of human excreta in

sexual pleasure. Philosophically, he makes the simplistic assumption that sexual deviation and criminality appear in nature, so therefore they must be 'natural'. He urges people to act spontaneously, according to one's instincts. His writings are credited with giving rise to the terms 'sadism' and 'masochism'.

The Marquis de Sade in Charenton asylum, where he was sent in 1803 to live out the remainder of his life.

During his imprisonment, De Sade penned a number of infamous pornographic texts. His major works include: *The 120 Days of Sodom* (1785), *Justine* (1791), *Juliette* (1798) and *The Philosophy of the Bedroom* (1795). In *The 120 Days of Sodom* he lists approximately 600 sexual perversions inflicted upon a group of enslaved adolescents. It is extremely graphic. *Justine*, his most famous work, has been described as being capable 'of corrupting the devil.' It outlines the misfortunes of a girl who believes in the goodness of God. The companion novel *Juliette* narrates the adventures of Justines's sister, Juliette, who rejects the church, espouses hedonism and consequently has a successful and happy life. *The Philosophy of the Bedroom* describes the sexual awakening of an adolescent woman of privilege.

Citizen Sade

On his release from prison in 1790 de Sade was able to resurrect his career and was elected to the National Convention as a member of the radical left. He re-invented himself as 'Citizen Sade' and he cleverly avoided execution during the heyday of the French Revolution by writing a eulogy in support of Marat, one of the key revolutionaries. De Sade's pornographic writings, however, landed him in trouble. According to popular opinion, after reading *Justine* and *Juliette* in 1801 Napoleon Bonaparte ordered de Sade's arrest. He was first sent to prison, then to a fortress. Finally, in 1803, he was declared insane and sent to the Charenton mental asylum.

Despite being incarcerated in the asylum, de Sade continued to write but was forced to smuggle out his jottings and publish under a pseudonym. He also managed to have an affair with a 13-year-old employee of the asylum, Madoleine

Le Clerk. The affair lasted from 1810 until his death in 1814. The Minister of the Interior banned de Sade from writing. He wrote to the governor of the asylum, demanding that 'the greatest care (must) be taken to prevent any use by him of pencils, ink and paper'.

Historically, de Sade is an interesting figure. His writings have provoked intense debate. To some, he is considered to be the harbinger of sexual and political freedom. He has even been hailed as 'the freest spirit that ever lived'. Others see him as the precursor to surrealism, psychoanalysis and existentialism. Then there are those who consider him to be the greatest degenerate in the history of French literature. The fact that he is capable of polarising opinion so violently points, if nothing else, to a startling and effervescent originality. To silence him is to invoke dogma and autocracy. If nothing else, he makes the point that by trying almost everything as human beings, we can come to an understanding of who we are, what we believe in, what we like and what we repudiate.

> Justine *is the most abominable book ever engendered by the most depraved imagination.*
>
> – Napoleon Bonaparte

MOTIVATION

anger

charity

envy

faith

gluttony

greed

hope

lust

pride

sloth

A WHIP AND A COUNTRY GARDEN: PERCY GRAINGER

MAIN CULPRIT:
Percy Grainger (1882–1961), Australian composer

SCANDAL:
A sado-masochist and racist, he died largely forgotten and loathing his own most popular compositions

WHY:
Had a dominating mother who alternately spoilt him and whipped him

Apart from sex I am not such a bad fellow. But as I am really not interested in anything else but sex it just boils down to this: that I hardly think of anything but sex and that all my sex thoughts are full of evil and cruelty.

– Percy Grainger

The Australian composer Percy Grainger was a gifted and experimental musician, who also had a keen interest in self-flagellation as well as the racist concept of Nordic supremacy.

Percy Grainger brought a boundless energy to everything he did, whether it was composing music, playing the piano, spouting absurd racial theories, revising the written English language or whipping himself – and others – until the blood flowed. The Australian-born composer had a hugely successful career during the first half of the 20th century, but it was one that came with more than its fair share of eccentric behaviour and sexual perversity. For Grainger, though, the music and the perversity were inseparable.

Grainger was born in Melbourne, Australia, on 8 July 1882. His father, John Grainger, was a successful architect who had designed many public buildings across the country. However, he was also an alcoholic who caught syphilis from a prostitute and passed it on to his wife, Rose. In 1891 he went to London 'for his health'. John Grainger and Rose never lived together again.

Percy suffered 3 months of bullying at school before his mother, Rose, took over his education, teaching him English, history and the piano at home. He was forbidden to associate with children of his own age. The relationship between mother and son became a suffocatingly close one, with Rose sitting by Percy's side as he practised on the piano for at least 2 hours a day.

Rose was a cultured woman who loved art, literature and music. She was also strong willed and domineering, and took control of every aspect of her son's life. She had often taken a horsewhip to her philandering husband, and now she whipped Percy if he neglected his lessons. The whip was kept in the front hallway – a constant reminder that he must improve himself.

Rose expected great things from her son. While pregnant with him, she had spent time each day contemplating a statuette of a Greek god, in the hope that something similar would emerge from her womb. The strategy seemed to have paid off, for Percy became a brilliant pianist. He gave his first public performance when he was 12 years old, and the critics hailed a new prodigy. The following year, after raising £50 at a benefit concert, mother and son travelled to Germany so that Percy could study at Dr Hoch's famous conservatorium in Frankfurt.

Nordic Superiority

It was in Germany that Grainger began to develop his racial theories – another legacy from Rose. She had introduced him to the Scandinavian myths and legends, which he adored. Her family, who were all fair haired and blue eyed, were proud of their 'Nordic' heritage and Rose taught her son to be wary of people with dark eyes – John Grainger had dark brown eyes, which must have contributed to this theory.

Percy applied his belief in Nordic superiority to music. He thought that German and Italian composers had far too much influence and that music had become hopelessly sterile and divorced from life. He believed a renaissance would come from the Anglo-Saxons and Scandinavians. His own compositions, using irregular rhythms and odd time signatures, were already startlingly original and years ahead of their time.

The Jogging Pianist

In 1901 Rose and Percy moved to London. He became known as the 'jogging pianist' because of his habit of racing through the streets to get to his concerts, bounding on stage at the last minute (he liked to be in a state of exhaustion before he played). His manic energy was legendary. Once, while touring in South Africa, he played in one town, then walked 105 kilometres to his next engagement, arriving there at 6 pm the following evening. While performing, his body would move and twitch strangely, and he sometimes talked over the music. He was even known to move the piano around during a recital. Most concert pianists take excessive care of their hands but if Grainger was travelling by ship, he thought nothing of stripping off all his clothes and helping to shovel coal in the boiler room.

Grainger was a striking individual physically as well. He had piercing blue eyes and a great shock of brilliant orange hair. He never wore a hat and could sometimes be seen wearing shorts, which in those days was almost enough to get you arrested. Grainger was, in fact, twice arrested in the United States after police mistook him for a vagrant. After touring New Zealand and getting inspiration from the Maoris, he asked his mother to make him shirts and shorts out of brightly coloured pieces of towelling.

Touring constantly, Grainger met the leading composers and musicians of the day and was courted by society wherever he went. In 1915 he and his mother sailed to the United States for a concert tour, and decided to stay. When the United States entered the war, he enlisted in the army and became a bandsman, playing in front of the US president and composing rousing marches.

Grainger wanted to shake up the musical world and became an early champion of folk music. In 1906, he had hiked around Britain recording folk songs on Edison wax cylinders, becoming the first person in the country to make field recordings like this. In 1918, he released a piano setting of an old English dance tune that he had been tinkering with for years, called *Country Gardens*. This jaunty piece became incredibly popular all around the world and hundreds of thousands of copies of the sheet music were sold. It completely eclipsed all Grainger's other musical achievements, and audiences at his concerts would never leave until he had played it. He grew to loathe it.

He was now earning a fortune from concerts, recordings and sheet music sales, and he and Rose moved into a large house in White Plains, outside New York City. He had two fireproof vaults installed in the cellar to store his papers.

Grainger was hailed as a genius in the United States, just as he had been in Britain. But he was a genius known almost as much for his eccentricities as his musical abilities. He travelled everywhere by train, never booking a sleeping car, preferring to sleep upright in his seat. He rarely wore an overcoat, even in the coldest weather, as if kept warm by the creative fires that burned within him. He only ate when he was hungry, and wore the same clothes for days. He never ironed his shirts – concert audiences, he explained, couldn't tell the difference. He also gave most of his money away.

Grainger was a keen self-publicist, and would sometimes play up his own idiosyncrasies for the benefit of the press, but there is no doubt that he was unconventional in almost everything he said or did.

Whippings and Rumours

Rose continued to dominate Percy, and dictated when his friends could see him. She did accept that one day he would have to marry, and occasionally sanctioned girlfriends for him. After a while though, she usually found a reason for him to end these relationships. Grainger always obeyed.

Grainger's sexual life was as unusual as everything else about him. All those lashings administered by his loving mother – which had continued until he was 15 or 16 years old – had turned him into a keen flagellant who found his most intense pleasure whipping women and being whipped in return. We know about all this because he detailed it in hundreds of uninhibited letters to his friends. In one of them, he described how he had once come across some books about flagellation openly displayed in a Dutch bookshop. 'It was a few days before my first recital in Holland, and I put the books aside – unread – until after my concert. I didn't wish to weaken myself before the concert. After the concert I read the books all night. The happiest night of my life, I suppose.' Grainger never went on tour without packing an assortment of twenty or so whips.

He wrote to one girlfriend, a Danish student of his, named Karen Holton, describing the flagellation sessions he hoped to have with her. 'You should not have a single stitch of clothing on your body, but I, "as man", must be allowed to wear a shield for the tediously easily destroyed parts of a man's body. [Grainger had designed a number of protective devices for the eyes and genitals.] I think it must be furiously painful for you to be whipped on your breasts, don't you think?' He also wrote to her that he wanted to have children, and dreamed of whipping

THE GRAINGER MUSEUM

Percy Grainger's 'autobiographical' museum officially opened in 1935, in Melbourne, Australia, but it wasn't really accessible to researchers until the early 1960s. It houses Grainger's extensive collection of manuscript scores, musical instruments (including the 'kangaroo-pouch free music machine') and even some of the clothes of composers who were his friends. But it also stands as a monument to his love of flagellation, containing eighty-three whips made of leather, bamboo and other materials; crotch protectors; a pair of bloodstained shorts and photographs of Percy's pink, whipped buttocks.

them too. 'It must be wonderful to hurt this soft, unspoiled skin … & when my girls begin to awaken sexually I would gradually like to have carnal knowledge with them …' Grainger – fortunately, it must be said – never had children.

Grainger's most intense relationship continued to be with his mother. Despite the ravages of syphilis, which was then incurable, she remained a good-looking woman, and they were often mistaken for husband and wife. In 1922 a rumour went around that their relationship was an incestuous one. It seems that this was started by a number of young women who were infatuated with Grainger and

resented his mother's domination over him. She was suffering from nightmares and hallucinations, and the rumour may have proved too much for her to bear. Rose's mental and physical health had been declining rapidly. One day she went to the office of Grainger's American agent, Antonia Sawyer, on the 18th floor of the Aeolian Building in New York City. When Rose complained of feeling ill, Sawyer went to a chemist to get her some medicine. While she was away, Rose stood on a chair and threw herself out of a window, landing on the roof of the adjoining building, fourteen floors below. She was still conscious when a doctor arrived, but died soon afterwards. Grainger had just come off stage after a sold-out concert in the Los Angeles Philharmonic Auditorium when he was handed a telegram telling him the devastating news.

Grainger toured constantly, met the leading artists of the day and was courted by society wherever he went. He is pictured here with Mexican actor and star of *The Flying Fleet*, Ramon Novarro, in 1929.

Going through her papers later, Grainger found a letter Rose had written to him the day before she died. It read in part: 'You must tell the truth – that in spite of everything that I said – I have never for one moment loved you wrongly – or you me – not for one moment or thought of doing so. The whole thing has driven me insane and I have accused myself of something I have never thought of. You and I have never loved one another anything but purely and right. No-one will believe – but it is the truth as you know.' It was signed, 'Your poor insane mother'. Grainger kept the letter in a container hanging around his neck for years. On an impulse, he destroyed many hundreds of other letters between himself and his mother, an act he came to bitterly regret.

While incest with his mother might seem to have been well within Percy Grainger's repertoire, there was no basis to the rumour. Apart from anything else, Rose would never have risked giving her son syphilis.

Grainger was distraught after his mother's death. He consoled himself by compiling an album of photographs of Rose – including two of her in her coffin – and some of her writings. He had thousands of copies printed and sent it to all their friends. Then he threw himself into touring.

Apart from Sex, Not Such a Bad Fellow

In 1926, Grainger was on a ship returning to the United States after a tour of Australia, when he met a 37-year-old Swedish poet and painter named Ella Viola Strom. She was a blue-eyed Nordic of the type that he so admired, and she also bore a resemblance to his mother. Grainger said it was love at first sight. Two years later, in a typical piece of self-promotion, he married her at a concert in the Hollywood Bowl, in front of about 20,000 people. Grainger played his new composition, *To a Nordic Princess*, which he dedicated to his bride.

Just before their marriage, Grainger had sent Ella a long letter detailing all his sexual tastes. She was shocked, but she loved him and if she wanted to stay with him, she had no choice but to participate – with enthusiasm. Grainger wrote another letter and sealed it with instructions that it was to be opened only if he or Ella, or indeed both of them, died during one of their flagellation sessions.

For Grainger, flagellation was not a mere aberration. It was the wellspring of his talent. 'Many children are cruel to animals and many little boys harsh to girls', he wrote, 'but this fierceness wanes as they grow up. But I never grew up in this respect & fierceness is the keynote of my music ...'. He spent a lot of time analysing his sadomasochism, and identified the central paradox in his nature. 'Apart from sex I am not such a bad fellow. But as I am really not interested in anything else but sex it just boils down to this: that I hardly think of anything but sex and that all my sex thoughts are full of evil and cruelty.'

Far from being ashamed of his mania for whipping, Grainger thought it important that every aspect of it be documented so that future generations could study it. A keen amateur photographer, he recorded the effects of the lash on himself and his wife. He had mirrors set up on the walls and ceiling so he could photograph himself from every angle. On the back of each photograph he noted the date and location of the session and the number of strokes applied.

Everything that deals with sexual matters absolutely knocks me over. I love to simply wade and swim in a sea of overwrought, ceaseless sexual thought ... That is how I live, following my lusts, and composing now and then on the side.

– Percy Grainger

Grainger's desire to celebrate his own life – and all its quirks – culminated in the founding of a museum devoted to himself. He gave the University of Melbourne most of his earnings from 1934–35 for the creation and maintenance of this museum. He designed the semi-circular building, laid some of the stones, donated a vast collection of memorabilia, and commissioned life-sized plaster and wood dummies of himself and Ella to stand guard over it all.

Blue-eyed English and Beatless Music

Grainger continued to embrace enough oddball ideas to keep several crackpots in business. He was, as always, a mass of contradictions. He was a socialist who mixed with high society, an anti-Semite who had many Jewish friends, a Nordic supremacist who donated to African American causes and thought that Duke Ellington was one of the greatest composers who had ever lived. He was even a vegetarian who hated vegetables – he lived chiefly on boiled rice and milk, nuts, cereals and oranges eaten whole.

Grainger's racial beliefs led him to the creation of what he called 'blue-eyed English', in which words with Latin, Greek, French or Italian roots were replaced by purely Anglo-Saxon words. In his letters, a composer is a 'tonesmith', a piano a 'keyed-hammer-string', a restaurant an 'eatshop', and so on. He also hated the Italian terms traditionally used in music scores, and *poco a poco crescendo molto* became 'louden lots bit by bit'.

A MATTER OF TASTE

True to character until the end, in his will, Grainger asked that his skeleton be stripped of flesh and put on display in the museum devoted to himself, but the University of Melbourne declined, on the grounds of taste.

During the 1930s, Grainger taught at several US universities, but twice declined offers of honorary doctorates of music, saying, 'I feel that my music must be regarded as the product of non-education'. His career as a composer and concert-pianist was in decline, however. Critics ridiculed him for popular works like *Country Gardens*, his sheet music went out of print and other musicians stopped performing his works. Desperate for his music to be heard, he offered to play for little or no fee, provided he could include some of his own compositions in the program. As a result, his income from concerts dried up almost completely.

After World War II he devoted himself to what he called 'free' or 'beatless' music, based on the sounds of nature. He had dreamed of creating such music since he was a young boy, and began to build a series of extraordinary machines on which to play it. He used brown paper and string, milk bottles, cotton reels, ping pong balls, a hair dryer and whatever else came to hand. One of them, 'the kangaroopouch free music machine', was a 3-metre tall contraption featuring two rolls of carpet which unrolled vertically. Grainger and the faithful Ella ventured out at night to scavenge for materials (wearing their best clothes to avoid being arrested). He also used rudimentary electronics in some of them, and has been hailed as a pioneer of electronic music. At the time, most people just thought he was a nut. None of the machines was completed.

Grainger in his sixties still had the energy of a man half his age, but in his last few years he suffered pain from abdominal cancer, which eventually killed him in 1961. He died largely forgotten by the music world.

There is no doubt that Grainger, with his endless eccentricities and determination to follow his own path, made a mess of his career, and that all his idiosyncrasies can be traced back to his mother (his relationship with her was, he wrote towards the end, 'the only truly passionate love affair of my life'). But without his mother, there would have been no career. Asked once whether he had inherited his musical talent, Grainger said he didn't believe in musical talent, and he in particular didn't have any. His career was 'entirely due to my mother's influence and her wish to see me as a composer'. And, he might have added, her ever-present whip.

MOTIVATION

anger
charity
envy
faith
gluttony
greed
hope
lust
pride
sloth

Howard Hughes at the peak of his career in 1938.
The American aircraft manufacturer and film magnate,
sustained severe injuries in a plane crash in 1946 and
gradually became a recluse until his death in 1976.

THE OBSESSIVE-COMPULSIVE BILLIONAIRE: HOWARD HUGHES

MAIN CULPRIT:
Howard Robert Hughes Jr (1905–76), industrialist, aviator
and movie producer

SCANDAL:
From a handsome billionaire, he regressed to become a
tortured, decrepit old man with no friends or family

WHY:
Obsessive-compulsive disorder with addiction to opiates

*I'm not a paranoid derranged millionaire. Goddamit, I'm
a billionaire.*
– Howard Hughes

In April 1976 Robert Maheu, once industrialist Howard Hughes's right-hand man, was telephoning around in an attempt to find out if the rumours were true – was Hughes, the richest man in the world, actually dead? Or were the rumours just another attempt at subterfuge by Hughes's inner circle, to put the media off his trail? It seemed that just about every week a new rumour enveloped the reclusive billionaire. Maheu had contacts in the FBI and CIA and he was determined to distinguish fact from fiction. His contacts had told him that a body thought to be Hughes's was under examination by the coroner. However, the complication was that Hughes had not appeared in public for almost 20 years, and the appearance of the body was so different from what the FBI had on file that they had been forced to fingerprint the corpse to determine its true identity. With a 2-billion dollar fortune up for grabs, there was no room for error.

The following day Maheu received the information he was after. Howard Hughes was indeed dead. Apparently he had died a couple of days earlier on 5 April, in his private plane en route to Houston Hospital. He had been in a coma for 3 days before medical help was sought. Maheu got angry. He was seething when he declared, 'If sheer neglect qualifies as a weapon, they [the Mormon inner circle] had killed him'. Maheu hadn't seen Hughes for nearly a decade, but he was still shaken. According to his contacts, when Hughes died he was a pathetic shadow of his once dapper self. Although he was a tall 1.9 metres, at his autopsy he weighed little more than 40 kilograms due to severe malnourishment and dehydration. He was dirty and dishevelled and had a Rip Van Winkle-style long beard. His hair, worn long halfway down his back was greasy and stank. His fingernails were 20 centimetres long and curled inwards. His toenails were black and about 10 centimetres long. Apparently, Hughes had been living on a diet of sweets, cake and TV dinners. He never brushed his teeth so they had become rotten. It was obvious that he hadn't washed in well over a year, so naturally, he was incredibly smelly and greasy. The autopsy also revealed the startling fact that he had dozens of broken-off hypodermic needle tips embedded in both arms, and even in his legs. It was also apparent that he had a fatal level of codeine (1.9 micrograms) in his bloodstream. His overall physical state showed abject neglect.

In Maheu's mind there was no doubt; they had killed him. This would never have happened if he still had been in charge. But Maheu had lost the battle in 1966 when Hughes, choosing his Mormon inner circle over Maheu, had escaped in the middle of the night to Las Vegas. Maheu had then been unceremoniously sacked. What a sad way to go, thought Maheu.

Hughes had been a larger-than-life, comic-book figure – the cowboy aviator, Hollywood producer and playboy, patriotic military contractor, maverick financier and mob buster. And now, through neglect, he was dead.

Film-maker Extraordinaire

Howard Robert Hughes Jr was born on 24 December 1905. His father, who invented a drill bit that revolutionised the mining business, patented his invention in 1909, and in doing so became a millionaire. Unfortunately, he had little time for his only son, so Hughes's mother became the major influence in the young boy's life. Like her husband, she died early in Howard's life. By the time Hughes was 19 years old he had lost both parents. It was his mother, however, who left an indelible mark on her son. As a sufferer of obsessive-compulsive disorder she was terrified of germs and insisted that Howard wash his hands dozens of times each day. She established a multitude of rituals to avoid the impact of germs and bacteria. She even discouraged Howard from playing with other children, believing

Time Life cover, 13 December 1976, tragically depicting a decrepit and profoundly neglected Howard Hughes.

they were infested with potential diseases. Apparently, if Howard so much as sneezed or coughed, she would take him to visit their local doctor. In latter years, Howard would develop many of his mother's eccentricities and from the 1950s onwards was severely affected by obsessive-compulsive disorder.

With the death of Howard Hughes Senior in 1924 just after Howard Junior's 18th birthday, the young Hughes inherited 75 per cent of his father's tool business. Angered by the interference of relatives who were the minority shareholders of the business, Hughes went to the courts and had himself legally declared an adult. He then bought out the shareholdings of his relatives.

With his parents no longer on the scene, Howard sought advice from an uncle who was a writer for Goldwyn's Movie Studios. As a result, Hughes decided to go into the filmmaking business. Like everything in his life, Hughes devoted himself passionately to this new project. In 1925, he married Ella Rice and moved to Hollywood where he could start working on a number of films. His first movie, *Everybody's Acting*, was a commercial flop. However, in an astute move, Hughes hired Noah Dietrich to head his movie subsidiary, and Dietrich delivered outstanding profits (in excess of $50 million per year), year after year. Hughes's next film, *Arabian Nights*, was completed in 1928. It was a box-office hit and delivered Hughes's first Academy Award. His next film, *Hell's Angels* (1930), about dog fighters in World War I, caused him much grief. Hughes, an obsessive perfectionist, spent $3.8 million on the film, making it the most expensive movie ever made. Fortunately it was a box office hit, but it was still unable to recoup its costs. Hughes was a stickler for detail. For example, he delayed the filming of *Hells Angels* for weeks until there were near-perfect weather patterns that provided abundant fluffy clouds in the sky – without the clouds, he argued, the aeroplanes appeared static and unrealistic. By the time *Hells Angels* had been completed, three pilots had lost their lives. A debonair Hughes, having procured his pilot's licence, ended up flying a plane himself and shot some of the crucial and most difficult scenes. He also managed to crash his plane during the shoot.

Hughes produced a number of other successful movies, the most important of which were *Scarface* (1932), *Billy the Kid* (1942) and *The Outlaw* (1943). From the 1930s onwards, Hughes found himself obstinately arguing with the censors, often causing major delays in the release of his movies. *Scarface*, for instance, could not be released until Hughes successfully sued the censors who were arguing that the film glorified violence and crime. *The Outlaw* also became scandalous due to its sexual content and because it implied a sexual relation between the male and female leads. Although completed in 1941, the film was not released until 1946. *The Outlaw* was also a showcase for Hughes's extraordinary attention to detail. While watching the filming of the movie, Hughes became convinced that the blouse worn by leading actress, Jane Russell, was bunching up in such a way as to suggest that she had two nipples on each side of her chest. To fix this problem, Hughes invented the half-cup bra, which appeared natural and sexy.

OBSESSIVE-COMPULSIVE DISORDER

This is an anxiety disorder which is characterised by recurrent and unwanted thoughts (obsessions) and/or repetitive behaviours (compulsions). Repetitive behaviours such as persistent hand washing, checking and cleaning are performed in an attempt to remove the compulsions. These rituals, however, provide only temporary relief and when the sufferer stops performing them, the result is a dramatic increase in anxiety.

Around this time, it became apparent that Hughes was increasingly affected by obsessive-compulsive disorder. At home, he instructed his cooks and servants that all peas – one of his favourite foods – had to be measured and must be of exactly the same size. He even invented a special fork so they could be properly measured. Hughes would explode in a fit of rage if he found a pea on his plate that was larger or smaller than the others.

Hughes's marriage to Ella Rice ended in 1929 and he began entering into affairs with many of Hollywood's starlets. He now considered himself a player and is rumoured to have slept with Katharine Hepburn, Bette Davis, Gene Tierney, Ava Gardner and Besse Love. Evidence also suggests that he may have been bisexual. He is said to have had sexual relations with Ben Lyon, Cary Grant and Jack Bueler. Around this time Hughes caught syphilis from one of his sexual partners. Lesions appeared on his hands. From the time he was diagnosed with syphilis, Hughes vehemently refused to shake anyone's hand – this created the impression that he was haughty, snobbish and above his peers. In reality he was trying to protect others from this virulent disease. In his later years it was difficult to tell whether Hughes's eccentric behaviour was caused by a progression of his obsessive-compulsive disorder or tertiary-stage syphilis.

Hughes the Aviator and Plane Manufacturer

After obtaining his pilot's licence during *Hells Angels*, Hughes became obsessed with all aspects of flying, aeronautical engineering and establishing speed and distance records. In 1932 he formed Hughes Aircraft, a division of the Hughes Tool Company and dedicated himself to engineering and manufacturing state-of-the-art aeroplanes and breaking existing aeronautical records. In 1934 he won the All-America Air Meet in Miami. Between 1934 and 1935 he built and personally tested the world's most advanced aeroplane, the H-1. By September 1935 he had set a new world speed record, clocking an impressive 566 kilometres per hour. The H-1 was renowned for its technical innovations: it had retractable landing gear and its rivets and joins were set flush into the steel, thereby reducing wind resistance. Between 1935 and 1937, Hughes set two transcontinental records. On 10 July 1938, flying a Lockheed Super Electra, he set a new world record for completing a flight around the world in 3 days and 19 hours. This time he beat the previous record by a staggering 4 days. He was also able to cut Lindbergh's Paris to New York record by half. Hughes was honoured by his peers and received multiple aviation awards.

From the 1940s onwards, Hughes devoted himself to designing passenger aircraft with pressurised cabins. All went well until July 1946 when he was almost killed in a crash while flying an experimental US-army spy plane called the XF-11 over Los Angeles. In a desperate attempt at saving himself, he tried to land on the Los Angeles County Golf Course. Unable to control his plane, he ended up crashing into three adjoining homes. Hughes was lucky to survive. He broke his collarbone and suffered six broken ribs, a punctured lung and extensive burns to his hands, arms and legs. Fortunately for Hughes, he was pulled from the wreckage by a local marine named William Durkin. During his stay in hospital, Hughes was given large doses of intravenous morphine. As a result, he would be addicted to opiates for the remainder of his life.

With World War II imminent, Hughes devoted his time to military planes. His desire for secrecy, in addition to his aversion of military protocols, meant that he was not always commercially successful. Twice he was unable to fulfil his contractual obligations and was ridiculed publicly as a result. His biggest embarrassment lay in the construction and delivery of the HK-1, which came to be known as the 'Spruce Goose'. Intended to be a 'flying boat', it was constructed primarily from birch and was a gargantuan wooden cargo plane. Unfortunately for Hughes, the prototype was not developed until 1947 when the war was already over. Due to its peculiar design and construction, few aviators believed it was capable of flying. In November 1947, Hughes agreed to give the plane a test run himself. He managed to fly the plane for just over 1.6 kilometres at a height of 21 metres above the water at Long Beach Harbour. Hughes's Aircraft performed so poorly during the war that Hughes was questioned by the Senate War Investigating Committee as to why so many military contracts failed.

By 1954 most of Hughes's top executives had left the fold. The reason given was invariably the same. Hughes was accused of being obsessively controlling, yet hopelessly indecisive. This was a major problem given the scope of his business activities. By the 1950s he was involved in many projects including the design and manufacture of planes, helicopters, satellites, radios and other electrical components, weapons guidance systems, armaments and philanthropy. In addition, he lent support to the CIA by allowing his businesses to be used as fronts whenever required. In 1954 he was ordered by the Secretary of the Air Force to step down and appoint a suitable manager. Afraid of losing his lucrative defence contracts, Hughes appointed Lawrence 'Pat' Hyland to take over.

Hughes in the cockpit of his plane, the Spruce Goose, Los Angeles, November 1947.

Hughes was desperate to find a trustworthy and competent right-hand man. By 1957 he had become hopelessly drug addicted and reclusive. He would sit for days in darkened rooms, avoiding human contact and communicating with his staff via memos. That year he had actually married the actress Jean Peters, but within a matter of months they were living apart. Hughes, after much procrastination, appointed Robert Maheu to run his affairs. With Maheu coming from an FBI background, Hughes felt comfortable with him. He paid him a yearly salary of $520,000, gave him access to a private jet and provided him with an open-book expense account. Maheu described the circumstances: 'He [Hughes] decided that he wanted me to become his alter ego so he would never have to make a public appearance'.

Around this time Howard Hughes vanished from public view. The tabloids published anything they could find on the man, especially his behaviour and whereabouts. Newspapers alternatively reported him as terminally ill, dead, mentally deranged, physically crippled and sexually perverted.

According to most biographers, Hughes's actions were becoming increasingly strange. He stored his urine in jars, which he then kept in a cupboard. He would only pick up objects with paper towels, being terrified of germs. Paradoxically, he stopped washing – it seems that he was worried about the germs others may spread, rather than his own. Sometimes he wore tissue boxes as makeshift shoes. He blacked out rooms and would sit naked watching television for hours on end. Although he regularly visited doctors, he was obstinate and would rarely heed their advice.

The Mormon Circle and Las Vegas

In 1966 Hughes sold his interest in Transworld Airways for $546 million. He wanted a new challenge but was terrified of dealing personally with the media, other executives and people in general. Gradually, he began to lose faith in Maheu and increasingly relied on a new inner circle comprising a number of astute Mormon businessmen including Bill Gay, Chester Davis and Raymond Holliday. Although Hughes was not a member of the Latter Day Saints Movement, he considered them trustworthy and dynamic. His opinion of Maheu had changed drastically. He described him as 'a no-good, dishonest son-of-a-bitch who stole me blind'. Without the knowledge of Maheu, Hughes decided to move his entourage from hotel to hotel. After visiting the Bahamas and London, he decided that his future lay in Las Vegas. Without informing Maheu of his whereabouts, Hughes's entourage arrived in Las Vegas on 27 November 1966. Having fired Maheu, he developed a vision of improving the sleazy image of Las Vegas while buying up casinos and hotels. As he put it: 'I like to think of Las Vegas in terms of a well-dressed man in a dinner jacket and a beautifully jewelled and furred female getting out of an expensive car'.

NUCLEAR TERROR

Hughes was so petrified of nuclear radiation that he told Maheu to offer both Nixon and Johnson $1 million if they would cease underground nuclear testing in Nevada. Maheu, worried at the reaction Hughes would receive from the press if the information was leaked, decided not to make the offers known to either presidential candidate.

Hughes arrived in Las Vegas on a special Union Pacific Train late at night and took up residence on the top floor of the Desert Inn hotel. After he had been staying there for 10 days, the owners of the casino, Moe Dalitz and Ruby Kolod, began to get impatient. The top floor had been reserved for high-roller gamblers and it appeared Hughes had no intention of leaving. Dalitz angrily informed Hughes's inner circle: 'Get the hell out of here or we'll throw your butt out'. Hughes called union leader and mobster Jimmy Hoffa and asked him to intervene. The same day, Hoffa rang Dalitz and not-so-gently asked him 'to leave my friends alone'. In the end, Hughes decided that the best solution to the problem was to buy the Desert Inn — he bought it for $13.25 million, which was well above the current valuation. He then went on a major shopping spree and bought a number of hotels and casinos including Castaways, New Frontier, The Landmark Hotel and the Silver Slipper. Hughes is attributed with cleaning up Las Vegas and wrestling control from the mob.

Once ensconced in the penthouse of the Desert Inn, Hughes refused to leave the premises and remained in his darkened rooms for over 4 years. He did, however, visit London in 1970. While he was there he fell and fractured his hip. He refused to accept the recommendations of doctors and did not exercise after his operation, thereby rendering himself bedridden. During this time his apartment was never cleaned. He had become so mentally unhinged that he often urinated on the floor.

He had also developed a penchant for lazing around his apartment completely naked – day and night. By this stage he had developed a phobia of telephones so that all correspondence with his employees was through written memos, which were often detailed and bizarre. Hughes spent most of his time watching movies in a drug-induced haze. As a chronic insomniac he liked to watch television late into the night. Frustrated that local television stopped transmission at 1 am he contacted the owner of KLAS-TV and demanded that it broadcast westerns and war flicks. Frustrated by these seemingly unreasonable requests, media mogul and partner in KLAS-TV Hank Greenspun is said to have exclaimed: 'Why doesn't he buy the damn thing and run it the way he pleases'. When told of Greenspun's reaction, Hughes bought the channel for $3.65 million – double its valuation price. Now, if Hughes dozed off during a movie he was watching, he would instruct an employee to ring the station and demand that the scene be shown again. Sometimes he would watch the same movie over and over. He is rumoured to have watched his favourite movie, *Ice Station Zebra*, over 150 times.

By April 1976 Hughes was on his deathbed and had become so apathetic that he did not bother to write a will. His death on 5 April was at first treated with suspicion – the tabloids worldwide had been reporting his death for over 2 decades. But this time it was for real. His $2 billion fortune was fought out in the courts and, in the end, approximately twenty-two cousins received a cut. Sadly, and ironically, the once brilliant, dynamic and innovative businessmen, died alone – he was surrounded by puppets, but devoid of close friends or relatives.

PERSONAL INSULATION

Hughes gave his domestic staff complex and detailed instructions. For example, before handing Hughes an eating utensil such as a fork or spoon, the object was to be wrapped in tissue paper. It was then sealed with adhesive tape. A second layer of tissue paper was then wrapped around the first protective layer. Employees were also told to hold between six and eight tissues when turning a doorknob.

FURTHER READING

Political Misconduct

A QUESTION OF PATERNITY: THOMAS JEFFERSON AND SALLY HEMINGS

Brody, Fawn M., *Thomas Jefferson: An Intimate History*, Bantam Books, New York, 1974

Ellis, Joseph J., *American Sphinx: The Character of Thomas Jefferson*, Vintage Books, New York, 1998

Foster, Eugene A. et al., 'Jefferson Fathered Slave's Last Child', *Nature*, 5 November 1998

Gordon-Reed, Annette, *Thomas Jefferson and Sally Hemings: An American Controversy*, The University Press of Virginia, Charlottesville, Virginia, 1997

Jefferson-Hemings DNA Testing: An On-Line Resource (www.monticello.org)

McLaughlin, Jack, *Jefferson and Monticello: The Biography of a Builder*, Henry Holt, New York, 1988

Miller, John Chester, *The Wolf by the Ears: Thomas Jefferson and Slavery*, Collier Macmillan Publishers, London, 1977

The Monticello Association (www.monticello-assoc.org)

TEMPERANCE IN ALL THINGS: JABEZ SPENCER BALFOUR

McKie, David, *Jabez: The Rise and Fall of a Victorian Scoundrel*, Atlantic, London, 2004

Rock, David, 'Jabez Spencer Balfour a Fraud Abroad', *History Today*, vol. 49, August 1999

THE WORST PRESIDENT IN AMERICAN HISTORY: WARREN G. HARDING

Adams, Samuel Hopkins, *The Incredible Era*, Houghton Mifflin Company, Boston, 1939

Mee, Charles L. Jr, *The Ohio Gang: The World of Warren G. Harding*, M. Evans and Co., New York, 1981

Russell, Francis, *The Shadow of Blooming Grove: Warren G. Harding in His Times*, McGraw-Hill, New York, 1968

Sferrazza, Carl, *Florence Harding: The First Lady, the Jazz Age, and the Death of America's Most Scandalous President*, Willliam Morrow, New York, 1988

A PECULIAR KIND OF LOVE: EDWARD VIII AND WALLIS SIMPSON

Blackwood, Caroline, *The Last of the Duchess*, Pantheon Books, New York, 1995

Bloch, Michael (ed.), *Wallis and Edward: Letters 1931–1937*, Simon & Schuster, New York, 1986

Craughwell-Varda, Kathleen 'Wallis Warfield Spencer Simpson', *Looking for Jackie: American Fashion Icons*, Hearst Books, New York, 1999

Dennis, Geoffrey, *Coronation Commentary*, Dodd, Mead & Company, New York, 1937

Ziegler, Philip, *King Edward VIII: A Biography*, Alfred A. Knopf, New York, 1991

'I AM NOT A CROOK': RICHARD NIXON AND WATERGATE

Ervin, Sam J. Jr, *The Whole Truth: The Watergate Conspiracy*, Random House, New York, 1980

Lukas, J. Anthony, *Night-Mare: The Underside of the Nixon Years*, Viking, New York, 1976

Nixon, Richard M., *RN: The Memoirs of Richard Nixon*, Warner Books, New York, 1978

Reeves, Richard: *President Nixon: Alone in the White House*, Simon & Schuster, New York, 2001

Woodward, Bob, *The Secret Man: The Story of Watergate's Deep Throat*, Simon & Schuster, New York, 2005

Woodward, Bob, Bernstein, Carl, *All the President's Men*, Simon & Schuster, New York, 1974

AN AFFAIR TO REMEMBER: JOHN PROFUMO AND THE FALL OF A GOVERNMENT

Cowell, Alan, 'John Profumo, British Minister Ruined by Sex Scandal, Dies', *New York Times*, 10 March, 2006

Keeler, Christine, with Thompson, Douglas, *The Truth at Last*, Sidgewick & Jackson, London, 2001

Sandbrook, Dominic, *Never Had It So Good*, Little Brown, London, 2005

THE PRIME MINISTER WHO GOT THE SACK: GOUGH WHITLAM

Kelly, Paul, *The Dismissal: Australia's Most Sensational Power Struggle – The Dramatic Fall of Gough Whitlam*, Angus and Robertson, Sydney, 1983

Whitlam, E. Gough, *The Truth of the Matter*, Penguin, London, 1979

Whitlam, E. Gough, *The Whitlam Government, 1972–75*, Viking, Sydney, 1986

Whitlam, E. Gough, *Abiding Interests: Memoirs*, University of Queensland Press, Brisbane, 1997

ALL THE PRESIDENT'S WOMEN: FERDINAND AND IMELDA MARCOS

Bonner, Raymond, *Waltzing with a Dictator: The Marcoses and the Making of American Policy*, Times Books, New York, 1987

Ellison, Katherine, *Imelda, Steel Butterfly of the Philippines*, McGraw-Hill, New York, 1988

Karnow, Stanley, *In Our Image: America's Empire in the Philippines*, Random House, New York, 1989

Romulo, Beth Day, *Inside the Palace: The Rise and Fall of Ferdinand & Imelda Marcos*, Putnam, New York, 1987

THE LIBERAL AND THE UNSTABLE STABLE BOY: JEREMY THORPE

Freeman, Simon, Penrose, Barrie, *Rinkagate: Rise and Fall of Jeremy Thorpe*, Bloomsbury, London, 1996

Thorpe, Jeremy, *In My Own Time: Reminiscences of a Liberal Leader*, Politico's Publishing, London, 1999

Waugh, Auberon, *The Last Word: An Eye-Witness Account of the Thorpe Trial*, Michael Joseph, London, 1980

'I DID NOT HAVE SEXUAL RELATIONS WITH THAT WOMAN!': BILL CLINTON

Clinton, Bill, *My Life*, Arrow, London, 2005

Harris, John F., *The Survivor: Bill Clinton in the White House*, Random House, New York, 2005

Klein, Joe, *The Natural: The Misunderstood Presidency of Bill Clinton*, Coronet Books, Philadelphia, 2002

Morris, Dick, *Behind the Oval Office: Getting Reelected Against All Odds*, Renaissance Books, London, 1999

Murder and Mystery

THE ENLIGHTENED DESPOT: CATHERINE THE GREAT

Alexander, John T., *Catherine the Great: Life and Legend*, Oxford University Press, Oxford, New York, 1989

Madariaga, Isabel de, *Catherine the Great: A Short History*, Yale University, New Haven, Connecticut, 2002

Troyat, Henri, *Catherine the Great* (English translation), Penguin, London, 1980

'THE INTERVIEW': AARON BURR JR AND THE DEATH OF A FOUNDING FATHER

Fleming, Thomas J., *Duel: Alexander Hamilton, Aaron Burr, and the Future of America*, Basic Books, New York, 1999

Kennedy, Roger G., *Burr, Hamilton, and Jefferson: a Study in Character*, Oxford University Press, Oxford, New York, 2000

Lomask, Milton, *Aaron Burr/Milton Lomask*, Farrar, Straus & Giroux, New York, 1979

THE STAR-SPANGLED KILLER: HOW DANIEL SICKLES GOT AWAY WITH MURDER

Beckman, W. Robert, 'Daniel Edgar Sickles', in *Encyclopedia of the American Civil War: A Political, Social, and Military History*, Heidler, David S., Heidler, Jeanne T. (eds), W. W. Norton & Company, New York, 2000

Eicher, John H., Eicher, David J., *Civil War High Commands*, Stanford University Press, Palo Alto, California, 2001

Keneally, Thomas, *American Scoundrel: Murder, Love and Politics in Civil War America*, Vintage Australia, Sydney, 2003

THE MAESTRO'S MELANCHOLIA: PYOTR TCHAIKOVSKY'S STORMY LIFE

Brown, David, *Tchaikowsky: A Biographical and Critical Study*, Gollancz, London, 1978

Evans, Edwin, *Tchaikowsky: A Biography*, Collier Books, New York, 1963

Poznansky, Alexander, *Tchaikowsky: The Quest for the Inner Man*, Schirmer Books, New York, 1991

Tchaikowsky, Pyotr I., *Letters to His Family: An Autobiography*, Stein and Day, New York, 1981

THE FAT MAN IN THE BATHROOM:
FATTY ARBUCKLE

Anger, Kenneth, *Hollywood Babylon: The Legendary Underground Classic of Hollywood's Darkest and Best Kept Secrets*, Dell Publishing, New York, 1981

Oderman, Stuart, *Roscoe 'Fatty' Arbuckle: A Biography of the Silent Film Comedian, 1887–1933*, McFarland & Company, North Carolina, 1994

Yallop, David, *The Day the Laughter Stopped: The True Story of Fatty Arbuckle*, St. Martin's Press, New York, 1976

False Prophets

THE PREACHER AND THE PROSTITUTE:
JIMMY SWAGGART

Barnhart, Joe E., *Jim and Tammy*, Prometheus, Amherst, New York, 1988

Bruce, Steve, *Pray TV: Televangelism in America*, Routledge, London, 1990

Seaman, Anne Rowe, *Swaggart: the Unauthorised Biography of an American Evangelist*, Continuum, New York, 1999

Swaggart, Jimmy, *Pornography: America's Dark Stain*, Jimmy Swaggart Ministries, Baton Rouge, 1985

'MAN RAPED BY BANANA':
THE REVEREND CANAAN BANANA

'Canaan Banana, Clergyman, Politician and Rapist', *Economist*, 29 November 2003

McNeil, Donald G. Jr, 'Former President of Zimbabwe Convicted of Sodomy', *New York Times*, 27 November 1998

Meldrum, Andrew, 'The Reverend Canaan Banana: Zimbabwe's First President, Whose Reputation Was Ruined by Sexual Scandal', *Guardian*, 12 November 2003

PRAISE THE LORD AND PASS THE LOOT:
JIM BAKKER'S FALL FROM GRACE

Bakker, Jim, *I Was Wrong*, Nelson Books, Nashville, 1996

Shephard, Charles E., *Forgiven: The Rise and Fall of James Bakker and the PTL Ministry*, Atlantic Monthly Press, Boston, 1989

On the Lam

THE FUGITIVE: CARAVAGGIO'S
LIFE ON THE RUN

Friedlaender, Walter, *Caravaggio Studies*, Princeton University Press, Princeton, New Jersey, 1974

Gregori, Mina, *Caravaggio*, Electa, Milan, 1994

Langdon, Helen, *Caravaggio: A Life*, Chatto & Windus, London, 1998

Macadam, Alta, *Rome*, A & C Black, London, 1998

Po-Chia Hsia, R., *The World of Catholic Renewal 1540–1770*, Cambridge University Press, Cambridge, 1998

Shoham, S. Giora, 'Caravaggio: The Violent Enlightenment', *Journal of Criminal Justice and Popular Culture*, vol. 6, 1999, pp. 67–82

'HE WOULDN'T TAKE NO FOR AN ANSWER':
ROMAN POLANSKI

Bugliosi, Vincent, with Gentry, Curt, *Helter Skelter: The True Story of the Manson Murders*, W. W. Norton & Co., New York, 1974

Campbell, Duncan, 'Rape Victim Backs Polanski', *Age* (Australia), 3 March, 2003

Cronin, Paul (ed.), *Roman Polanski: Interviews*, University of Mississippi Press, Jackson, Mississippi, 2005

Geimer, Samantha, 'Judge the Movie, Not the Man', *Los Angeles Times*, 23 February 2003

Internet Movie Database (imdb.com)

Leaming, Barbara, *Polanski, A Biography: The Filmmaker As Voyeur*, Simon & Schuster, New York, 1981

'Polanski Named in Rape Charge', *Washington Post*, 13 March 1977

THE CASE OF THE VANISHING ARISTOCRAT:
LORD LUCAN

MacLaughlin, Duncan with Hall, William, *Dead Lucky: Lord Lucan: The Final Truth*, John Blake Publishing, London, 2003

Marnham, Patrick, *Trail of Havoc*, Viking, London, 1987

Langley, William, 'Lord Lucan's Ghost', *Australian Women's Weekly*, September 2002

Double Lives

THE SCAM ARTISTE EXTRAORDINAIRE: THERESE HUMBERT

Herzog, Don, *Cunning*, Princeton University Press, Princeton, New Jersey, 2006

Miller, William Ian, *Faking It*, Cambridge University Press, Cambridge, 2005

Spurling, Hilary, *La Grande Thérèse*, Harper Collins, London, 2000

PORTRAIT OF A SHADOW: THE SECRETS OF ANTHONY BLUNT

Carter, Amanda, *Anthony Blunt: His Lives*, Farrar, Straus and Giroux, New York, 2002

Newton, Vern W., *The Cambridge Spies*, Madison Books, New York, 1991

Steiner, George, *George Steiner: A Reader*, Oxford University Press, Oxford; New York, 1987

GOOD VERSUS EVIL: THE PETROV AFFAIR

Manne, Robert, *The Petrov Affair: Politics and Espionage*, Australian National University Press, Canberra, 1987

Petrov, Vladimir, *My Retreat from Russia*, Yale University Press, New Haven, Conneticut, 1950

Petrov, Vladimir & Evdokia, *Empire of Fear*, Deutsch, New York, 1956

Whitlam, Nicholas, *Nest of Traitors: The Petrov Affair*, Australian National University Press, Canberra, 1985

THE PSEUDOCIDAL POLITICIAN: JOHN STONEHOUSE

Haigh, John, *Taking Chances, Winning with Probability*, Oxford University Press, Oxford, New York, 2000

Stonehouse, John, *Death of an Idealist*, W. H. Allen, London, 1975

Private Perversions

PLEASURE THROUGH PAIN: THE MARQUIS DE SADE

du Plessix Gray, Francine, *At Home With the Marquis De Sade: A Life*, Penguin, London, 1999

Gillette, Paul J., (translator), *The Complete Marquis De Sade*, Holloway House Publishing, Los Angeles, 2006

Hayman, Ronald, *Marquis de Sade: The Genius of Passion*, Tauris Parke Paperbacks, London, 2003

Thomas, Donald Serrell, *The Marquis De Sade: A New Biography*, Citadel Press, New York, 1992

A WHIP AND A COUNTRY GARDEN: PERCY GRAINGER

Bird, John, *Percy Grainger*, Currrency Press, Sydney, 1998

Gillies, Malcolm, *Self-Portrait of Percy Grainger*, Oxford University Press, Oxford, New York, 2006

Wilfrid Mellers, Wilfred, *Percy Grainger*, (Oxford Studies of Composers) Oxford University Press, Oxford, New York, 1992

THE OBSESSIVE-COMPULSIVE BILLIONAIRE: HOWARD HUGHES

Barlett, Donald L., Steele, James, *Howard Hughes: His Life and Madness*, W. W. Norton & Company, New York, 2004

Brown, Peter Harry, Broeske, Pat H., *Howard Hughes: The Untold Story*, Da Capo Press, New York, 2004

Hack, Richard, *Hughes: The Private Diaries, Memos and Letters*, New Millennium Entertainment, New York, 2001

Real, Jack G., Yenne, Bill, *The Asylum of Howard Hughes*, Xlibris Corporation, 2003

Thunder Bay Press
An imprint of the Baker & Taylor Publishing Group
10350 Barnes Canyon Road, San Diego, CA 92121
www.thunderbaybooks.com

All notations of errors or omissions should be addressed to Thunder Bay Press, Editorial Department, at the
above address. All other correspondence (author inquiries, permissions) concerning the content of this book
should be addressed to Murdoch Books Pty Limited, 83 Alexander St, Crows Nest, NSW 2065, Australia.

ISBN-13: 978-1-60710-862-7
ISBN-10: 1-60710-862-3

Library of Congress Cataloging-in-Publication Data available upon request.

Printed by 1010 Printing International Limited, CHINA

1 2 3 4 5 17 16 15 14 13